GW00390885

METROPOLITAN WRITINGS

ᴍ Hᴀᴢʟɪᴛᴛ was born in Maidstone, Kent in 1778, the son
Unitarian minister. After a short period in America, the
.y settled in the village of Wem, Shropshire. Hazlitt was
cated at the Unitarian College in Hackney from 1793 to
5, although he decided against the religious life, and began
move in the political and literary circles of Coleridge,
rdsworth, Lamb and Godwin. He wrote on philosophy and
tics before becoming increasingly involved in literature
journalism. In 1814 he became the *Morning Chronicle*
amentary reporter and theatre critic, while also writing
ys for journals, including the *Edinburgh Review* and Leigh
t's *Examiner*. His works on literature include the *Characters
akespeare's Plays* (1817), dedicated to Lamb and admired by
s; *Lectures on the English Poets* (1818); *The Round Table*, in
aboration with Leigh Hunt (1818); and *Lectures on the
sh Comic Writers* (1819). His *Political Essays* were also
ished in 1819, and *Table Talk* in 1821–2. In 1825 and 1826
of his best work was collected in two volumes of essays,
Spirit of the Age and *The Plain Speaker*. In the last ten years
s life Hazlitt experienced emotional turmoil and poverty,
ugh he continued to publish until his death in 1830.

Ry Dᴀʀᴛ was educated at Clare College, Cambridge,
en 1986 and 1993. He taught English Literature at the
rsity of York from 1993 to 2000, and is now teaching the
subject at University College London. He also writes for
LS and contributes programme notes for the Royal Opera
e, Covent Garden. He has published two books, *Rousseau,
Ro pierre and English Romanticism* (Cambridge, 1999) and
Unrequited Love: On Stalking and Being Stalked (Short Books,
2003).

Fyfield*Books* aim to make available some of the great classics of British and European literature in clear, affordable formats, and to restore often neglected writers to their place in literary tradition.

Fyfield*Books* take their name from the Fyfield elm in Matthew Arnold's 'Scholar Gypsy' and 'Thyrsis'. The tree stood not far from the village where the series was originally devised in 1971.

Roam on! The light we sought is shining still.
Dost thou ask proof? Our tree yet crowns the hill,
Our Scholar travels yet the loved hill-side

from 'Thyrsis'

WILLIAM HAZLITT

Metropolitan Writings

Edited with an introduction by
GREGORY DART

SURREY LIBRARIES	
Askews & Holts	13-Mar-2012
824.7 LIT	£12.95

Fyfield*Books*

CARCANET

To Vibeche Standal

First published in Great Britain in 2005 by
Carcanet Press Limited
Alliance House
Cross Street
Manchester M2 7AQ

Introduction and editorial matter © Gregory Dart 2005

The right of Gregory Dart to be identified as the editor
of this work has been asserted by him in accordance with
the Copyright, Designs and Patents Act of 1988
All rights reserved

A CIP catalogue record for this book is available from the British Library
ISBN 1 85754 758 6

The publisher acknowledges financial assistance from Arts Council England

Typeset by XL Publishing Services, Tiverton
Printed and bound in England by SRP Ltd, Exeter

Contents

Introduction

A real Cockney, Hazlitt wrote, in his superbly entertaining essay
'On Londoners and Country People', ventures outside the city 'as
a cat crosses a gutter', and finds that the countryside has a very
blank appearance, because 'it is not lined with houses all the way,
like London'. He 'lives in a go-cart of local prejudices and positive
illusions', the essayist continues, 'and when he is turned out of it,
hardly knows how to stand or move' (p. 85). By the late Victorian
period the word 'Cockney' had come to signify a salt-of-the-earth
representative of the East End working class, but in 1823, when
Hazlitt wrote this piece, it still had a rather more satirical flavour,
and signified not so much a class as a condition:

> The true Cockney has never travelled beyond the purlieus of the
> Metropolis, either in the body or the spirit. Primrose-hill is the
> Ultima Thule of his most romantic desires; Greenwich Park
> stands him in stead of the Vales of Arcady. Time and Space are
> lost to him. He is confined to one spot, and to the present
> moment. He sees everything near, superficial, little, in hasty
> succession. The world turns round, and his head with it, like a
> roundabout at a fair, till he becomes stunned and giddy with the
> motion. Figures glide by as in a *camera obscura*. There is a glare,
> a perpetual hubbub, a noise, a crowd about him; he sees and
> hears a vast number of things, and knows nothing. He is pert,
> raw, ignorant, conceited, ridiculous, shallow, contemptible. His
> senses keep him alive, and he knows, inquires, and cares for
> nothing farther. He meets the Lord Mayor's coach, and treats
> himself to an imaginary ride in it. He notices the people going
> to court or to a city-feast, and is quite satisfied with the show.
> (pp. 82–3)

This caricature draws on a long tradition, which goes back to late
medieval times, of the Cockney as a cock's egg, a mother's darling,
a pampered and effeminate child. But what distinguishes Hazlitt's
treatment from that of previous writers is the extraordinary
intellectual pressure, at once psychological and sociological, that
he brings to this comic stereotype, seeing it as an ideal opportunity
to investigate the influence of the metropolis upon mental life. In
his analysis, the city accelerates and spectacularises experience. It

destroys all sense of process or perspective. Hence for the Cockney, life is like a wall of advertisements in which all elements and values have been flattened, so that 'everything is vulgarised in his mind'. 'Nothing dwells long enough on it to produce an interest,' Hazlitt suggests, 'nothing is contemplated sufficiently at a distance to excite curiosity or wonder. *Your true Cockney is your only true leveller.* Let him be as low as he will, he fancies he is as good as anybody else' (p. 83).

Launching a full-scale attack on metropolitan vanity in 'On Londoners', Hazlitt argues that the Cockney 'comes so often in contact with fine persons and things' that he becomes 'surcharged with a sort of second-hand, vapid, tingling, troublesome self-importance'. With his imagination ensnared by the urban spectacle of celebrity, wealth and power, he soars forth in a bubble of false consciousness, and has a very high opinion of himself regardless of his actual condition:

> He resides in a garret or in a two pair of stairs' back room; yet he talks of the magnificence of London, and gives himself airs in consequence upon it, as if all the houses in Portman or in Grosvenor Square were his by right or in reversion [...] Let us suppose him to be a lawyer's clerk at half-a guinea a week: but he knows the Inns of Court, the Temple Gardens and Gray's Inn Passage, sees the lawyers in their wigs walking up and down Chancery Lane, and has advanced within half-a dozen yards of the Chancellor's chair: – who can doubt that he understands (by implication) every point of law (however intricate) better than the most expert country practitioner? He is a shopman, and nailed all day behind the counter: but he sees hundreds of thousands of gay, well-dressed people pass – an endless phantasmagoria – and enjoys their liberty and gaudy fluttering pride. He is a footman – but he rides behind beauty, through a crowd of carriages, and visits a thousand shops. (pp. 84–5)

Cockneyism's true home, Hazlitt suggests, is in the uneasy, interstitial realm between the polite and the plebeian, among shopkeepers, servants, tailors and lawyer's clerks – if only because such types best exemplify the tantalising proximity of ambition and achievement that is the central feature of metropolitan life. 'A real Cockney is the poorest creature in the world,' he insists, 'the most literal, the most mechanical, and yet he too lives in a world of romance – a fairy-land of his own' (p. 84).

Hazlitt had been living in London for many years when he wrote these lines, and was a life-long champion of the people, so it surprised some of his fellow radicals to witness him launching such an attack. The situation was further complicated by the fact that, for six years previously, the Edinburgh-based Tory magazine *Blackwood's* had been waging war on London literary culture, and had repeatedly accused Hazlitt of being an ignorant, vulgar Cockney. There was no doubt in the essayist's mind that these attacks were politically motivated, but that didn't stop him becoming interested in the concept of Cockneyism himself. Throughout his career as a radical journalist, essayist and literary critic, he always considered truth to be plural, the product of a continuing dialectic, and never the sole preserve of any one position or party. 'The mind strikes out truth by collision', he wrote in 'On the Aristocracy of Letters', 'as steel strikes fire from the flint!' (p. 59). He was an oppositional thinker on principle, and in the absence of any external combatant, liked nothing better than to overturn his own convictions, and argue with himself. And it is this, as much as his brilliant use of language, that gives life and form to his essays. They are strongly argued and yet supple, self-questioning without being self-contradictory. They openly exploit the opportunity for free inquiry that is inherent in the genre.

'On Londoners and Country People' is a case in point. Culturally, Hazlitt was contemptuous of Cockney vulgarity, because of its ignorant, levelling tendencies. But in political terms, he approved of it, seeing it as a source of democratic feeling. What distinguishes 'On Londoners' is the skill with which Hazlitt negotiates between these two positions, moving sinuously from the former to the latter via some vivid vignettes of Cockney life. The essay concludes with a return to the abstract style of the opening, but in a significantly different spirit from before. Citing Wordsworth's assertion in *The Excursion* that all city-dwellers are 'shut up in cells of ignorance, without natural affections', Hazlitt offers the most passionate counter to the Lake poet's rural bias:

> In London there is a *public*; and each man is part of it. We are gregarious, and affect the kind. We have a sort of abstract existence; and a community of ideas and knowledge (rather than local proximity) is the bond of society and good fellowship. This is one great cause of the tone of political feeling in large and populous cities. There is here a visible body-politic, a type and

image of that vast Leviathan the State. We comprehend that vast denomination, the *People*, of which we see a tenth part moving daily before us; and by having our imaginations emancipated from petty interests and concerns, we learn to venerate ourselves as men, and to respect the rights of human nature. (p. 94)

Hazlitt offers a character of the ideal citizen of London to set against the rabid anti-metropolitanism of Wordsworth and the Blackwoodsmen, and by using the first person plural, he identifies both himself and his readers with this new urban type. Less overt, but no less significant, is the way he draws on his earlier Cockney caricature, while reinventing many of its terms. Like the Cockney, Hazlitt's ideal Londoner is imaginatively seduced by the metropolis, and takes his identity from the street. But seen from a political perspective, this process of abstraction now looks more virtuous than vulgar, since it promotes a first-hand feeling for the rights of man.

Much of the richness of 'On Londoners and Country People' lies in its tripartite structure, which enables the essay to be in two minds about metropolitan culture without ever seeming indecisive. This powerful ambivalence is a recurrent feature of Hazlitt's London writing, which is characteristically modern in its sense of the city as simultaneously the best and worst place in the world. In the Regency period there was real money to be made as a periodical essayist, and Hazlitt was one of the more successful, but the career of the freelance was still very uncertain, especially when pursued in defiance of the literary establishment. 'There is not a more helpless or more despised animal than a mere author', he wrote in his essay 'On the Aristocracy of Letters', 'without any extrinsic advantages of birth, breeding or fortune to set him off [...] the best wits, like the handsomest faces *upon the town*, lead a harassing, precarious life' (p. 61). Hazlitt was a man of immortal longings, who had spent much of his early youth struggling unsuccessfully to be a painter, but he also had a retiring, scholarly side, which had been heavily indulged during long years of philosophical contemplation in his twenties. When he first began to concentrate on writing reflective essays in the 1820s, he was still full of high ambition, but he did also feel worn down by the incessant Tory attacks upon him, and intermittently doubtful of his chosen genre's lasting value. Hence, like many Londoners before and since, he felt torn between a passionate involvement in the professional life of the capital, and an equally heightened sense of it as a place of inevitable disappointment. This tension that is admirably caught in the superbly unreconciled essay 'On Living to One's Self', which begins with the day-dream of becoming 'a silent spectator of the mighty scene of things' (p. 16) but all too soon finds itself back in the metropolitan market-place, railing energetically against the *Quarterly Review* and that 'mean, stupid, dastardly, pitiful, spiteful, envious, ungrateful animal... the Public' (p. 24).

Even in his oft-professed love of the country, Hazlitt showed himself to be a true Londoner. In 'On Going a Journey', for example, there is a subtle tension between Hazlitt the Shropshire lad, for whom nature is, potentially at least, a place of real significance, a philosophical and moral resting-place, a *home*, and Hazlitt the Cockney holiday-maker, for whom it is only ever a kind of touristic spectacle, a temporary antidote to the city. A true Romantic at heart, Hazlitt was a great admirer of the work of William Wordsworth, whose poetry of solitude and sublime landscape was one of the glories of the age, but he was also, as a periodical essayist, naturally drawn to Steele and Addison's *Tatler* and *Spectator*, and to the Augustan tradition of middle-class politeness and urbanity that they helped bring into being. Hence in his review of *The Excursion* Hazlitt mingles profound admiration for the philosophical depth of Wordsworth's poetry with a deep mistrust for its preoccupation with rural society, arguing famously that 'all country people hate each other' and that if there is anything good to be had in the country 'they will not let you have it' (p. 78). And significantly, in the essay 'Of Persons One Would Wish to Have Seen', an essentially Romantic fascination with the fate of genius in history is both indulged and controlled by its context, a *Spectator*-type group discussion in which social and conversational values take precedence over the claims of individual brilliance.

In Hazlitt the country is ideal but uninhabitable; the city compromised but convivial. The former is associated with the utopian aspirations of the revolutionary decade, as can be seen in 'On Going a Journey' where Hazlitt remembers his youthful pilgrimage to see Wordsworth and Coleridge in Somerset in 1798; the latter with professional disappointments and their consolations, a place where 'life is short, but full of mirth and pastime', to borrow a phrase from 'On Coffee-House Politicians' (p. 45). London is a milieu where it is almost impossible to hang on to distant dreams, but where the very nearness of others has, paradoxically enough, a reconciling effect. In 'On Why Distant Objects Please' Hazlitt argues that while places and things have a more romantic effect when viewed from a distance, people gain from being seen close-up. 'Ignorance alone makes monsters and bugbears,' he writes, 'we can scarcely hate any one that we know' (p. 74).

Certainly, the theory tallies well with Hazlitt's own literary practice. In the middle section of 'On Londoners and Country People' Hazlitt shifts from a satirical critique of Cockneyism to some pen portraits of individual Cockney acquaintances, Dr Goodman, Mr Dunster and Richard Pinch, and the essay becomes softer and more sympathetic as it moves from the abstract to the particular, in a way that prepares the ground perfectly for its final generalising flourish. The essay 'On Coffee-House Politicians' has a similar structure. Hazlitt begins by railing bad-temperedly against the ephemerality and superficiality of London pub conversation, in which 'light and worthless materials float on the surface,' and 'the solid and sterling [...] often sink to the bottom' (p. 41); he then slides slowly, almost involuntarily, into celebrating the sheer friendliness, if not intellectual effervescence, of his old cronies at the Southampton Tavern. And as with 'On Londoners', when the essayist finally returns to the level of abstract argument at the end of the piece, it is in a very different spirit from its opening, one that has benefited enormously from rubbing shoulders with individuals, and has laid itself open to being cheered and consoled. 'I like the country very well', Hazlitt concludes, 'if I want to enjoy my own company: but London is the only place for equal society' (p. 53). Structured as they are, these metropolitan sketches don't merely assert the value of dropping one's *blasé* front and rediscovering a common urbanity, they dramatise the process taking place in the mind of the essayist himself. Moreover, they do so in a way that lets the force of the original critique, whether it be of Cockneys or Coffee-House Politicians, remain as compelling as ever. They are openly dialectical and dialectically open.

One of the best examples of this technique is 'The Indian Jugglers'. This essay begins as a celebration of the theatrical entertainer who can perform his task to a level of mechanical perfection that will never be possible in writing. 'A single error of a hair's-breadth, of the smallest conceivable portion of time, would be fatal', Hazlitt says of the juggler in question: 'the precision of the movements must be like a mathematical truth, their rapidity is like lightning' (p. 1). But in the next section he confesses that however much he might admire performers like Richer the rope dancer at Sadler's Wells, he still has far more respect for an artist such as Sir Joshua Reynolds, 'the latter was but a bungler in his profession to the other, it is true; but then he had a harder task-master to obey' (pp. 5–6). Presently Hazlitt works this up into a distinction between genius – the great power that produces great effects – and mere mechanical talent, that lower species of accomplishment that a rope-dancer, Indian juggler or gentleman fencer might be deemed to possess. It is a very Romantic distinction that has its roots in the aspiration to transcend the physical world and ascend to a timeless realm of immortality: 'No act terminating in itself constitutes greatness', Hazlitt writes, 'This will apply to all displays of power or trials of skill, which are confined to the momentary, individual effort, and construct no permanent trophy of themselves without them' (p. 9).

There is something very satisfying to lovers of high culture in this valorising of intellectual genius – the kind of genius displayed by poets and painters – over and above mere physical excellence, and it is entirely in keeping with the élitist tendency of High Romantic aesthetics. But the really surprising and refreshing thing is that Hazlitt doesn't end the essay there, but dives back suddenly, 'apparently between jest and earnest', into a posthumous celebration of one of the age's great sportsmen, John Cavanagh the fives player. Hazlitt's celebration of Cavanagh is energetic and heart-felt, and calls into question his previous conclusions. A few pages earlier it had seemed clear that sport was incompatible with true greatness, but the example of Cavanagh is so heroic and inspiring that it threatens to overturn this prejudice. Was Cavanagh a genius? One of the best things about 'The Indian Jugglers' is that the essayist does not answer this question directly – but such is the passion with which he eulogises his champion's achievements, that the earlier distinction between genius and talent is fruitfully troubled as a result.

The almost involuntary enthusiasm Hazlitt shows for sport and circus performance in 'The Indian Jugglers' is another example of his complicated attitude to the city; and also it reminds us that, as a place of entertainment, London had never been more spectacular than during the Regency. In addition to exhibitions of Indian juggling and rope-dancing, there was also cricket, riding and boxing, and new 'houses of melodrama' such as the Royal Coburg (now the Old Vic) to challenge the traditional theatres at Covent Garden, Drury Lane and the Haymarket. There were pleasure gardens at Vauxhall and Chelsea; and Barker's Panorama, which was a kind of precursor of the modern cinema, was already firmly established in the north-east corner of Leicester Square. With the construction of Regent Street, Regent's Park, Piccadilly Circus and the Burlington Arcade, the West End streets had never looked more elegant, and Beau Brummell and his fellow Regency dandies took full advantage of its wide, clean pavements. And yet, elsewhere, elements of the old street life of the capital survived. Raree-shows (little box theatres exhibiting freaks and rarities) were still to be seen on Fleet Street and Whitechapel; and strolling players, wrestlers, dwarfs and fire-eaters continued to entertain the throng at Smithfield's notorious Bartholomew Fair.

In Book VII of his autobiographical epic _The Prelude_ Wordsworth expressed a kind of horror at London's theatrical nature, seeing it as a place where 'Folly, vice, / Extravagance in gesture, mien and dress, / And all the strife of singularity' had become universal. And he saw Bartholomew Fair as a perfect symbol of the 'blank confusion' of the metropolis, with everyone caught up in a 'perpetual flow of trivial objects, melted and reduced / To one identity, by differences that have no law, no meaning and no end' (1805 text, lines 572–7, 696–707). In his essay 'On Fashion' Hazlitt took a similar view. 'Fashion', he wrote, 'constantly begins and ends in the two things it abhors most, singularity and vulgarity' (p. 100). Like Wordsworth, he deplored the vain striving after status and identity through dress; unlike him he welcomed the extent to which the Industrial Revolution showed signs of democratising the clothes market: 'the ideas of natural equality and the Manchester steam-engines together have, like a double battery, levelled the high towers and artificial structures of fashion in dress, and a white muslin gown is now the common costume of the mistress and the maid' (p. 103). So, too, in his essay 'On Footmen', Hazlitt scoffed at the pride of liveried servants, a pride entirely based on the flaunting of manners and fine clothes that had been borrowed from their masters. Footmen were perfect symbols of the aristocratic spirit in metropolitan society in that their status, their very being, was based on imitation, and Hazlitt could not help but see them as self-complacent dupes, Cockneys without the virtue, as it were. Hazlitt's grudging admiration for Beau Brummell is no contradiction to this position, for as is clear from the short piece 'Brummelliana', he saw the famous dandy as a secret enemy of the aristocracy. What Brummell demonstrated, through his extraordinary wit and cheek, was the fact that social superiority was all about style and not substance, and that anyone – even a commoner like himself – could perform it.

Both Wordsworth and Hazlitt were preoccupied with the role of the imagination, in life and in art. Wordsworth considered London as an imaginative lure, a set of delusive representations, a place of intoxication and disenchantment, and was only too ready to swap its shifting phantasmagoria for the stability and beauty of the mountains. Hazlitt saw the superficiality and shiftingness of the city too, but did not deplore it, considering the metropolis to be the perfect place to contemplate the imagination and its limits. Many of Hazlitt's most enjoyable essays reflect upon this theme. Drawn from the essayist's own personal experience, 'On the Want of Money' is a very droll, dreamy account of what it's like to be cash-poor in the metropolis and it shows imagination prevailing – temporarily at least – over adverse circumstances. It also uses a wealth of delightful, digressive anecdotes to demonstrate how such circumstances might in themselves act as spurs to the fancy, while finally being forced to acknowledge that real poverty is no joke at all. So, too, in his late essay 'The Sick-Chamber' there is a wonderful exploration of the power and weakness of the mind – its utter debility in the face of physical illness, and its triumphant forgetfulness on recovery. 'No sooner does our disorder turn its back upon us,' Hazlitt writes, 'than we laugh at it. The state we have been in, sounds like a dream, a fable.' Strikingly, given his poor health at the time, Hazlitt shows the imagination to be an all-conquering faculty, if only to itself.

One of Hazlitt's most characteristic pieces on the role of imagination and memory is 'The Letter-Bell', the last essay he ever wrote. In Wordsworth mountains and daffodils, rural ruins and inscriptions left on yew trees are typical inducements to retrospection. The letter-bell is very man-made and mechanical in comparison, and yet it fulfils exactly the same function in Hazlitt's mind: 'it has a lively, pleasant sound with it,' he writes, 'and not only fills the street with its importunate clamour, but rings clear through the length of many half-forgotten years' (pp. 177–8). Its tinkling sound reminds him of the road from Wem to Shrewsbury, by which he first set out on his journey through life; it brings back memories of the revolutionary decade, and of the time immediately preceding his first acquaintance with Wordsworth and Coleridge. 'At this time the light of the French Revolution circled my head like a glory', he says, 'though dabbled with drops of crimson gore' (p. 178). Going further, the letter-bell also reminds him that, in spite of all that these two poets have had to say about the swarming restlessness of city dwellers, he himself has remained far more politically consistent than they. 'This is the reason I can write an article on the *Letter-Bell'*, he explains, 'and other such subjects; I have never given the lie to my own soul. If I have felt any impression once, I feel it more strongly a second time; and I have no wish to revile or discard my best thoughts' (p. 179). The letter-bell chimes the present with the past, but it also serves as a link between the town and the country, prompting Hazlitt into fond recollections of seeing the mail-coaches pouring out of West London of an evening, and of reading the marvellous description of the rural post-boy in Cowper. Taking its cue from the letter-bell itself, Hazlitt's essay is a powerful 'conductor of the imagination', with an associative reach that spreads in all directions, from Wem to ancient Greece via Wordsworth, Coleridge, Piccadilly coach-station, the French Revolution of 1830 and 1780s pastoral.

Like many of Hazlitt's more reflective essays, 'The Letter-Bell' is full of allusions to Wordsworth's 'Tintern Abbey', and, more especially, to his celebrated ode 'On Intimations of Immortality', one of the greatest poems on imagination and memory in the English language. This ode was a favourite work of Hazlitt's: his writings are littered with references to it, so much so, indeed, that it functions as a kind of *leitmotif* in his work. There are two main reasons for this. One is that the poem's description of youthful optimism slowly giving way to disenchantment was a perfect summing up of how Hazlitt felt about his own life; another is that he saw it as providing a kind of philosophical allegory of the failure of the French Revolution. The narrative of Wordsworth's poem is essentially the narrative of life itself, offering what is, at one and the same time, a universal description of every child's development from infancy to adulthood, and a very personal account of the poet's own journey from visionary idealism to reflective maturity. The story it tells is essentially entropic, even tragic. When we are born we are in a very real sense part of nature's immortal oneness, the poet says, but we gradually grow out of this paradisal state as we become aware of our own mortality:

The Youth, who daily farther from the east
Must travel, still is Nature's priest,
And by the vision splendid
Is on his way attended;
At length the Man perceives it die away
And fade into the light of common day. (ll. 71–6)

Our only consolation, Wordsworth says, is in our common humanity, and in the dim recollections we may continue to entertain of our glorious, visionary past.

In his essay 'On the Feeling of Immortality in Youth' Hazlitt rewrites Wordsworth's Ode in his own deeply metropolitan, although no less Romantic, terms, just as he had in a sense rewritten the latter's 'Tintern Abbey' in his earlier piece 'On Going a Journey'. It is a beautiful piece of prose, and a fitting complement to Wordsworth's famous work. Commencing with the assertion that 'no young man believes he shall ever die' Hazlitt's narrative of life follows the same entropic trajectory as Wordsworth's, blazing with visionary energy at the beginning, and then slowly dwindling down into disappointment and retrospection. The difference is that, whereas for Wordsworth there is a real and objective bond between man and nature, which time might splinter but never completely sever, for Hazlitt that early sense we have of being at home in the universe is only ever a kind of delusion, albeit an enchanting one:

> Our first and strongest impressions are taken from the mighty scene that is opened to us, and we very innocently transfer its durability as well as its magnificence to ourselves. Like a rustic at a fair, we are full of amazement and rapture, and have no thoughts of going home, or that it will soon be night […] We do not go from a play till the scene is ended, and the lights are ready to be extinguished. But the fair face of nature still shines on; shall we be called away, before the curtain falls, or ere we have scarce had a glimpse of what is going on? Like children, our step-mother Nature holds us up to see the raree-show of the universe; and then, as if life were a burthen to support, lets us instantly down again. Yet in that short interval, what 'brave sublunary things' does not the spectacle unfold; like a bubble, at one minute reflecting the universe, and the next, shook to air! (pp. 123–4)

This is a passage about life, not London, but metropolitan metaphors are woven through it. In *The Prelude* Wordsworth had seen Bartholomew Fair as a symbol of all that was most artificial and alienating about the city; but for Hazlitt the image of a naïve rustic wandering awe-struck among the booths at Smithfield is a poignant image of both the festivity and the fragility of our all-too-brief dream of life. Life promises to be a long-running performance, he suggests, and yet it is more like an afternoon matinée. Most striking of all is the image of 'our step-mother Nature' temporarily holding us up to see the 'raree-show' of the universe (supplying the step, as it were, and then taking it away again), so that all we catch is a quick glimpse of the wonders on display. 'To have it all snatched from one,' Hazlitt complains, 'like a juggler's ball or a phantasmagoria; there is something revolting and incredible to sense in the transition, and no wonder that, aided by youth and warm blood, and the flush of enthusiasm, the mind contrives for a long time to reject it with disdain and loathing as a monstrous and improbable fiction' (pp. 125–6).

By describing the progress of life in terms of a metropolitan dynamic of intoxication and disenchantment, Hazlitt does two things. He extracts a certain wry comedy out of the otherwise poignant drama of disappointed expectations, a comedy that recalls the absurd gap between the Cockney's unbounded imaginings and his cribbed and confined setting. But he also emphasises the shared nature of this predicament, the fact that, however separately and subjectively we might experience this narrowing of our prospects, the experience itself is a common one, and 'appears like a fable'.

From this perspective, life takes on the quality of a shifting panorama or phantasmagoria; it is beaten to a thinness, and becomes mere representation: 'it is only as the pageant of life passes by and the masques turn their backs upon us,' Hazlitt says, 'that we see through the deception, or believe that the train will have an end' (pp. 128–9). And this is precisely what renders the metropolis such a perfect place to contemplate existence, with its richly theatrical sense of life balanced by its innate sociality. The point is made most forcibly in another late essay, 'The Free Admission', in which Hazlitt engages in an extended meditation on the theatre as 'a discipline of humanity' (pp. 165–6).

No, a play is nothing without an audience, it is a satisfaction too great and too general not to be shared with others [...] let the eager crowd beset the theatre-doors 'like bees in spring-time, when the sun with Taurus rides' – let the boxes be filled with innocence and beauty like beds of lilies on the first night of *Isabella* or *Belvidera*, see the flutter, the uneasy delight of expectation, see the big tear roll down the cheek of sensibility as the story proceeds – let us listen to the deep thunder of the pit, or catch the gallery's shout at some true master-stroke of passion; and we feel that a thousand hearts are beating in our bosoms, and hail the sparkling illusion reflected in a thousand eyes.

A Note on the Text

This text is based on *The Complete Works of William Hazlitt*, 21 vols, edited by P.P. Howe (London: Dent, 1930–4).

Responding to constraints of space, and also in order to preserve a clean, readable text, I have restricted myself to supplying endnotes only in cases when further information seemed necessary to support the meaning of a particular passage, or, in the case of Hazlitt's frequent allusions to other literary works, when the reference itelf seemed significant and worthy of note. Only the endnotes in this edition have been supplied by the editor; the footnotes, which are marked throughout by an asterisk, are Hazlitt's own.

Of the essays collected here, only a few are currently available in paperback. However, many of them are to be found in Duncan Wu's *Selected Writings* (London: Pickering and Chatto, 1998), and all of them in Howe's complete edition.

Gregory Dart
University College London

The Indian Jugglers

Having given up his early ambition to be a painter, Hazlitt was best known in the 1810s as a political journalist, a theatre critic, and a public lecturer on literature. But from 1820 he began increasingly to concentrate on writing original essays. This splendidly double-handed piece on mechanical skill, art and sport is taken from the first volume of *Table-Talk* (London: John Warren, 1821). The Indian Jugglers of the title had appeared at the Olympic New Theatre, Newcastle Street, the Strand, in 1815, and were one of the highlights of the winter season. The concluding obituary of Cavanagh the fives player, 'written apparently between jest and earnest', is, of course, by Hazlitt himself.

Coming forward and seating himself on the ground in his white dress and tightened turban, the chief of the Indian Jugglers begins with tossing up two brass balls, which is what any of us could do, and concludes with keeping up four at the same time, which is what none of us could do to save our lives, nor if we were to take our whole lives to do it in. Is it then a trifling power we see at work, or is it not something next to miraculous? It is the utmost stretch of human ingenuity, which nothing but the bending the faculties of body and mind to it from the tenderest infancy with incessant, ever-anxious application up to manhood, can accomplish or make even a slight approach to. Man, thou art a wonderful animal, and thy ways past finding out! Thou canst do strange things, but thou turnest them to little account! – To conceive of this effort of extraordinary dexterity distracts the imagination and makes admiration breathless. Yet it costs nothing to the performer, any more than if it were a mere mechanical deception with which he had nothing to do but to watch and laugh at the astonishment of the spectators. A single error of a hair's-breadth, of the smallest conceivable portion of time, would be fatal: the precision of the movements must be like a mathematical truth, their rapidity is like lightning. To catch four balls in succession in less than a second of time, and deliver them back so as to return with seeming consciousness to the hand again, to make them revolve round him at certain intervals, like the planets in their spheres, to make them chase one another like sparkles of fire, or shoot up like flowers or meteors, to throw them behind his back and twine them round his neck like ribbons or like serpents, to do what appears an impossibility, and to do it with all the ease, the grace, the carelessness imaginable, to laugh at, to play with the glittering mockeries, to follow them with his eye as if he could fascinate them with its lambent fire, or as if he had only to see that they kept time with the music on the stage – there is something in all this which he who does not admire may be quite sure he never really admired any thing in the whole course of his life. It is skill surmounting difficulty, and beauty triumphing over skill. It seems as if the difficulty once mastered naturally resolved itself into ease and grace, and as if to be overcome at all, it must be overcome without an effort. The smallest awkwardness or want of pliancy or self-possession would stop the whole process. It is the work of witchcraft, and yet sport for children. Some of the other feats are quite as curious and wonderful, such as the balancing the artificial tree and shooting a bird from each branch through a quill; though none of them have the elegance or facility of the keeping up of the brass balls. You are in pain for the result, and glad when the experiment is over; they are not accompanied with the same unmixed, unchecked delight as the former; and I would not give much to be merely astonished without being pleased at the same time. As to the swallowing of the sword, the police ought to interfere to prevent it. When I saw the Indian Juggler do the same things before, his feet were bare, and he had large rings on the toes, which kept turning round all the time of the performance, as if they moved of themselves. – The hearing a speech in Parliament, drawled or stammered out by the Honourable Member or the Noble Lord, the ringing the changes on their common-places, which any one could repeat after them as well as they, stirs me not a jot, shakes not my good opinion of myself: but the seeing the Indian Jugglers does. It makes me ashamed of myself. I ask what there is that I can do as well as this? Nothing. What have I been doing all my life? Have I been idle, or have I nothing to shew for all my labour and pains? Or have I passed my time in pouring words like water into empty sieves, rolling a stone up a hill and then down again, trying to prove an argument in the teeth of facts, and looking for causes in the dark, and not finding them? Is there no one thing in which I can challenge competition, that I can bring as an instance of exact perfection, in which others cannot find a flaw? The utmost I can pretend to is to write a description of what this fellow can do. I can write a book: so can many others who have not even learned to spell. What abortions are these Essays! What errors, what ill-pieced transitions, what crooked reasons, what lame conclusions! How little is made out, and that little how ill! Yet they are the best I can do. I endeavour to recollect all I have ever observed or thought upon a subject, and to express it as nearly as I can. Instead of writing on four subjects at a time, it is as much as I can manage to keep the thread of one discourse clear and unentangled. I have also time on my hands to correct my opinions, and polish my periods: but the one I cannot, and the other I will not do. I am fond of arguing: yet with a good deal of pains and practice it is often as much as I can do to beat my man; though he may be a very indifferent hand. A common fencer would disarm his adversary in the twinkling of an eye, unless he were a professor like himself. A stroke of wit will sometimes produce this effect, but there is no such power or superiority in sense or reasoning. There is no complete mastery of execution to be shown there: and you hardly know the professor from the impudent pretender or the mere clown.*

I have always had this feeling of the inefficacy and slow progress of intellectual compared to mechanical excellence, and it has always made me somewhat dissatisfied. It is a great many years since I saw Richer, the famous rope-dancer, perform at Sadler's Wells. He was matchless in his art, and added to his extraordinary skill exquisite ease, and unaffected natural grace. I was at that time employed in copying a half-length picture of Sir Joshua Reynolds's; and it put me out of conceit with it. How ill this part was made out in the drawing! How heavy, how slovenly this other

---

* The celebrated Peter Pindar (Dr Wolcot) first discovered and brought out the talents of the late Mr Opie, the painter. He was a poor Cornish boy, and was out at work in the fields, when the poet went in search of him. 'Well, my lad, can you go and bring me your very best picture?' The other flew like lightning, and soon came back with what he considered as his master-piece. The stranger looked at it, and the young artist, after waiting for some time without his giving any opinion, at length exclaimed eagerly, 'Well, what do you think of it?' – 'Think of it?' said Wolcot, 'why I think you ought to be ashamed of it – that you who might do so well, do no better!' The same answer would have applied to this artist's latest performances, that had been suggested by one of his earliest efforts.

was painted! I could not help saying to myself, 'If the rope-dancer had performed his task in this manner, leaving so many gaps and botches in his work, he would have broke his neck long ago; I should never have seen that vigorous elasticity of nerve and precision of movement!' – Is it then so easy an undertaking (comparatively) to dance on a tight-rope? Let any one, who thinks so, get up and try. There is the thing. It is that which at first we cannot do at all, which in the end is done to such perfection. To account for this in some degree, I might observe that mechanical dexterity is confined to doing some one particular thing, which you can repeat as often as you please, in which you know whether you succeed or fail, and where the point of perfection consists in succeeding in a given undertaking. – In mechanical efforts, you improve by perpetual practice, and you do so infallibly, because the object to be attained is not a matter of taste or fancy or opinion, but of actual experiment, in which you must either do the thing or not do it. If a man is put to aim at a mark with a bow and arrow, he must hit it or miss it, that's certain. He cannot deceive himself, and go on shooting wide or falling short, and still fancy that he is making progress. The distinction between right and wrong, between true and false, is here palpable; and he must either correct his aim or persevere in his error with his eyes open, for which there is neither excuse nor temptation. If a man is learning to dance on a rope, if he does not mind what he is about, he will break his neck. After that, it will be in vain for him to argue that he did not make a false step. His situation is not like that of Goldsmith's pedagogue –

> In argument they own'd his wondrous skill,
> And e'en though vanquish'd, he could argue still.[1]

Danger is a good teacher, and makes apt scholars. So are disgrace, defeat, exposure to immediate scorn and laughter. There is no opportunity in such cases for self-delusion, no idling time away, no being off your guard (or you must take the consequences) – neither is there any room for humour or caprice or prejudice. If the Indian Juggler were to play tricks in throwing up the three case-knives, which keep their positions like the leaves of a crocus in the air, he would cut his fingers. I can make a very bad antithesis without cutting my fingers. The tact of style is more ambiguous than that of double-edged instruments. If the Juggler were told that by flinging himself under the wheels of the Jaggernaut,[2] when the idol issues forth on a gaudy day, he would immediately be transported into Paradise, he might believe it, and nobody could disprove it. So the Brahmins may say what they please on that subject, may build up dogmas and mysteries without end, and not be detected: but their ingenious countryman cannot persuade the frequenters of the Olympic Theatre that he performs a number of astonishing feats without actually giving proofs of what he says. – There is then in this sort of manual dexterity, first a gradual aptitude acquired to a given exertion of muscular power, from constant repetition, and in the next place, an exact knowledge how much is still wanting and necessary to be supplied. The obvious test is to increase the effort or nicety of the operation, and still to find it come true. The muscles ply instinctively to the dictates of habit. Certain movements and impressions of the hand and eye, having been repeated together an infinite number of times, are unconsciously but unavoidably cemented into closer and closer union; the limbs require little more than to be put in motion for them to follow a regular track with ease and certainty; so that the mere intention of the will acts mathematically, like touching the spring of a machine, and you come with Locksley in Ivanhoe, in shooting at a mark, 'to allow for the wind'.

Farther, what is meant by perfection in mechanical exercises is the performing certain feats to a uniform nicety, that is, in fact, undertaking no more than you can perform. You task yourself, the limit you fix is optional, and no more than human industry and skill can attain to: but you have no abstract, independent standard of difficulty or excellence (other than the extent of your own powers). Thus he who can keep up four brass balls does this *to perfection*; but he cannot keep up five at the same instant, and would fail every time he attempted it. That is, the mechanical performer undertakes to emulate himself, not to equal another.* But the artist undertakes to imitate another, or to do what nature has done, and this it appears is more difficult, *viz.* to copy what she has set before us in the face of nature or 'human face divine,' entire and without a blemish, than to keep up four brass balls at the same instant; for the one is done by the power of human skill and industry, and the other never was nor will be. Upon the whole, therefore, I have more respect for Reynolds, than I have for Richer: for, happen how it will, there have been more people in the world who could dance on a rope like the one than who could paint like Sir Joshua. The latter

* If two persons play against each other at any game, one of them necessarily fails.

was but a bungler in his profession to the other, it is true; but then he had a harder task-master to obey, whose will was more wayward and obscure, and whose instructions it was more difficult to practise. You can put a child apprentice to a tumbler or rope-dancer with a comfortable prospect of success, if they are but sound of wind and limb: but you cannot do the same thing in painting. The odds are a million to one. You may make indeed as many H[ayman]s and H[ighmore]s, as you put into that sort of machine, but not one Reynolds amongst them all, with his grace, his grandeur, his blandness of *gusto*, 'in tones and gestures hit', unless you could make the man over again. To snatch this grace beyond the reach of art is then the height of art – where fine art begins, and where mechanical skill ends. The soft suffusion of the soul, the speechless breathing eloquence, the looks 'commercing with the skies,' the ever-shifting forms of an eternal principle, that which is seen but for a moment, but dwells in the heart always, and is only seized as it passes by strong and secret sympathy, must be taught by nature and genius, not by rules or study. It is suggested by feeling, not by laborious microscopic inspection: in seeking for it without, we lose the harmonious clue to it within: and in aiming to grasp the substance, we let the very spirit of art evaporate. In a word, the objects of fine art are not the objects of sight but as these last are the objects of taste and imagination, that is, as they appeal to the sense of beauty, of pleasure, and of power in the human breast, and are explained by that finer sense, and revealed in their inner structure to the eye in return. Nature is also a language. Objects, like words, have a meaning; and the true artist is the interpreter of this language, which he can only do by knowing its application to a thousand other objects in a thousand other situations. Thus the eye is too blind a guide of itself to distinguish between the warm or cold tone of a deep blue sky, but another sense acts as a monitor to it, and does not err. The colour of the leaves in autumn would be nothing without the feeling that accompanies it; but it is that feeling that stamps them on the canvas, faded, seared, blighted, shrinking from the winter's flaw, and makes the sight as true as touch –

> And visions, as poetic eyes avow,
> Cling to each leaf and hang on every bough.[3]

The more ethereal, evanescent, more refined and sublime part of art is the seeing nature through the medium of sentiment and passion, as each object is a symbol of the affections and a link in the chain of our endless being. But the unravelling this mysterious web of thought and feeling is alone in the Muse's gift, namely, in the power of that trembling sensibility which is awake to every change and every modification of its ever-varying impressions, that,

Thrills in each nerve, and lives along the line.

This power is indifferently called genius, imagination, feeling, taste; but the manner in which it acts upon the mind can neither be defined by abstract rules, as is the case in science, nor verified by continual unvarying experiments, as is the case in mechanical performances. The mechanical excellence of the Dutch painters in colouring and handling is that which comes the nearest in fine art to the perfection of certain manual exhibitions of skill. The truth of the effect and the facility with which it is produced are equally admirable. Up to a certain point, every thing is faultless. The hand and eye have done their part. There is only a want of taste and genius. It is after we enter upon that enchanted ground that the human mind begins to droop and flag as in a strange road, or in a thick mist, benighted and making little way with many attempts and many failures, and that the best of us only escape with half a triumph. The undefined and the imaginary are the regions that we must pass like Satan, difficult and doubtful, 'half flying, half on foot'.[4] The object in sense is a positive thing, and execution comes with practice.

Cleverness is a certain *knack* or aptitude at doing certain things, which depend more on a particular adroitness and off-hand readiness than on force or perseverance, such as making puns, making epigrams, making extempore verses, mimicking the company, mimicking a style, &c. Cleverness is either liveliness and smartness, or something answering to *sleight of hand*, like letting a glass fall sideways off a table, or else a trick, like knowing the secret spring of a watch. Accomplishments are certain external graces, which are to be learnt from others, and which are easily displayed to the admiration of the beholder, *viz.* dancing, riding, fencing, music, and so on. These ornamental acquirements are only proper to those who are at ease in mind and fortune. I know an individual[5] who if he had been born to an estate of five thousand a year, would have been the most accomplished gentleman of the age. He would have been the delight and envy of the circle in which he moved –

would have graced by his manners the liberality flowing from the openness of his heart, would have laughed with the women, have argued with the men, have said good things and written agreeable ones, have taken a hand at piquet or the lead at the harpsichord, and have set and sung his own verses – *nugæ canoræ* – with tenderness and spirit; a Rochester without the vice, a modern Surrey! As it is, all these capabilities of excellence stand in his way. He is too versatile for a professional man, not dull enough for a political drudge, too gay to be happy, too thoughtless to be rich. He wants the enthusiasm of the poet, the severity of the prose-writer, and the application of the man of business. – Talent is the capacity of doing any thing that depends on application and industry, such as writing a criticism, making a speech, studying the law. Talent differs from genius, as voluntary differs from involuntary power. Ingenuity is genius in trifles, greatness is genius in undertakings of much pith and moment. A clever or ingenious man is one who can do any thing well, whether it is worth doing or not: a great man is one who can do that which when done is of the highest importance. Themistocles said he could not play on the flute, but that he could make of a small city a great one. This gives one a pretty good idea of the distinction in question.

Greatness is great power, producing great effects. It is not enough that a man has great power in himself, he must shew it to all the world in a way that cannot be hid or gainsaid. He must fill up a certain idea in the public mind. I have no other notion of greatness than this two-fold definition, great results springing from great inherent energy. The great in visible objects has relation to that which extends over space: the great in mental ones has to do with space and time. No man is truly great, who is great only in his life-time. The test of greatness is the page of history. Nothing can be said to be great that has a distinct limit, or that borders on something evidently greater than itself. Besides, what is short-lived and pampered into mere notoriety, is of a gross and vulgar quality in itself. A Lord Mayor is hardly a great man. A city orator or patriot of the day only shew, by reaching the height of their wishes, the distance they are at from any true ambition. Popularity is neither fame nor greatness. A king (as such) is not a great man. He has great power, but it is not his own. He merely wields the lever of the state, which a child, an idiot, or a madman can do. It is the office, not the man we gaze at. Any one else in the same situation would be just as much an object of abject curiosity. We laugh at the country girl who having seen a king expressed her disappointment by saying, 'Why, he is only a man!' Yet, knowing this, we run to see a king as if he was something more than a man. – To display the greatest powers, unless they are applied to great purposes, makes nothing for the character of greatness. To throw a barley-corn through the eye of a needle, to multiply nine figures by nine in the memory, argues infinite dexterity of body and capacity of mind, but nothing comes of either. There is a surprising power at work, but the effects are not proportionate, or such as take hold of the imagination. To impress the idea of power on others, they must be made in some way to feel it. It must be communicated to their understandings in the shape of an increase of knowledge, or it must subdue and overawe them by subjecting their wills. Admiration, to be solid and lasting, must be founded on proofs from which we have no means of escaping; it is neither a slight nor a voluntary gift. A mathematician who solves a profound problem, a poet who creates an image of beauty in the mind that was not there before, imparts knowledge and power to others, in which his greatness and his fame consists, and on which it reposes. Jedediah Buxton will be forgotten; but Napier's bones will live.[6] Lawgivers, philosophers, founders of religion, conquerors and heroes, inventors and great geniuses in arts and sciences, are great men; for they are great public benefactors, or formidable scourges to mankind. Among ourselves, Shakespear, Newton, Bacon, Milton, Cromwell, were great men; for they shewed great power by acts and thoughts, which have not yet been consigned to oblivion. They must needs be men of lofty stature, whose shadows lengthen out to remote posterity. A great farce-writer may be a great man; for Molière was but a great farce-writer. In my mind, the author of *Don Quixote* was a great man. So have there been many others. A great chess-player is not a great man, for he leaves the world as he found it. No act terminating in itself constitutes greatness. This will apply to all displays of power or trials of skill, which are confined to the momentary, individual effort, and construct no permanent image or trophy of themselves without them. Is not an actor then a great man, because 'he dies and leaves the world no copy'? I must make an exception for Mrs Siddons, or else give up my definition of greatness for her sake.[7] A man at the top of his profession is not therefore a great man. He is great in his way, but that is all, unless he shews the marks of a great moving intellect, so that we trace the master-mind, and can sympathise with the springs that urge him

on. The rest is but a craft or *mystery*. John Hunter was a great man
– *that* any one might see without the smallest skill in surgery. His
style and manner shewed the man. He would set about cutting up
the carcase of a whale with the same greatness of *gusto* that Michael
Angelo would have hewn a block of marble. Lord Nelson was a
great naval commander; but for myself, I have not much opinion
of a sea-faring life. Sir Humphry Davy is a great chemist, but I am
not sure that he is a great man. I am not a bit the wiser for any of
his discoveries, nor I never met with any one that was. But it is in
the nature of greatness to propagate an idea of itself, as wave
impels wave, circle without circle. It is a contradiction in terms for
a coxcomb to be a great man. A really great man has always an idea
of something greater than himself. I have observed that certain
sectaries and polemical writers have no higher compliment to pay
their most shining lights than to say that 'Such a one was a
considerable man in his day.' Some new elucidation of a text sets
aside the authority of the old interpretation, and a 'great scholar's
memory outlives him half a century', at the utmost. A rich man is
not a great man, except to his dependents and his steward. A lord
is a great man in the idea we have of his ancestry, and probably of
himself, if we know nothing of him but his title. I have heard a story
of two bishops, one of whom said (speaking of St Peter's at Rome)
that when he first entered it, he was rather awe-struck, but that as
he walked up it, his mind seemed to swell and dilate with it, and
at last to fill the whole building – the other said that as he saw more
of it, he appeared to himself to grow less and less every step he
took, and in the end to dwindle into nothing. This was in some
respects a striking picture of a great and little mind – for greatness
sympathises with greatness, and littleness shrinks into itself. The
one might have become a Wolsey; the other was only fit to become
a Mendicant Friar – or there might have been court-reasons for
making him a bishop. The French have to me a character of
littleness in all about them; but they have produced three great men
that belong to every country, Molière, Rabelais, and Montaigne.

To return from this digression, and conclude the Essay. A
singular instance of manual dexterity was strewn in the person of
the late John Cavanagh, whom I have several times seen. His death
was celebrated at the time in an article in the *Examiner* newspaper
(Feb. 7, 1819), written apparently between jest and earnest: but as
it is *pat* to our purpose, and falls in with my own way of considering
such subjects, I shall here take leave to quote it.

'Died at his house in Burbage-street, St Giles's, John Cavanagh, the famous hand fives-player.[8] When a person dies, who does any one thing better than any one else in the world, which so many others are trying to do well, it leaves a gap in society. It is not likely that any one will now see the game of fives played in its perfection for many years to come – for Cavanagh is dead, and has not left his peer behind him. It may be said that there are things of more importance than striking a ball against a wall – there are things indeed which make more noise and do as little good, such as making war and peace, making speeches and answering them, making verses and blotting them; making money and throwing it away. But the game of fives is what no one despises who has ever played at it. It is the finest exercise for the body, and the best relaxation for the mind. The Roman poet said that "Care mounted behind the horseman and stuck to his skirts." But this remark would not have applied to the fives-player. He who takes to playing at fives is twice young. He feels neither the past nor future "in the instant". Debts, taxes, "domestic treason, foreign levy, nothing can touch him further". He has no other wish, no other thought, from the moment the game begins, but that of striking the ball, of placing it, of *making* it! This Cavanagh was sure to do. Whenever he touched the ball, there was an end of the chase. His eye was certain, his hand fatal, his presence of mind complete. He could do what he pleased, and he always knew exactly what to do. He saw the whole game, and played it; took instant advantage of his adversary's weakness, and recovered balls, as if by a miracle and from sudden thought, that every one gave for lost. He had equal power and skill, quickness, and judgment. He could either out-wit his antagonist by finesse, or beat him by main strength. Sometimes, when he seemed preparing to send the ball with the full swing of his arm, he would by a slight turn of his wrist drop it within an inch of the line. In general, the ball came from his hand, as if from a racket, in a straight horizontal line; so that it was in vain to attempt to overtake or stop it. As it was said of a great orator that he never was at a loss for a word, and for the properest word, so Cavanagh always could tell the degree of force necessary to be given to a ball, and the precise direction in which it should be sent. He did his work with the greatest ease; never took more pains than was necessary; and while others were fagging themselves to death, was as cool and collected as if he had just entered the court. His style of play was as remarkable as his power of execution. He had no affectation, no trifling. He did not throw away the game to show off an attitude, or try an experiment. He was a fine, sensible, manly player, who did what he could, but that was more than any one else could even affect to do. His blows were not undecided and ineffectual – lumbering like Mr Wordsworth's epic poetry, nor wavering like Mr Coleridge's lyric prose, nor short of the mark like Mr Brougham's speeches, nor wide of it like Mr Canning's wit, nor foul like the *Quarterly*, not *let* balls like the *Edinburgh Review*.[9] Cobbett and Junius together would have made a Cavanagh. He was the best *up-hill* player in the world; even when his adversary was fourteen, he would play on the same or better, and as he never flung away the game through carelessness and conceit, he never gave it up through laziness or want of heart. The only peculiarity of his play was that he never *volleyed*, but let the balls hop; but if they rose an inch from the ground, he never missed having them. There was not only nobody equal, but nobody second to him. It is supposed that he could give any other player half the game, or beat him with his left hand. His service was tremendous. He once played Woodward and Meredith together (two of the best players in England) in the Fives-court, St Martin's-street, and made seven and twenty aces following by services alone – a thing unheard of. He another time played Peru, who was considered a first-rate fives-player, a match of the best out of five games, and in the three first games, which of course decided the match, Peru got only one ace. Cavanagh was an Irishman by birth, and a house-painter by profession. He had once laid aside his working-dress, and walked up, in his smartest clothes, to the Rosemary Branch to have an afternoon's pleasure. A person accosted him, and asked him if he would have a game. So they agreed to play for half-a-crown a game, and a bottle of cider. The first game began – it was seven, eight, ten, thirteen, fourteen, all. Cavanagh won it. The next was the same. They played on, and each game was hardly contested. "There," said the unconscious fives-player, "there was a stroke that Cavanagh could not take: I never played better in my life, and yet I can't win a game. I don't know how it is." However, they played on, Cavanagh winning every game, and the by-standers drinking the cider, and laughing all the time. In the twelfth game, when Cavanagh was only four, and the stranger thirteen, a person came in, and said, "What! are you here, Cavanagh?" The words were no sooner pronounced than the astonished player let the ball drop from his hand, and saying, "What! have I been breaking my heart all this time to beat Cavanagh?" refused to make another effort. "And yet, I give you my word," said Cavanagh, telling the story with some triumph, "I played all the while with my clenched fist." – He used frequently to play matches at Copenhagen-house for wagers and dinners. The wall against which they play is the same that supports the kitchen-chimney, and when the wall resounded louder than usual, the cooks exclaimed, "Those are the Irishman's balls," and the joints trembled on the spit! – Goldsmith consoled himself that there were places where he too was admired: and Cavanagh was the admiration of all the fives-courts, where he ever played. Mr Powell, when he played matches in the Court in St Martin's-street, used to fill his gallery at half a crown a head, with amateurs and admirers of talent in whatever department it is shown. He could not have shown himself in any ground in England, but he would have been immediately surrounded with inquisitive gazers, trying to find out in what part of his frame his unrivalled skill lay, as politicians wonder to see the balance of Europe suspended in Lord Castlereagh's face, and admire the trophies of the British Navy lurking under Mr Croker's hanging brow.[10] Now Cavanagh was as good-looking a man as the Noble Lord, and much better looking than the Right Hon. Secretary. He had a clear, open countenance, and did not look sideways or down, like Mr Murray the bookseller. He was a young fellow of sense, humour, and courage. He once had a quarrel with a waterman at Hungerford-stairs, and, they say, served him out in great style. In a word, there are hundreds at this day, who cannot mention his name without admiration, as the best fives player that perhaps ever lived (the greatest excellence of which they have any notion) – and the noisy shout of the ring happily stood him in stead of the unheard voice of posterity! – The only person who seems to have excelled as much in another way as Cavanagh did in his, was the late John Davies, the racket-player. It was remarked of him that he did not seem to follow the ball, but the ball seemed to follow him. Give him a foot of wall, and he was sure to make the ball. The four best racket-players of that day were Jack Spines, Jem Harding, Armitage, and Church. Davies could give any one of these two hands a time, that is, half the game, and each of these, at their best, could give the best player now in London the same odds. Such are the gradations in all exertions of human skill and art. He once played four capital players together, and beat them. He was also a first-rate tennis-player, and an excellent fives-player. In the Fleet or King's Bench, he would have stood against Powell, who was reckoned the best open-ground player of his time.[11] This last-mentioned player is at present the keeper of the Fives-court, and we might recommend to him for a motto over his door – "Who enters here, forgets himself, his country, and his friends." And the best of it is, that by the calculation of the odds, none of the three are worth remembering! – Cavanagh died from the bursting of a blood-vessel, which prevented him from playing for the last two or three years. This, he was often heard to say, he thought hard upon him. He was fast recovering, however, when he was suddenly carried off, to the regret of all who knew him. As Mr Peel made it a qualification of the present Speaker, Mr Manners Sutton, that he was an excellent moral character, so Jack Cavanagh was a zealous Catholic, and could not be persuaded to eat meat on a Friday, the day on which he died. We have paid this willing tribute to his memory.

> Let no rude hand deface it,
> And his forlorn "*Hic Jacet*"[12]

On Living to One's-Self*

From the first volume of *Table-Talk* (1821). Winterslow Hut was a cottage owned by Hazlitt's estranged wife Sarah in the remote village of Winterslow, near Salisbury. The essayist used to resort to it on a regular basis during the 1820s, as a place to write, paint and go walking. 'On Living to One's Self' comes at the beginning of a highly creative period for Hazlitt, but his morale was at a very low ebb when he was penning it. He was angry with his enemies in the Tory press for having all but destroyed his literary reputation, and he was angry with his friends, most notably Hunt and Lamb, for their lack of public support. He was also conscious of the failure of his marriage, which had resulted in separation the year before. In 'On Living to One's Self' Hazlitt fantasises the possibility of retreating completely from professional and personal ties to become 'a silent spectator of the mighty scene of things'. But in the conclusion he shows himself to be as full of worldly passion as ever, railing energetically against the *Quarterly Review* and that 'mean, stupid, dastardly, pitiful, spiteful, envious, ungrateful animal … the Public'. More ominously still, in the section which describes the dangers of falling in love, there is an early reference to the disastrous infatuation the forty-two-year-old Hazlitt had recently conceived for his landlord's twenty-year-old daughter Sarah Walker, the full story of which was later told in the excruciatingly confessional *Liber Amoris* (1823).

> Remote, unfriended, melancholy, slow,
> Or by the lazy Scheldt or wandering Po.[1]

I never was in a better place or humour than I am at present for writing on this subject. I have a partridge getting ready for my supper, my fire is blazing on the hearth, the air is mild for the season of the year, I have had but a slight fit of indigestion to-day

---

*   Written at Winterslow Hut, January 18th–19th, 1821.

(the only thing that makes me abhor myself), I have three hours good before me, and therefore I will attempt it. It is as well to do it at once as to have it to do for a week to come.

If the writing on this subject is no easy task, the thing itself is a harder one. It asks a troublesome effort to ensure the admiration of others: it is a still greater one to be satisfied with one's own thoughts. As I look from the window at the wide bare heath before me, and through the misty moon-light air see the woods that wave over the top of Winterslow,

> While Heav'n's chancel-vault is blind with sleet,[2]

my mind takes its flight through too long a series of years, supported only by the patience of thought and secret yearnings after truth and good, for me to be at a loss to understand the feeling I intend to write about; but I do not know that this will enable me to convey it more agreeably to the reader.

Lady G. in a letter to Miss Harriet Byron, assures her that 'her brother Sir Charles lived to himself': and Lady L. soon after (for Richardson was never tired of a good thing) repeats the same observation; to which Miss Byron frequently returns in her answers to both sisters – 'For you know Sir Charles lives to himself', till at length it passes into a proverb among the fair correspondents.[3] This is not, however, an example of what I understand by *living to one's-self*, for Sir Charles Grandison was indeed always thinking of himself; but by this phrase I mean never thinking at all about one's-self, any more than if there was no such person in existence. The character I speak of is as little of an egotist as possible: Richardson's great favourite was as much of one as possible. Some satirical critic has represented him in Elysium 'bowing over the *faded* hand of Lady Grandison' (Miss Byron that was) – he ought to have been represented bowing over his own hand, for he never admired any one but himself, and was the god of his own idolatry. Neither do I call it living to one's-self to retire into a desert (like the saints and martyrs of old) to be devoured by wild beasts, nor to descend into a cave to be considered as a hermit, nor to get to the top of a pillar or rock to do fanatic penance and be seen of all men. What I mean by living to one's-self is living in the world, as in it, not of it: it is as if no one knew there was such a person, and you wished no one to know it: it is to be a silent spectator of the mighty scene of things, not an object of attention or curiosity in it; to take a thoughtful, anxious interest in what is passing in the world, but not to feel the slightest inclination to make or meddle with it. It is such a life as a pure spirit might be supposed to lead, and such an interest as it might take in the affairs of men, calm, contemplative, passive, distant, touched with pity for their sorrows, smiling at their follies without bitterness, sharing their affections, but not troubled by their passions, not seeking their notice, nor once dreamt of by them. He who lives wisely to himself and to his own heart, looks at the busy world through the loop-holes of retreat, and does not want to mingle in the fray. 'He hears the tumult, and is still.'[4] He is not able to mend it, nor willing to mar it. He sees enough in the universe to interest him without putting himself forward to try what he can do to fix the eyes of the universe upon him. Vain the attempt! He reads the clouds, he looks at the stars, he watches the return of the seasons, the falling leaves of autumn, the perfumed breath of spring, starts with delight at the note of a thrush in a copse near him, sits by the fire, listens to the moaning of the wind, pores upon a book, or discourses the freezing hours away, or melts down hours to minutes in pleasing thought. All this while he is taken up with other things, forgetting himself. He relishes an author's style, without thinking of turning author. He is fond of looking at a print from an old picture in the room, without teasing himself to copy it. He does not fret himself to death with trying to be what he is not, or to do what he cannot. He hardly knows what he is capable of, and is not in the least concerned whether he shall ever make a figure in the world. He feels the truth of the lines –

> The man whose eye is ever on himself,
> Doth look on one, the least of nature's works;
> One who might move the wise man to that scorn
> Which wisdom holds unlawful ever[5] –

he looks out of himself at the wide extended prospect of nature and takes an interest beyond his narrow pretensions in general humanity. He is free as air, and independent as the wind. Woe be to him when he first begins to think what others say of him. While a man is contented with himself and his own resources, all is well. When he undertakes to play a part on the stage, and to persuade the world to think more about him than they do about themselves, he is got into a track where he will find nothing but briars and thorns, vexation and disappointment. I can speak a little to this point. For many years of my life I did nothing but think. I had nothing else to do but solve some knotty point, or dip in some abstruse author, or look at the sky, or wander by the pebbled sea-side –

> To see the children sporting on the shore,
> And hear the mighty waters rolling evermore.[6]

I cared for nothing, I wanted nothing. I took my time to consider whatever occurred to me, and was in no hurry to give a sophistical answer to a question – there was no printer's devil waiting for me. I used to write a page or two perhaps in half a year; and remember laughing heartily at the celebrated experimentalist Nicholson, who told me that in twenty years he had written as much as would make three hundred octavo volumes. If I was not a great author, I could read with ever fresh delight, 'never ending, still beginning', and had no occasion to write a criticism when I had done. If I could not paint like Claude,[7] I could admire 'the witchery of the soft blue sky' as I walked out, and was satisfied with the pleasure it gave me. If I was dull, it gave me little concern: if I was lively, I indulged my spirits. I wished well to the world, and believed as favourably of it as I could. I was like a stranger in a foreign land, at which I looked with wonder, curiosity, and delight, without expecting to be an object of attention in return. I had no relations to the state, no duty to perform, no ties to bind me to others: I had neither friend nor mistress, wife or child. I lived in a world of contemplation, and not of action.

This sort of dreaming existence is the best. He who quits it to go in search of realities, generally barters repose for repeated disappointments and vain regrets. His time, thoughts, and feeling are no longer at his own disposal. From that instant he does not survey the objects of nature as they are in themselves, but looks asquint at them to see whether he cannot make them the instruments of his ambition, interest, or pleasure; for a candid, undesigning, undisguised simplicity of character, his views become jaundiced, sinister, and double: he takes no farther interest in the great changes of the world but as he has a paltry share in producing them: instead of opening his senses, his understanding, and his heart to the resplendent fabric of the universe, he holds a crooked mirror before his face, in which he may admire his own person and pretensions, and just glance his eye aside to see whether others are not admiring him too. He no more exists in the impression which 'the fair variety of things' makes upon him, softened and subdued by habitual contemplation, but in the feverish sense of his own upstart self-importance. By aiming to fix, he is become the slave of opinion. He is a tool, a part of a machine that never stands still, and is sick and giddy with the ceaseless motion. He has no satisfaction but in the reflection of his own image in the public gaze, but in the repetition of his own name in the public ear. He himself is mixed up with, and spoils every thing. I wonder Buonaparte was not tired of the N.N.s stuck all over the Louvre and throughout France. Goldsmith[8] (as we all know), when in Holland, went out into a balcony with some handsome Englishwomen, and on their being applauded by the spectators, turned round, and said peevishly – 'There are places where I also am admired.' He could not give the craving appetite of an author's vanity one day's respite. I have seen a celebrated talker of our own time turn pale and go out of the room when a showy-looking girl has come into it, who for a moment divided the attention of his hearers. Infinite are the mortifications of the bare attempt to emerge from obscurity; numberless the failures; and greater and more galling still the vicissitudes and tormenting accompaniments of success –

> – Whose top to climb
> Is certain falling, or so slippery, that
> The fear's as bad as falling.[9]

'Would to God,' exclaimed Oliver Cromwell, when he was at any time thwarted by the Parliament, 'that I had remained by my wood-side to tend a flock of sheep, rather than have been thrust on such a government as this!' When Buonaparte got into his carriage to proceed on his Russian expedition, carelessly twirling his glove, and singing the air – 'Malbrook to the wars is going' – he did not think of the tumble he has got since, the shock of which no one could have stood but himself. We see and hear chiefly of the favourites of Fortune and the Muse, of great generals, of first-rate actors, of celebrated poets. These are at the head; we are struck with the glittering eminence on which they stand, and long to set out on the same tempting career: – not thinking how many discontented half-pay lieutenants are in vain seeking promotion all their lives, and obliged to put up with 'the insolence of office, and the spurns which patient merit of the unworthy takes';[10] how many half-starved strolling-players are doomed to penury and tattered robes in country-places, dreaming to the last of a London engagement; how many wretched daubers shiver and shake in the ague-fit of alternate hopes and fears, waste and pine away in the atrophy of genius, or else turn drawing-masters, picture-cleaners, or newspaper critics; how many hapless poets have sighed out their souls to the Muse in vain, without ever getting their effusions farther known than the Poet's-Corner of a country newspaper, and looked and looked with grudging, wistful eyes at the envious horizon that bounded their provincial fame! Suppose an actor, for instance, 'after the heart-aches and the thousand natural pangs that flesh is heir to', *does* get at the top of his profession, he can no longer bear a rival near the throne; to be second or only equal to another, is to be nothing: he starts at the prospect of a successor, and retains the mimic sceptre with a convulsive grasp: perhaps as he is about to seize the first place which he has long had in his eye, an unsuspected competitor steps in before him, and carries off the prize, leaving him to commence his irksome toil again: he is in a state of alarm at every appearance or rumour of the appearance of a new actor: 'a mouse that takes up its lodging in a cat's ear'* has a mansion of peace to him: he dreads every hint of an objection, and least of all can forgive praise mingled with censure: to doubt is to insult, to discriminate is to degrade: he dare hardly look into a criticism unless some one has *tasted* it for him, to see that there is no offence in it: if he does not draw crowded houses every night, he can neither eat nor sleep; or if all these terrible inflictions are removed, and he can 'eat his meal in peace', he then becomes surfeited with applause and dissatisfied with his profession: he wants to be something else, to be distinguished as an author, a collector, a classical scholar, a man of sense and information, and weighs every word he utters, and half retracts it before he utters it, lest if he were to make the smallest slip of the tongue, it should get buzzed abroad that *Mr —— was only clever as an actor*! If ever there was a man who did not derive more pain than pleasure from his vanity, that man, says Rousseau, was no other than a fool. A country-gentleman near Taunton spent his whole life in making some hundreds of wretched copies of second-rate pictures, which were bought up at his death by a neighbouring Baronet, to whom

Some demon whisper'd, L[ethbridge], have a taste!

A little Wilson[11] in an obscure corner escaped the man of *virtù*, and was carried off by a Bristol picture-dealer for three guineas, while

* Webster's *Duchess of Malfy*.

the muddled copies of the owner of the mansion (with the frames) fetched thirty, forty, sixty, a hundred ducats a piece. A friend of mine found a very fine Canaletto in a state of strange disfigurement, with the upper part of the sky smeared over and fantastically variegated with English clouds; and on enquiring of the person to whom it belonged whether something had not been done to it, received for answer 'that a gentleman, a great artist in the neighbourhood, had retouched some parts of it'. What infatuation! Yet this candidate for the honours of the pencil might probably have made a jovial fox-hunter or respectable justice of the peace, if he could only have stuck to what nature and fortune intended him for. Miss —— can by no means be persuaded to quit the boards of the theatre at [Salisbury], a little country town in the West of England. Her salary has been abridged, her person ridiculed, her acting laughed at; nothing will serve – she is determined to be an actress, and scorns to return to her former business as a milliner. Shall I go on? An actor in the same company was visited by the apothecary of the place in an ague-fit, who, on asking his landlady as to his way of life, was told that the poor gentleman was very quiet and gave little trouble, that he generally had a plate of mashed potatoes for his dinner, and lay in bed most of his time, repeating his part. A young couple, every way amiable and deserving, were to have been married, and a benefit-play was bespoke by the officers of the regiment quartered there, to defray the expense of a license and of the wedding-ring, but the profits of the night did not amount to the necessary sum, and they have, I fear, 'virgined it e'er since!' Oh for the pencil of Hogarth or Wilkie to give a view of the comic strength of the company at [Salisbury], drawn up in battle-array in the *Clandestine Marriage*, with a *coup d'œil* of the pit, boxes, and gallery, to cure for ever the love of the *ideal*, and the desire to shine and make holiday in the eyes of others, instead of retiring within ourselves and keeping our wishes and our thoughts at home!

Even in the common affairs of life, in love, friendship, and marriage, how little security have we when we trust our happiness in the hands of others! Most of the friends I have seen have turned out the bitterest enemies, or cold, uncomfortable acquaintance. Old companions are like meats served up too often that lose their relish and their wholesomeness. He who looks at beauty to admire, to adore it, who reads of its wondrous power in novels, in poems, or in plays, is not unwise: but let no man fall in love, for from that moment he is 'the baby of a girl'. I like very well to repeat such lines as these in the play of *Mirandola* –

> – With what a waving air she goes
> Along the corridor. How like a fawn!
> Yet statelier. Hark! No sound, however soft,
> Nor gentlest echo telleth when she treads,
> But every motion of her shape doth seem
> Hallowed by silence[12] –

but however beautiful the description, defend me from meeting with the original!

> The fly that sips treacle
> Is lost in the sweets;
> So he that tastes woman
> Ruin meets.

The song is Gay's, not mine, and a bitter-sweet it is. [13] – How few out of the infinite number of those that marry and are given in marriage, wed with those they would prefer to all the world; nay, how far the greater proportion are joined together by mere motives of convenience, accident, recommendation of friends, or indeed not unfrequently by the very fear of the event, by repugnance and a sort of fatal fascination: yet the tie is for life, not to be shaken off but with disgrace or death: a man no longer lives to himself, but is a body (as well as mind) chained to another, in spite of himself –

> Like life and death in disproportion met.

So Milton (perhaps from his own experience) makes Adam exclaim, in the vehemence of his despair,

> For either
> He never shall find out fit mate, but such
> As some misfortune brings him or mistake;
> Or whom he wishes most shall seldom gain
> Through her perverseness, but shall see her gain'd
> By a far worse; or if she love, withheld
> By parents; or his happiest choice too late
> Shall meet, already link'd and wedlock-bound
> To a fell adversary, his hate and shame;
> Which infinite calamity shall cause
> To human life, and household peace confound.[14]

If love at first sight were mutual, or to be conciliated by kind offices; if the fondest affection were not so often repaid and chilled by indifference and scorn; if so many lovers both before and since the madman in *Don Quixote* had not 'worshipped a statue, hunted the wind, cried aloud to the desert'; if friendship were lasting; if merit were renown, and renown were health, riches, and long life; or if the homage of the world were paid to conscious worth and the true aspirations after excellence, instead of its gaudy signs and outward trappings: – then indeed I might be of opinion that it is better to live to others than one's-self: but as the case stands, I incline to the negative side of the question* –

> I have not loved the world, nor the world me;
> I have not flattered its rank breath, nor bow'd
> To its idolatries a patient knee –
> Nor coin'd my cheek to smiles – nor cried aloud
> In worship of an echo; in the crowd
> They could not deem me one of such; I stood
> Among them, but not of them; in a shroud
> Of thoughts which were not their thoughts, and still could,
> Had I not filed my mind which thus itself subdued.
>
> I have not loved the world, nor the world me –
> But let us part fair foes; I do believe,
> Though I have found them not, that there may be
> Words which are things – hopes which will not deceive,
> And virtues which are merciful nor weave
> Snares for the failing: I would also deem
> O'er others' griefs that some sincerely grieve;
> That two, or one, are almost what they seem –
> That goodness is no name, and happiness no dream.[15]

Sweet verse embalms the spirit of sour misanthropy: but woe betide the ignoble prose-writer who should thus dare to compare notes with the world, or tax it roundly with imposture.

---

* Shenstone and Gray were two men, one of whom pretended to live to himself, and the other really did so. Gray shrunk from the public gaze (he did not even like his portrait to be prefixed to his works) into his own thoughts and indolent musings; Shenstone affected privacy, that he might be sought out by the world; the one courted retirement in order to enjoy leisure and repose, as the other coquetted with it, merely to be interrupted with the importunity of visitors and the flatteries of absent friends.

If I had sufficient provocation to rail at the public, as Ben Jonson did at the audience in the Prologues to his plays, I think I should do it in good set terms, nearly as follows. There is not a more mean, stupid, dastardly, pitiful, selfish, spiteful, envious, ungrateful animal than the Public. It is the greatest of cowards, for it is afraid of itself. From its unwieldy, overgrown dimensions, it dreads the least opposition to it, and shakes like isinglass at the touch of a finger. It starts at its own shadow, like the man in the Hartz mountains,[16] and trembles at the mention of its own name. It has a lion's mouth, the heart of a hare, with ears erect and sleepless eyes. It stands 'listening its fears'. It is so in awe of its own opinion, that it never dares to form any, but catches up the first idle rumour, lest it should be behind-hand in its judgment, and echoes it till it is deafened with the sound of its own voice. The idea of what the public will think prevents the public from ever thinking at all, and acts as a spell on the exercise of private judgment, so that in short the public ear is at the mercy of the first impudent pretender who chooses to fill it with noisy assertions, or false surmises, or secret whispers. What is said by one is heard by all; the supposition that a thing is known to all the world makes all the world believe it, and the hollow repetition of a vague report drowns the 'still, small voice' of reason. We may believe or know that what is said is not true: but we know or fancy that others believe it – we dare not contradict or are too indolent to dispute with them, and therefore give up our internal, and, as we think, our solitary conviction to a sound without substance, without proof, and often without meaning. Nay more, we may believe and know not only that a thing is false, but that others believe and know it to be so, that they are quite as much in the secret of the imposture as we are, that they see the puppets at work, the nature of the machinery, and yet if any one has the art or power to get the management of it, he shall keep possession of the public ear by virtue of a cant-phrase or nickname; and, by dint of effrontery and perseverance, make all the world believe and repeat what all the world know to be false. The ear is quicker than the judgment. We know that certain things are said; by that circumstance alone we know that they produce a certain effect on the imagination of others, and we conform to their prejudices by mechanical sympathy, and for want of sufficient spirit to differ with them. So far then is public opinion from resting on a broad and solid basis, as the aggregate of thought and feeling in a community, that it is slight and shallow and variable to the last

degree – the bubble of the moment – so that we may safely say the
public is the dupe of public opinion, not its parent. The public is
pusillanimous and cowardly, because it is weak. It knows itself to
be a great dunce, and that it has no opinions but upon suggestion.
Yet it is unwilling to appear in leading-strings, and would have it
thought that its decisions are as wise as they are weighty. It is hasty
in taking up its favourites, more hasty in laying them aside, lest it
should be supposed deficient in sagacity in either case. It is
generally divided into two strong parties, each of which will allow
neither common sense nor common honesty to the other side. It
reads the *Edinburgh* and *Quarterly Reviews*, and believes them both
– or if there is a doubt, malice turns the scale. Taylor and Hessey
told me that they had sold nearly two editions of the *Characters of
Shakespear's Plays* in about three months, but that after the *Quarterly
Review* of them came out, they never sold another copy. The public,
enlightened as they are, must have known the meaning of that
attack as well as those who made it. It was not ignorance then but
cowardice that led them to give up their own opinion. A crew of
mischievous critics at Edinburgh having fixed the epithet of the
Cockney School to one or two writers born in the metropolis, all the
people in London became afraid of looking into their works, lest
they too should be convicted of cockneyism.[17] Oh brave public!
This epithet proved too much for one of the writers in question,
and stuck like a barbed arrow in his heart. Poor Keats! What was
sport to the town was death to him. Young, sensitive, delicate, he
was like

> A bud bit by an envious worm,
> Ere he could spread his sweet leaves to the air,
> Or dedicate his beauty to the sun[18] –

and unable to endure the miscreant cry and idiot laugh, withdrew
to sigh his last breath in foreign climes. – The public is as envious
and ungrateful as it is ignorant, stupid, and pigeon-livered –

> A huge-sized monster of ingratitudes.

It reads, it admires, it extols only because it is the fashion, not from
any love of the subject or the man. It cries you up or runs you down
out of mere caprice and levity. If you have pleased it, it is jealous
of its own involuntary acknowledgment of merit, and seizes the
first opportunity, the first shabby pretext, to pick a quarrel with
you, and be quits once more. Every petty caviller is erected into a

judge, every tale-bearer is implicitly believed. Every little low paltry creature that gaped and wondered only because others did so, is glad to find you (as he thinks) on a level with himself. An author is not then, after all, a being of another order. Public admiration is forced, and goes against the grain. Public obloquy is cordial and sincere: every individual feels his own importance in it. They give you up bound hand and foot into the power of your accusers. To attempt to defend yourself is a high crime and misdemeanour, a contempt of court, an extreme piece of impertinence. Or, if you prove every charge unfounded, they never think of retracting their error, or making you amends. It would be a compromise of their dignity; they consider themselves as the party injured, and resent your innocence as an imputation on their judgment. The celebrated Bub Doddington, when out of favour at court, said 'he would not *justify* before his sovereign: it was for Majesty to be displeased, and for him to believe himself in the wrong!' The public are not quite so modest. People already begin to talk of the Scotch Novels as overrated. How then can common authors be supposed to keep their heads long above water? As a general rule, all those who live by the public starve, and are made a bye-word and a standing jest into the bargain. Posterity is no better (not a bit more enlightened or more liberal), except that you are no longer in their power, and that the voice of common fame saves them the trouble of deciding on your claims. The public now are the posterity of Milton and Shakespear. Our posterity will be the living public of a future generation. When a man is dead, they put money in his coffin, erect monuments to his memory, and celebrate the anniversary of his birthday in set speeches. Would they take any notice of him if he were living? No! – I was complaining of this to a Scotchman who had been attending a dinner and a subscription to raise a monument to Burns. He replied, he would sooner subscribe twenty pounds to his monument than have given it him while living; so that if the poet were to come to life again, he would treat him just as he was treated in fact. This was an honest Scotchman. What *he* said, the rest would do.

Enough: my soul, turn from them, and let me try to regain the obscurity and quiet that I love, 'far from the madding strife', in some sequestered corner of my own, or in some far-distant land! In the latter case, I might carry with me as a consolation the passage in Bolingbroke's *Reflections on Exile*, in which he describes in glowing colours the resources which a man may always find within himself, and of which the world cannot deprive him.

'Believe me, the providence of God has established such an order in the world, that of all which belongs to us, the least valuable parts can alone fall under the will of others. Whatever is best is safest; lies out of the reach of human power; can neither be given nor taken away. Such is this great and beautiful work of nature, the world. Such is the mind of man, which contemplates and admires the world whereof it makes the noblest part. These are inseparably ours, and as long as we remain in one we shall enjoy the other. Let us march therefore intrepidly wherever we are led by the course of human accidents. Wherever they lead us, on what coast soever we are thrown by them, we shall not find ourselves absolutely strangers. We shall feel the same revolution of seasons, and the same sun and moon* will guide the course of our year. The same azure vault, bespangled with stars, will be every where spread over our heads. There is no part of the world from whence we may not admire those planets which roll, like ours, in different orbits round the same central sun; from whence we may not discover an object still more stupendous, that army of fixed stars hung up in the immense space of the universe, innumerable suns whose beams enlighten and cherish the unknown worlds which roll around them; and whilst I am ravished by such contemplations as these, whilst my soul is thus raised up to heaven, imports me little what ground I tread upon.'

---

*   Plutarch, *Of Banishment*. He compares those who cannot live out of their own country, to the simple people who fancied the moon of Athens was a finer moon than that of Corinth.

         – *Labentem cœlo quæ ducitis annum.*

                              Virgil, *Georgics*

On Going a Journey

First published in *The New Monthly Magazine*, January 1822, as 'Table-Talk No. 1', signed 'T.', and with an editorial note: 'These essays are by the well-known author of 'Table-Talk,' in 1 vol., 8vo. Published during the last year.' Included in the second volume of *Table-Talk* (London: Colburn, 1822).

This is an essay about how one may lose oneself in space – in the countryside, or in foreign lands – but find oneself in time, in remembered landscapes, and in the dear, disappointed prospects of the past. Of the many journeys discussed here, two were of particular significance to Hazlitt, both for personal reasons, and because they called to mind the lost idealism of the revolutionary decade. The first is the pilgrimage he made as a twenty-year-old from his home in Wem in Shropshire to Alfoxden in Somerset, to visit the two young poets William Wordsworth and Samuel Taylor Coleridge, who were then at the height of their powers. This was in 1798. The second is the trip he made to Napoleonic France in 1802 during the short-lived peace of Amiens, when he saw the Louvre, which was the first major art gallery of its kind to be open to the general public. 'I was at no loss for language,' he writes of this first trip to Paris, 'for that of all the great schools of painting was open to me.'

One of the pleasantest things in the world is going a journey; but I like to go by myself. I can enjoy society in a room; but out of doors, nature is company enough for me. I am then never less alone than when alone.

The fields his study, nature was his book.[1]

I cannot see the wit of walking and talking at the same time. When I am in the country, I wish to vegetate like the country. I am not for criticising hedge-rows and black cattle. I go out of town in order to forget the town and all that is in it. There are those who for this purpose go to watering-places, and carry the metropolis with them. I like more elbow-room, and fewer incumbrances. I like solitude, when I give myself up to it, for the sake of solitude; nor do I ask for

> – a friend in my retreat,
> Whom I may whisper solitude is sweet.[2]

The soul of a journey is liberty, perfect liberty, to think, feel, do just as one pleases. We go a journey chiefly to be free of all impediments and of all inconveniences; to leave ourselves behind, much more to get rid of others. It is because I want a little breathing-space to muse on indifferent matters, where Contemplation

> May plume her feathers and let grow her wings,
> That in the various bustle of resort
> Were all too ruffled, and sometimes impair'd,[3]

that I absent myself from the town for awhile, without feeling at a loss the moment I am left by myself. Instead of a friend in a post-chaise or in a tilbury, to exchange good things with, and vary the same stale topics over again, for once let me have a truce with impertinence. Give me the clear blue sky over my head, and the green turf beneath my feet, a winding road before me, and a three hours' march to dinner – and then to thinking! It is hard if I cannot start some game on these lone heaths. I laugh, I run, I leap, I sing for joy. From the point of yonder rolling cloud, I plunge into my past being, and revel there, as the sun-burnt Indian plunges headlong into the wave that wafts him to his native shore. Then long-forgotten things, like 'sunken wrack and sumless treasuries', burst upon my eager sight, and I begin to feel, think, and be myself again. Instead of an awkward silence, broken by attempts at wit or dull common-places, mine is that undisturbed silence of the heart which alone is perfect eloquence. No one likes puns, alliterations, antitheses, argument, and analysis better than I do; but I sometimes had rather be without them. 'Leave, oh, leave me to my repose!' I have just now other business in hand, which would seem idle to you, but is with me 'the very stuff of the conscience'. Is not this wild rose sweet without a comment? Does not this daisy leap to my heart, set in its coat of emerald? Yet if I were to explain to you the circumstance that has so endeared it to me, you would only smile. Had I not better then keep it to myself, and let it serve me to brood over, from here to yonder craggy point, and from thence onward to the far-distant horizon? I should be but bad company all that way, and therefore prefer being alone. I have heard it said that you may, when the moody fit comes on, walk or ride on by yourself, and indulge your reveries. But this looks like a breach of manners, a neglect of others, and you are thinking all the time that you ought to rejoin your party. 'Out upon such half-faced fellowship,' say I. I like to be either entirely to myself, or entirely at the disposal of others; to talk or be silent, to walk or sit still, to be sociable or solitary. I was pleased with an observation of Mr Cobbett's, that 'he thought it a bad French custom to drink our wine with our meals, and that an Englishman ought to do only one thing at a time.' So I cannot talk and think, or indulge in melancholy musing and lively conversation by fits and starts. 'Let me have a companion of my way,' says Sterne, 'were it but to remark how the shadows lengthen as the sun goes down.' It is beautifully said: but in my opinion, this continual comparing of notes interferes with the involuntary impression of things upon the mind, and hurts the sentiment. If you only hint what you feel in a kind of dumb show it is insipid: if you have to explain it, it is making a toil of a pleasure. You cannot read the book of nature, without being perpetually put to the trouble of translating it for the benefit of others. I am for the synthetical method on a journey, in preference to the analytical. I am content to lay in a stock of ideas then, and to examine and anatomise them afterwards. I want to see my vague notions float like the down of the thistle before the breeze, and not to have them entangled in the briars and thorns of controversy. For once, I like to have it all my own way; and this is impossible unless you are alone, or in such company as I do not covet. I have no objection to argue a point with any one for twenty miles of measured road, but not for pleasure. If you remark the scent of a beanfield crossing the road, perhaps your fellow-traveller has no smell. If you point to a distant object, perhaps he is short-sighted, and has to take out his glass to look at it. There is a feeling in the air, a tone in the colour of a cloud which hits your fancy, but the effect of which you are unprepared to account for. There is then no sympathy, but an uneasy craving after it, and a dissatisfaction which pursues you on the way, and in the end probably produces ill humour. Now I never quarrel with myself, and take all my own conclusions for granted till I find it necessary to defend them against objections. It is not merely that you may not be of accord on the objects and circumstances that present themselves before you – they may recall a number of ideas, and lead to associations too delicate and refined to be possibly communicated to others. Yet these I love to cherish, and sometimes still fondly clutch them, when I can escape from the throng to do so. To give way to our feelings before company, seems extravagance or affectation; on the other hand, to have to unravel this mystery of our being at every turn, and to make others take an equal interest in it (otherwise the end is not answered) is a task to which few are competent. We must 'give it an understanding, but no tongue'. My old friend C[oleridge], however, could do both. He could go on in the most delightful explanatory way over hill and dale, a summer's day, and convert a landscape into a didactic poem or a Pindaric ode. 'He talked far above singing.' If I could so clothe my ideas in sounding and flowing words, I might perhaps wish to have some one with me to admire the swelling theme; or I could be more content, were it possible for me still to hear his echoing voice in the woods of All-Foxden.[4] They had 'that fine madness in them which our first poets had'; and if they could have been caught by some rare instrument, would have breathed such strains as the following.

> – Here be woods as green
> As any, air likewise as fresh and sweet
> As when smooth Zephyrus plays on the fleet
> Face of the curled stream, with flow'rs as many
> As the young spring gives, and as choice as any;
> Here be all new delights, cool streams and wells,
> Arbours o'ergrown with woodbine, caves and dells:
> Choose where thou wilt, while I sit by and sing,
> Or gather rushes to make many a ring
> For thy long fingers; tell thee tales of love,
> How the pale Phœbe, hunting in a grove,
> First saw the boy Endymion, from whose eyes
> She took eternal fire that never dies;
> How she convey'd him softly in a sleep
> His temples bound with poppy, to the steep
> Head of old Latmos, where she stoops each night,
> Gilding the mountain with her brother's light,
> To kiss her sweetest.
>
> *The Faithful Shepherdess*[5]

Had I words and images at command like these, I would attempt to wake the thoughts that lie slumbering on golden ridges in the evening clouds: but at the sight of nature my fancy, poor as it is, droops and closes up its leaves, like flowers at sunset. I can make nothing out on the spot: – I must have time to collect myself.

In general, a good thing spoils out-of-door prospects: it should be reserved for Table-talk. L[amb] is for this reason, I take it, the worst company in the world out of doors; because he is the best within. I grant, there is one subject on which it is pleasant to talk on a journey; and that is, what one shall have for supper when we get to our inn at night. The open air improves this sort of conversation or friendly altercation, by setting a keener edge on appetite. Every mile of the road heightens the flavour of the viands we expect at the end of it. How fine it is to enter some old town, walled and turreted, just at the approach of night-fall, or to come to some straggling village, with the lights streaming through the surrounding gloom; and then after inquiring for the best entertainment that the place affords, to 'take one's ease at one's inn!' These eventful moments in our lives are in fact too precious, too full of solid, heartfelt happiness to be frittered and dribbled away in imperfect sympathy. I would have them all to myself, and drain them to the last drop: they will do to talk of or to write about afterwards. What a delicate speculation it is, after drinking whole goblets of tea,

The cups that cheer, but not inebriate,[6]

and letting the fumes ascend into the brain, to sit considering what we shall have for supper – eggs and a rasher, a rabbit smothered in onions, or an excellent veal-cutlet! Sancho in such a situation once fixed upon cow-heel; and his choice, though he could not help it, is not to be disparaged. Then in the intervals of pictured scenery and Shandean contemplation, to catch the preparation and the stir in the kitchen – *Procul, O procul este profani!* These hours are sacred to silence and to musing, to be treasured up in the memory, and to feed the source of smiling thoughts hereafter. I would not waste them in idle talk; or if I must have the integrity of fancy broken in upon, I would rather it were by a stranger than a friend. A stranger takes his hue and character from the time and place; he is a part of the furniture and costume of an inn. If he is a Quaker, or from the West Riding of Yorkshire, so much the better. I do not even try to sympathise with him, and he *breaks no squares.* I associate nothing with my travelling companion but present objects and passing events. In his ignorance of me and my affairs, I in a manner forget myself. But a friend reminds one of other things, rips up old grievances, and destroys the abstraction of the scene. He comes in ungraciously between us and our imaginary character. Something is dropped in the course of conversation that gives a hint of your profession and pursuits; or from having some one with you that knows the less sublime portions of your history, it seems that other people do. You are no longer a citizen of the world: but your 'unhoused free condition is put into circumscription and confine'. The *incognito* of an inn is one of its striking privileges – 'lord of one's-self, uncumber'd with a name'. Oh! it is great to shake off the trammels of the world and of public opinion – to lose our importunate, tormenting, everlasting personal identity in the elements of nature, and become the creature of the moment, clear of all ties – to hold to the universe only by a dish of sweet-breads, and to owe nothing but the score of the evening – and no longer seeking for applause and meeting with contempt, to be known by no other title than *the Gentleman in the parlour!* One may take one's choice of all characters in this romantic state of uncertainty as to one's real pretensions, and become indefinitely respectable and negatively right-worshipful. We baffle prejudice and disappoint conjecture; and from being so to others, begin to be objects of curiosity and wonder even to ourselves. We are no more those hackneyed commonplaces that we appear in the world: an inn restores us to the level of nature, and quits scores with society! I have certainly spent some enviable hours at inns – sometimes when I have been left entirely to myself, and have tried to solve some metaphysical problem, as once at Witham-common, where I found out the proof that likeness is not a case of the association of ideas – at other times, when there have been pictures in the room, as at St Neot's, (I think it was) where I first met with Gribelin's engravings of the Cartoons,[7] into which I entered at once; and at a little inn on the borders of Wales, where there happened to be hanging some of Westall's drawings, which I compared triumphantly (for a theory that I had, not for the admired artist) with the figure of a girl who had ferried me over the Severn, standing up in the boat between me and the fading twilight – at other times I might mention luxuriating in books, with a peculiar interest in this way, as I remember sitting up half the night to read Paul and Virginia, which I picked up at an inn at Bridgewater, after being drenched in the rain all day; and at the same place I got through two volumes of Madame D'Arblay's *Camilla*. It was on the tenth of April, 1798, that I sat down to a volume of the *New Eloise*,[8] at the inn at Llangollen, over a bottle of sherry and a cold chicken.

The letter I chose was that in which St Preux describes his feelings as he first caught a glimpse from the heights of the Jura of the Pays de Vaud, which I had brought with me as a *bonne bouche* to crown the evening with. It was my birthday, and I had for the first time come from a place in the neighbourhood to visit this delightful spot. The road to Llangollen turns off between Chirk and Wrexham; and on passing a certain point, you come all at once upon the valley, which opens like an amphitheatre, broad, barren hills rising in majestic state on either side, with 'green upland swells that echo to the bleat of flocks' below, and the river Dee babbling over its stony bed in the midst of them. The valley at this time 'glittered green with sunny showers', and a budding ash-tree dipped its tender branches in the chiding stream. How proud, how glad I was to walk along the high road that commanded the delicious prospect, repeating the lines which I have just quoted from Mr Coleridge's poems! But besides the prospect which opened beneath my feet, another also opened to my inward sight, a heavenly vision, on which were written, in letters large as Hope could make them, these four words, LIBERTY, GENIUS, LOVE, VIRTUE; which have since faded into the light of common day, or mock my idle gaze.

The beautiful is vanished, and returns not.[9]

Still I would return some time or other to this enchanted spot; but I would return to it alone. What other self could I find to share that influx of thoughts, of regret, and delight, the traces of which I could hardly conjure up to myself, so much have they been broken and defaced! I could stand on some tall rock, and overlook the precipice of years that separates me from what I then was. I was at that time going shortly to visit the poet whom I have above named. Where is he now? Not only I myself have changed; the world, which was then new to me, has become old and incorrigible. Yet will I turn to thee in thought, O sylvan Dee,[10] as then thou wert, in joy, in youth and gladness; and thou shalt always be to me the river of Paradise, where I will drink of the waters of life freely!

There is hardly any thing that shows the short-sightedness or capriciousness of the imagination more than travelling does. With change of place we change our ideas; nay, our opinions and feelings. We can by an effort indeed transport ourselves to old and long-forgotten scenes, and then the picture of the mind revives again; but we forget those that we have just left. It seems that we can think but of one place at a time. The canvas of the fancy has only a certain extent, and if we paint one set of objects upon it, they immediately efface every other. We cannot enlarge our conceptions; we only shift our point of view. The landscape bares its bosom to the enraptured eye; we take our fill of it; and seem as if we could form no other image of beauty or grandeur. We pass on, and think no more of it: the horizon that shuts it from our sight also blots it from our memory like a dream. In travelling through a wild barren country, I can form no idea of a woody and cultivated one. It appears to me that all the world must be barren, like what I see of it. In the country we forget the town, and in town we despise the country. 'Beyond Hyde Park,' says Sir Fopling Flutter, 'all is a desert.'[11] All that part of the map that we do not see before us is a blank. The world in our conceit of it is not much bigger than a nutshell. It is not one prospect expanded into another, county joined to county, kingdom to kingdom, lands to seas, making an image voluminous and vast; – the mind can form no larger idea of space than the eye can take in at a single glance. The rest is a name written on a map, a calculation of arithmetic. For instance, what is the true signification of that immense mass of territory and population, known by the name of China to us? An inch of paste-board on a wooden globe, of no more account than a China orange! Things near us are seen of the size of life: things at a distance are diminished to the size of the understanding. We measure the universe by ourselves, and even comprehend the texture of our own being only piece-meal. In this way, however, we remember an infinity of things and places. The mind is like a mechanical instrument that plays a great variety of tunes, but it must play them in succession. One idea recalls another, but it at the same time excludes all others. In trying to renew old recollections, we cannot as it were unfold the whole web of our existence; we must pick out the single threads. So in coming to a place where we have formerly lived and with which we have intimate associations, every one must have found that the feeling grows more vivid the nearer we approach the spot, from the mere anticipation of the actual impression: we remember circumstances, feelings, persons, faces, names, that we had not thought of for years; but for the time all the rest of the world is forgotten! – To return to the question I have quitted above.

I have no objection to go to see ruins, aqueducts, pictures, in company with a friend or a party, but rather the contrary, for the former reason reversed. They are intelligible matters, and will bear talking about. The sentiment here is not tacit, but communicable and overt. Salisbury Plain is barren of criticism, but Stonehenge will bear a discussion antiquarian, picturesque, and philosophical. In setting out on a party of pleasure, the first consideration always is where we shall go: in taking a solitary ramble, the question is what we shall meet with by the way. The mind then is 'its own place'; nor are we anxious to arrive at the end of our journey. I can myself do the honours indifferently well to works of art and curiosity. I once took a party to Oxford with no mean *éclat* – shewed them the seat of the Muses at a distance,

With glistering spires and pinnacles adorn'd[12] –

descanted on the learned air that breathes from the grassy quadrangles and stone walls of halls and colleges – was at home in the Bodleian; and at Blenheim quite superseded the powdered Cicerone that attended us, and that pointed in vain with his wand to common-place beauties in matchless pictures. – As another exception to the above reasoning, I should not feel confident in venturing on a journey in a foreign country without a companion. I should want at intervals to hear the sound of my own language. There is an involuntary antipathy in the mind of an Englishman to foreign manners and notions that requires the assistance of social sympathy to carry it off. As the distance from home increases, this relief, which was at first a luxury, becomes a passion and an appetite. A person would almost feel stifled to find himself in the deserts of Arabia without friends and countrymen: there must be allowed to be something in the view of Athens or old Rome that claims the utterance of speech; and I own that the Pyramids are too mighty for any single contemplation. In such situations, so opposite to all one's ordinary train of ideas, one seems a species by one's-self, a limb torn off from society, unless one can meet with instant fellowship and support. – Yet I did not feel this want or craving very pressing once, when I first set my foot on the laughing shores of France. Calais was peopled with novelty and delight. The confused, busy murmur of the place was like oil and wine poured into my ears; nor did the mariners' hymn, which was sung from the top of an old crazy vessel in the harbour, as the sun went down, send an alien sound into my soul. I breathed the air of general humanity. I walked over 'the vine-covered hills and gay regions of France', erect and satisfied; for the image of man was not cast down and chained to the foot of arbitrary thrones. I was at no loss for language, for that of all the great schools of painting was open to me. The whole is vanished like a shade. Pictures, heroes, glory, freedom, all are fled: nothing remains but the Bourbons and the French people! – There is undoubtedly a sensation in travelling into foreign parts that is to be had nowhere else: but it is more pleasing at the time than lasting. It is too remote from our habitual associations to be a common topic of discourse or reference, and, like a dream or another state of existence, does not piece into our daily modes of life. It is an animated but a momentary hallucination. It demands an effort to exchange our actual for our ideal identity; and to feel the pulse of our old transports revive very keenly, we must 'jump' all our present comforts and connexions. Our romantic and itinerant character is not to be domesticated. Dr Johnson remarked how little foreign travel added to the facilities of conversation in those who had been abroad. In fact, the time we have spent there is both delightful and in one sense instructive; but it appears to be cut out of our substantial, downright existence, and never to join kindly on to it. We are not the same, but another, and perhaps more enviable individual, all the time we are out of our own country. We are lost to ourselves, as well as to our friends. So the poet somewhat quaintly sings,

> Out of my country and myself I go.[13]

Those who wish to forget painful thoughts, do well to absent themselves for a while from the ties and objects that recall them: but we can be said only to fulfil our destiny in the place that gave us birth. I should on this account like well enough to spend the whole of my life in travelling abroad, if I could any where borrow another life to spend afterwards at home!

On Coffee-House Politicians

From volume two of *Table-Talk* (1822). This essay begins as an attack on the vanity and ephemerality of London pub conversation, lamenting that 'living knowledge is the tomb of the dead'. But then it softens into a series of affectionate reminiscences of Hazlitt's long-time local, the Southampton Coffee-House near Chancery Lane, before finally offering a rousing tribute to London as 'the only place for equal society'.

There is a set of people who fairly come under this denomination. They spend their time and their breath in coffee-houses and other places of public resort, hearing or repeating some new thing. They sit with a paper in their hands in the morning, and with a pipe in their mouths in the evening, discussing the contents of it. The *Times*, the *Morning Chronicle*, and the *Herald* are necessary to their existence: in them 'they live and move and have their being.' The Evening Paper is impatiently expected, and called for at a certain critical minute: the news of the morning become stale and vapid by the dinner-hour. A fresher interest is required, an appetite for the latest-stirring information is excited with the return of their meals; and a glass of old port or humming ale hardly relishes as it ought without the infusion of some lively topic that had its birth with the day, and perishes before night. 'Then come in the sweets of the evening:' – the Queen, the coronation, the last new play, the next fight, the insurrection of the Greeks or Neapolitans, the price of stocks, or death of kings, keep them on the alert till bed-time. No question comes amiss to them that is quite new – none is ever heard of that is at all old.

That of an hour's age doth hiss the speaker.[1]

The World before the Flood or the Intermediate State of the Soul are never once thought of – such is the quick succession of subjects, the suddenness and fugitiveness of the interest taken in them, that the Two-penny Post-Bag would be at present looked upon as an old-fashioned publication, and the Battle of Waterloo, like the proverb, is somewhat musty. It is strange that people should take so much interest at one time in what they so soon forget: – the truth is, they feel no interest in it at any time, but it does for something to talk about. Their ideas are served up to them, like their bill of fare, for the day; and the whole creation, history, war, politics, morals, poetry, metaphysics, is to them like a file of antedated newspapers, of no use, not even for reference, except the one which lies on the table! – You cannot take any of these persons at a greater disadvantage than before they are provided with their cue for the day. They ask with a face of dreary vacuity, 'Have you anything new?' – and on receiving an answer in the negative, have nothing farther to say. Talk of the Westminster Election, the Bridge-street Association, or Mr Cobbett's Letter to John Cropper of Liverpool, and they are alive again. Beyond the last twenty-four hours, or the narrow round in which they move, they are utterly to seek, without ideas, feelings, interests, apprehensions of any sort; so that if you betray any knowledge beyond the vulgar routine of SECOND EDITIONS and first-hand private intelligence, you pass with them for a dull fellow, not acquainted with what is going forward in the world or with the practical value of things. I have known a person of this stamp censure John Cam Hobhouse[2] for referring so often as he does to the affairs of the Greeks and Romans, as if the affairs of the nation were not sufficient for his hands: another asks you if a General in modern times cannot throw a bridge over a river without having studied Cæsar's *Commentaries*; and a third cannot see the use of the learned languages, as he has observed that the greatest proficients in them are rather taciturn than otherwise, and hesitate in their speech more than other people. A dearth of general information is almost necessary to the thorough-paced coffee-house politician; in the absence of thought, imagination, sentiment, he is attracted immediately to the nearest common-place, and floats through the chosen regions of noise and empty rumours without difficulty and without distraction. Meet 'any six of these men in buckram', and they will accost you with the same question and the same answer: they have seen it somewhere in print, or had it from some city-oracle, that morning; and the sooner they vent their opinions the better, for they will not keep. Like tickets of admission to the theatre for a particular evening, they must be used immediately, or they will be worth nothing: and the object is to find auditors for the one and customers for the other, neither of which is difficult; since people who have no ideas of their own are glad to hear what any one else has to say, as those who have not free admissions to the play will very obligingly take up with an occasional order. – It sometimes gives one a melancholy but mixed sensation to see one of the better sort of this class of politicians, not without talents or learning, absorbed for fifty years together in the all-engrossing topic of the day: mounting on it for exercise and recreation of his faculties, like the great horse at a riding-school, and after his short, improgressive, untired career dismounting just where he got up; flying abroad in continual consternation on the wings of all the newspapers; waving his arm like a pump-handle in sign of constant change, and spouting out torrents of puddled politics from his mouth; dead to all interests but those of the state; seemingly neither older nor wiser for age; unaccountably enthusiastic, stupidly romantic, and actuated by no other motive than the mechanical operations of the spirit of newsmongering!*

'What things,' exclaims Beaumont in his verses to Ben Jonson, 'have we not seen done at the Mermaid!

> – Then when there hath been thrown
> Wit able enough to justify the town
> For three days past, wit that might warrant be
> For the whole city to talk foolishly![3]

I cannot say the same of the S[outhampton], though it stands on classic ground, and is connected by local tradition with the great names of the Elizabethan age.[4] What a falling off is here! Our ancestors of that period seem not only to be older by two hundred

---

*   It is not very long ago that I saw two Dissenting Ministers (the *Ultima Thule* of the sanguine, visionary temperament in politics) stuffing their pipes with dried currant-leaves, calling it Radical tobacco, lighting it with a lens in the rays of the sun, and at every puff fancying that they undermined the Boroughmongers, as Trim blew up the army opposed to the Allies! They had *deceived the Senate*. Methinks I see them now, smiling as in scorn of Corruption.

> – Dream on, blest pair:
> Yet happier if you knew your happiness,
> And knew to know no more!

The world of Reform that you dote on, like Berkeley's material world, lives only in your own brain, and long may it live there! Those same Dissenting Ministers throughout the country (I mean the descendants of the old Puritans) are to this hour a sort of Fifth-monarchy men: very turbulent fellows, in my opinion altogether incorrigible, and according to the suggestions of others, should be hanged out of the way without judge or jury for the safety of church and state. Marry, hang them! they may be left to die a natural death: the race is nearly extinct of itself, and can do little more good or harm!

years, and proportionately wiser and wittier than we, but hardly a
trace of them is left, not even the memory of what has been. How
should I make my friend M[ounsey] stare,[5] if I were to mention the
name of my still better friend, old honest Signor Friscobaldo, the
father of Bellafront: – yet his name was perhaps invented, and the
scenes in which he figures unrivalled might for the first time have
been read aloud to thrilling ears on this very spot! Who reads
Deckar now? Or if by chance any one awakes the strings of that
ancient lyre, and starts with delight as they yield wild, broken
music, is he not accused of envy to the living Muse? What would
a linen-draper from Holborn think, if I were to ask him after the
clerk of St Andrew's, the immortal, the forgotten Webster? His
name and his works are no more heard of: though *these* were
written with a pen of adamant, 'within the red-leaved tables of the
heart', his fame was 'writ in water'. So perishable is genius, so swift
is time, so fluctuating is knowledge, and so far is it from being true
that men perpetually accumulate the means of improvement and
refinement. On the contrary, living knowledge is the tomb of the
dead, and while light and worthless materials float on the surface,
the solid and sterling as often sink to the bottom, and are
swallowed up for ever in weeds and quicksands! – A striking
instance of the short-lived nature of popular reputation occurred
one evening at the S[outhampton], when we got into a dispute, the
most learned and recondite that ever took place, on the
comparative merits of Lord Byron and Gray. A country-gentleman
happened to drop in, and thinking to show off in London company,
launched into a lofty panegyric on the *Bard* of Gray as the sublimest
composition in the English language. This assertion presently
appeared to be an anachronism, though it was probably the
opinion in vogue thirty years ago, when the gentleman was last in
town. After a little floundering, one of the party volunteered to
express a more contemporary sentiment, by asking in a tone of
mingled confidence and doubt – 'But you don't think, Sir, that Gray
is to be mentioned as a poet in the same day with my Lord Byron?'
The disputants were now at issue: all that resulted was that Gray
was set aside as a poet who would not go down among readers of
the present day, and his patron treated the works of the Noble Bard
as mere ephemeral effusions, and spoke of poets that would be
admired thirty years hence, which was the farthest stretch of his
critical imagination. His antagonist's did not even reach so far. This
was the most romantic digression we ever had; and the subject was

not afterwards resumed. – No one here (generally speaking) has the slightest notion of any thing that has happened, that has been said, thought, or done out of his own recollection. It would be in vain to hearken after those 'wit-skirmishes', those 'brave sublunary things', which were the employment and delight of the Beaumonts and Bens of former times: but we may happily repose on dulness, drift with the tide of nonsense, and gain an agreeable vertigo by lending an ear to endless controversies. The confusion, provided you do not mingle in the fray and try to disentangle it, is amusing and edifying enough. Every species of false wit and spurious argument may be learnt here by potent examples. Whatever observations you hear dropt, have been picked up in the same place or in a kindred atmosphere. There is a kind of conversation made up entirely of scraps and hearsay, as there are a kind of books made up entirely of references to other books. This may account for the frequent contradictions which abound in the discourse of persons educated and disciplined wholly in coffee-houses. There is nothing stable or well-grounded in it: it is 'nothing but vanity, chaotic vanity'. They hear a remark at the Globe which they do not know what to make of; another at the Rainbow in direct opposition to it; and not having time to reconcile them, vent both at the Mitre.[6] In the course of half an hour, if they are not more than ordinarily dull, you are sure to find them on opposite sides of the question. This is the sickening part of it. People do not seem to talk for the sake of expressing their opinions, but to maintain an opinion for the sake of talking. We meet neither with modest ignorance nor studious acquirement. Their knowledge has been taken in too much by snatches to digest properly. There is neither sincerity nor system in what they say. They hazard the first crude notion that comes to hand, and then defend it how they can; which is for the most part but ill. 'Don't you think,' says M[ounsey], 'that Mr ——— is a very sensible, well-informed man?' – 'Why no,' I say, 'he seems to me to have no ideas of his own, and only to wait to see what others will say in order to set himself against it. I should not think that is the way to get at the truth. I do not desire to be driven out of my conclusions (such as they are) merely to make way for his upstart pretensions.' – 'Then there is ——— : what of him?' – 'He might very well express all he has to say in half the time, and with half the trouble. Why should he beat about the bush as he does? He appears to be getting up a little speech, and practising on a smaller scale for a Debating Society – the lowest ambition a man can have. Besides, by his manner of drawling out his words, and interlarding his periods with inuendos and formal reservations, he is evidently making up his mind all the time which side he shall take. He puts his sentences together as printers set up types, letter by letter. There is certainly no principle of short-hand in his mode of elocution. He goes round for a meaning, and the sense waits for him. It is not conversation, but rehearsing a part. Men of education and men of the world order this matter better. They know what they have to say on a subject, and come to the point at once. Your coffee-house politician balances between what he heard last and what he shall say next; and not seeing his way clearly, puts you off with circumstantial phrases, and tries to gain time for fear of making a false step. This gentleman has heard some one admired for precision and copiousness of language; and goes away, congratulating himself that he has not made a blunder in grammar or in rhetoric the whole evening. He is a theoretical *Quidnunc* – is tenacious in argument, though wary; carries his point thus and thus, bandies objections and answers with uneasy pleasantry, and when he has the worst of the dispute, puns very emphatically on his adversary's name, if it admits of that kind of misconstruction.' G[eorge Kirkpatrick] is admired by the waiter, who is a sleek hand* for his temper in managing an argument. Any one else would perceive that the latent cause is not patience with his antagonist, but satisfaction with himself. I think this unmoved self-complacency, this cavalier smooth simpering indifference is more annoying than the extremest violence or irritability. The one shews that your opponent does care something about you, and may be put out of his way by your remarks; the other seems to announce that nothing you say can shake his opinion a jot, that he has considered the whole of what you have to offer beforehand, and that he is in all respects much wiser and more accomplished than you. Such persons talk to grown people with the same air of patronage and condescension that they do to children. 'They will explain' – is a familiar expression with them, thinking you can only differ from them in consequence of misconceiving what they say.

---

* William, our waiter, is dressed neatly in black, takes in the *Tickler*,[7] (which many of the gentlemen like to look into) wears, I am told, a diamond-pin in his shirt-collar, has a music-master to teach him to play on the flageolet two hours before the maids are up, complains of confinement and a delicate constitution, and is a complete Master Stephen in his way.[8]

Or if you detect them in any error in point of fact (as to acknowledged deficiency in wit or argument, they would smile at the idea) they add some correction to your correction, and thus have the whip-hand of you again, being more correct than you who corrected them. If you hint some obvious oversight, they know what you are going to say, and were aware of the objection before you uttered it: – 'So shall their anticipation prevent your discovery.' By being in the right you gain no advantage: by being in the wrong you are entitled to the benefit of their pity or scorn! It is sometimes curious to see a select group of our little Gotham[9] getting about a knotty point that will bear a wager, as whether Dr Johnson's Dictionary was originally published in quarto or folio. The confident assertions, the cautious overtures, the length of time demanded to ascertain the fact, the precise terms of the forfeit, the provisos for getting out of paying it at last, lead to a long and inextricable discussion. G[eorge] was however so convinced in his own mind that the *Mourning Bride* was written by Shakespear, that he ran headlong into the snare: the bet was decided, and the punch was drunk. He has skill in numbers, and seldom exceeds his sevenpence. – He had a brother once, no Michael Cassio, no great arithmetician: R[oger Kirkpatrick] was a rare fellow, of the driest humour, and the nicest tact, of infinite sleights and evasions, of a picked phraseology, and the very soul of mimicry. I fancy I have some insight into physiognomy myself, but he could often expound to me at a single glance the characters of those of my acquaintance that I had been most at fault about. The account as it was cast up and balanced between us was not always very favourable. How finely, how truly, how gaily he took off the company at the S[outhampton]! Poor and faint are my sketches compared to his! It was like looking into a *camera obscura* – you saw faces shining and speaking – the smoke curled, the lights dazzled, the oak wainscoating took a higher polish – there was old S[arratt], tall and gaunt, with his couplet from Pope and case at Nisi Prius, M[ounsey] eyeing the ventilator and lying *perdu* for a moral, and H[ume] and A[yrton] taking another friendly finishing glass![10] – These and many more wind-falls of character he gave us in thought, word, and action. I remember his once describing three different persons together to myself and M[artin] B[urney], *viz.* the manager of a country theatre, a tragic and a comic performer, till we were ready to tumble on the floor with laughing at the oddity of their humours, and at R[oger]'s extraordinary powers of ventriloquism, bodily and mental; and B[urney] said (such was the vividness of the scene) that when he awoke the next morning, he wondered what three amusing characters he had been in company with the evening before. Oh! it was a rich treat to see him describe M[udford], him of the *Courier*, the Contemplative Man, who wrote an answer to *Cœlebs*,[11] coming into a room, folding up his great coat, taking out a little pocket volume, laying it down to think, rubbing the calf of his leg with grave self-complacency, and starting out of his reverie when spoken to with an inimitable vapid exclamation of 'Eh!' M[udford] is like a man made of fleecy hosiery: R[oger] was lank and lean 'as is the ribbed sea-sand'. Yet he seemed the very man he represented, as fat, pert, and dull as it was possible to be. I have not seen him of late:

For Kais is fled, and our tents are forlorn.

But I thought of him the other day when the news of the death of Buonaparte came, whom we both loved for precisely contrary reasons, he for putting down the rabble of the people, and I because he had put down the rabble of kings. Perhaps this event may rouse him from his lurking-place, where he lies like Reynard, with head declined, in feigned slumbers!* –

* His account of Dr W[hittle] was prodigious – of his occult sagacity, of his eyes prominent and wild like a hare's, fugacious of followers, of the arts by which he had left the City to lure the patients that he wanted after him to the West-End, of the ounce of tea that he purchased by stratagem as an unusual treat to his guest, and of the narrow winding staircase, from the height of which he contemplated in security the imaginary approach of duns. He was a large, plain, fair-faced Moravian preacher, turned physician. He was an honest man, but vain of he knew not what. He was once sitting where Sarratt was playing a game at chess without seeing the board; and after remaining for some time absorbed in silent wonder, he turned suddenly to me and said, 'Do you know Mr H[azlitt], that I think there is something I could do?' 'Well, what is that?' 'Why perhaps you would not guess, but I think I could dance, I'm sure I could; ay, I could dance like Vestris!' – Sarratt, who was a man of various accomplishments, (among others one of the Fancy,) afterwards bared his arm to convince us of his muscular strength, and Mrs W[hittle] going out of the room with another lady said, 'Do you know, Madam, the Doctor is a great jumper!' Molière could not outdo this. Never shall I forget his pulling off his coat to eat beef-steaks on equal terms with Martin B[urney]. Life is short, but full of mirth and pastime, did we not so soon forget what we have laughed at, perhaps that we may not remember what we have cried at! – Sarratt, the chess-player, was an extraordinary man. He had the same tenacious, epileptic faculty in other things that he had at chess, and could no more get any other ideas out of his mind than he could those of the figures on the board. He was a great reader, but had not the least taste. Indeed the

I had almost forgotten the S[outhampton] Tavern. We for some time took C—— for a lawyer, from a certain arguteness of voice and slenderness of neck, and from his having a quibble and a laugh at himself always ready. On inquiry, however, he was found to be a patent-medicine seller, and having leisure in his apprenticeship, and a forwardness of parts, he had taken to study Blackstone and the Statutes at Large. On appealing to M[ounsey] for his opinion on this matter, he observed pithily, 'I don't like so much law: the gentlemen here seem fond of law, but I have law enough at chambers.' One sees a great deal of the humours and tempers of men in a place of this sort, and may almost gather their opinions from their characters. There is E——, a fellow that is always in the wrong – who puts might for right on all occasions – a Tory in grain – who has no one idea but what has been instilled into him by custom and authority – an everlasting babbler on the stronger side of the question – querulous and dictatorial, and with a peevish whine in his voice like a beaten school-boy. He is a great advocate for the Bourbons, and for the National Debt. The former he affirms to be the choice of the French people, and the latter he insists is necessary to the salvation of these kingdoms. This last point a little inoffensive gentleman among us, of a saturnine aspect but simple conceptions, cannot comprehend. 'I will tell you, Sir – I will make my proposition so clear that you will be convinced of the truth of my observation in a moment. Consider, Sir, the number of trades that would be thrown out of employ, if it were done away with: what would become of the porcelain manufacture without it?' Any stranger to overhear one of these debates would swear that the English as a nation are bad logicians. Mood and figure are unknown to them. They do not argue by the book. They arrive at conclusions through the force of prejudice, and on the principles of contradiction. Mr E—— having thus triumphed in argument, offers a flower to the notice of the company as a specimen of his flower-garden, a curious exotic, nothing like it to be found in this kingdom, talks of his carnations, of his country house, and old English hospitality, but never invites any of his friends to come

---

violence of his memory tyrannised over and destroyed all power of selection. He could repeat Ossian by heart, without knowing the best passage from the worst; and did not perceive he was tiring you to death by giving an account of the breed, education, and manners of fighting-dogs for hours together. The sense of reality quite superseded the distinction between the pleasurable and the painful. He was altogether a mechanical philosopher.

down and take their Sunday's dinner with him. He is mean and ostentatious at the same time; insolent and servile, does not know whether to treat those he converses with as if they were his porters or his customers: the prentice-boy is not yet wiped out of him, and his imagination still hovers between his mansion at ——, and the work-house. Opposed to him and to every one else, is K——, a radical reformer and logician, who makes clear work of the taxes and national debt, reconstructs the Government from the first principles of things, shatters the Holy Alliance[12] at a blow, grinds out the future prospects of society with a machine, and is setting out afresh with the commencement of the French Revolution five and twenty years ago, as if on an untried experiment. He minds nothing but the formal agreement of his premises and his conclusions, and does not stick at obstacles in the way nor consequences in the end. If there was but one side of a question, he would be always in the right. He casts up one column of the account to admiration, but totally forgets and rejects the other. His ideas lie like square pieces of wood in his brain, and may be said to be piled up on a stiff architectural principle, perpendicularly, and at right angles. There is no inflection, no modification, no graceful embellishment, no Corinthian capitals. I never heard him agree to two propositions together, or to more than half a one at a time. His rigid love of truth bends to nothing but his habitual love of disputation. He puts one in mind of one of those long-headed politicians and frequenters of coffee-houses mentioned in Berkeley's *Minute Philosopher*, who would make nothing of such old-fashioned fellows as Plato and Aristotle. He has the new light strong upon him, and he knocks other people down with its solid beams. He denies that he has got certain views out of Cobbett,[13] though he allows that there are excellent ideas occasionally to be met with in that writer. It is a pity that this enthusiastic and unqualified regard to truth should be accompanied with an equal exactness of expenditure and unrelenting eye to the main-chance. He brings a bunch of radishes with him for cheapness, and gives a band of musicians at the door a penny, observing that he likes their performance better than all the Opera-squalling. This brings the severity of his political principles into question if not into contempt. He would abolish the National Debt from motives of personal economy, and objects to Mr Canning's pension because it perhaps takes a farthing a year out of his own pocket. A great deal of radical reasoning has its source in this feeling. – He bestows no

small quantity of his tediousness upon M[ounsey], on whose mind
all these formulas and diagrams fall like seed on stony ground:
'while the manna is descending', he shakes his ears, and in the
intervals of the debate, insinuates an objection, and calls for
another half-pint. I have sometimes said to him – 'Any one to come
in here without knowing you, would take you for the most
disputatious man alive, for you are always engaged in an argument
with somebody or other.' The truth is, that M[ounsey] is a good-
natured, gentlemanly man, who notwithstanding, if appealed to,
will not let an absurd or unjust proposition pass without
expressing his dissent; and therefore he is a sort of mark for all
those (and we have several of that stamp) who like to teaze other
people's understandings, as wool-combers teaze wool. He is
certainly the flower of the flock. He is the oldest frequenter of the
place, the latest sitter-up, well-informed, inobtrusive, and that
sturdy old English character, a lover of truth and justice. I never
knew M[ounsey] approve of any thing unfair or illiberal. There is
a candour and uprightness about his mind which can neither be
wheedled nor browbeat into unjustifiable complaisance. He looks
strait-forward as he sits with his glass in his hand, turning neither
to the right nor the left, and I will venture to say that he has never
had a sinister object in view through life. Mrs Battle (it is recorded
in her *Opinions on Whist*) could not make up her mind to use the
word '*Go*'.[14] M[ounsey] from long practice has got over this
difficulty, and uses it incessantly. It is no matter what adjunct
follows in the train of this despised monosyllable: – whatever
liquid comes after this prefix is welcome. M[ounsey] without being
the most communicative, is the most conversible man I know. The
social principle is inseparable from his person. If he has nothing to
say, he drinks your health; and when you cannot from the rapidity
and carelessness of his utterance catch what he says, you assent to
it with equal confidence: you know his meaning is good. His
favourite phrase is 'We have all of us something of the cox-comb';
and yet he has none of it himself. Before I had exchanged half a
dozen sentences with M[ounsey], I found that he knew several of
my old acquaintance (an immediate introduction of itself, for the
discussing the characters and foibles of common friends is a great
sweetener and cement of friendship) – and had been intimate with
most of the wits and men about town for the last twenty years. He
knew Tobin, Wordsworth, Porson, Wilson, Paley, Erskine, and
many others.[15] He speaks of Paley's pleasantry and unassuming

manners, and describes Porson's long potations and long quotations formerly at the Cider-Cellar in a very lively way.[16] He has doubts, however, as to that sort of learning. On my saying that I had never seen the Greek Professor but once, at the Library of the London Institution, when he was dressed in an old rusty black coat, with cobwebs hanging to the skirts of it, and with a large patch of coarse brown paper covering the whole length of his nose, looking for all the world like a drunken carpenter, and talking to one of the Proprietors with an air of suavity, approaching to condescension, M[ounsey] could not help expressing some little uneasiness for the credit of classical literature. 'I submit, Sir, whether common sense is not the principal thing? What is the advantage of genius and learning if they are of no use in the conduct of life' – M[ounsey] is one who loves the hours that usher in the morn, when a select few are left in twos and threes like stars before the break of day, and when the discourse and the ale are 'aye growing better and better.' W[ells],[17] M[ounsey], and myself were all that remained one evening. We had sat together several hours without being tired of one another's company. The conversation turned on the Beauties of Charles the Second's Court at Windsor, and from thence to Count Grammont, their gallant and gay historian.[18] We took our favourite passages in turn – one preferring that of Killigrew's country-cousin, who having been resolutely refused by Miss Warminster (one of the Maids of Honour) when he found she had been unexpectedly brought to bed, fell on his knees and thanked God that now she might take compassion on him – another insisting that the Chevalier Hamilton's assignation with Lady Chesterfield, when she kept him all night shivering in an old out-house, was better. Jacob Hall's prowess was not forgotten, nor the story of Miss Stuart's garters. I was getting on in my way with that delicate *endroit*, in which Miss Churchill is first introduced at court and is besieged (as a matter of course) by the Duke of York, who was gallant as well as bigoted on system. His assiduities however soon slackened, owing (it is said) to her having a pale, thin face; till one day, as they were riding out hunting together, she fell from her horse, and was taken up almost lifeless. The whole assembled court were thrown by this event into admiration that such a body should belong to such a face* (so transcendent a pattern was she of the

---

* 'Ils ne pouvoient croire qu'un corps de cette beauté fût de quelque chose au visage de Mademoiselle Churchill.' – *Memoires de Grammont*, vol. II, p. 254.

female form) and the Duke was fixed. This I contended was striking, affecting, and grand, the sublime of amorous biography, and said I could conceive of nothing finer than the idea of a young person in her situation, who was the object of indifference or scorn from outward appearance, with the proud suppressed consciousness of a Goddess-like symmetry, locked up by 'fear and niceness, the hand-maids of all women', from the wonder and worship of mankind. I said so then, and I think so now: my tongue grew wanton in the praise of this passage, and I believe it bore the bell from its competitors. W[ells] then spoke of Lucius Apuleius and his *Golden Ass*, which contains the story of Cupid and Psyche, with other matter rich and rare, and went on to the romance of Heliodorus, Theagenes and Chariclea. This, as he affirmed, opens with a pastoral landscape equal to Claude, and in it the presiding deities of Love and Wine appear in all their pristine strength, youth and grace, crowned and worshipped as of yore. The night waned, but our glasses brightened, enriched with the pearls of Grecian story. Our cup-bearer slept in a corner of the room, like another Endymion, in the pale ray of an half-extinguished lamp, and starting up at a fresh summons for a farther supply, he swore it was too late, and was inexorable to entreaty. M[ounsey] sat with his hat on and with a hectic flush in his face while any hope remained, but as soon as we rose to go, he darted out of the room as quick as lightning, determined not to be the last that went. – I said some time after to the waiter, that 'Mr M[ounsey] was no flincher.' – 'Oh! Sir,' says he, 'you should have known him formerly, when Mr H[ume] and Mr A[yrton] used to be here. Now he is quite another man: he seldom stays later than one or two.' – 'Why, did they keep it up much later then?' – 'Oh! yes; and used to sing catches and all sorts.' – 'What, did Mr M[ounsey] sing catches?' – 'He joined chorus, Sir, and was as merry as the best of them. He was always a pleasant gentleman!' – This H[ume] and A[yrton] succumbed in the fight. A[yrton] was a dry Scotchman, H[ume] a good-natured, hearty Englishman. I do not mean that the same character applies to all Scotchmen or to all Englishmen. H[ume] was of the Pipe-Office (not unfitly appointed), and in his cheerfuller cups would delight to speak of a widow and a bowling-green, that ran in his head to the last.[19] 'What is the good of talking of those things now?' said the man of utility. 'I don't know,' replied the other, quaffing another glass of sparkling ale, and with a lambent fire playing in his eye and round his bald forehead – (he had a head that Sir Joshua would have made something bland and genial of) – 'I don't know, but they were delightful to me at the time, and are still pleasant to talk and think of.' – *Such a one*, in Touchstone's phrase, *is a natural philosopher*; and in nine cases out of ten that sort of philosophy is the best! I could enlarge this sketch, such as it is; but to prose on to the end of the chapter might prove less profitable than tedious.

I like very well to sit in a room where there are people talking on subjects I know nothing of, if I am only allowed to sit silent and as a spectator. But I do not much like to join in the conversation, except with people and on subjects to my taste. Sympathy is necessary to society. To look on, a variety of faces, humours, and opinions is sufficient: to mix with others, agreement as well as variety is indispensable. What makes good society? I answer, in one word, real fellowship. Without a similitude of tastes, acquirements, and pursuits (whatever may be the difference of tempers and characters) there can be no intimacy or even casual intercourse, worth the having. What makes the most agreeable party? A number of people with a number of ideas in common, 'yet so as with a difference'; that is, who can put one or more subjects which they have all studied in the greatest variety of entertaining or useful lights. Or in other words, a succession of good things said with good humour, and addressed to the understandings of those who hear them, make the most desirable conversation. Ladies, lovers, beaux, wits, philosophers, the fashionable or the vulgar, are the fittest company for one another. The discourse at Randall's is the best for boxers: that at Long's for lords and loungers. I prefer H[unt]'s conversation almost to any other person's, because, with a familiar range of subjects, he colours with a totally new and sparkling light, reflected from his own character. Elia, the grave and witty, says things not to be surpassed in essence: but the manner is more painful and less a relief to my own thoughts.[20] Some one conceived he could not be an excellent companion, because he was seen walking down the side of the Thames, *passibus iniquis*, after dining at Richmond. The objection was not valid. I will however admit that the said Elia is the worst company in the world in bad company, if it be granted me that in good company he is nearly the best that can be. He is one of those of whom it may be said, *Tell me your company, and I'll tell you your manners.* He is the creature of sympathy, and makes good whatever opinion you seem to entertain of him. He cannot outgo the apprehensions of the circle; and invariably acts up or down to the point of refinement or vulgarity at which they pitch him. He appears to take a pleasure in exaggerating the prejudices of strangers against him; a pride in confirming the prepossessions of friends. In whatever scale of intellect he is placed, he is as lively or as stupid as the rest can be for their lives. If you think him odd and ridiculous, he becomes more and more so every minute, *à la folie*, till he is a wonder gazed by all – set him against a good wit and a ready apprehension, and he brightens more and more –

> Or like a gate of steel
> Fronting the sun, receives and renders back
> Its figure and its heat.[21]

We had a pleasant party one evening at B[arry] C[ornwall]'s.[22] A young literary bookseller who was present went away delighted with the elegance of the repast, and spoke in raptures of a servant in green livery and a patent-lamp. I thought myself that the charm of the evening consisted in some talk about Beaumont and Fletcher and the old poets, in which every one took part or interest, and in a consciousness that we could not pay our host a better compliment than in thus alluding to studies in which he excelled, and in praising authors whom he had imitated with feeling and sweetness! – I should think it may be also laid down as a rule on this subject, that to constitute good company a certain proportion of hearers and speakers is requisite. Coleridge makes good company for this reason. He immediately establishes the principle of the division of labour in this respect, wherever he comes. He takes his cue as speaker, and the rest of the party theirs as listeners – a 'Circean herd' – without any previous arrangement having been gone through. I will just add that there can be no good society without perfect freedom from affectation and constraint. If the unreserved communication of feeling or opinion leads to offensive familiarity, it is not well. But it is no better where the absence of offensive remarks arises only from formality and an assumed respectfulness of manner.

I do not think there is any thing deserving the name of society to be found out of London: and that for the two following reasons. First, there is *neighbourhood* elsewhere, accidental or unavoidable acquaintance: people are thrown together by chance or grow together like trees; but you can pick your society nowhere but in London. The very persons that of all others you would wish to associate with in almost every line of life, (or at least of intellectual pursuit,) are to be met with there. It is hard if out of a million of people you cannot find half a dozen to your liking. Individuals may seem lost and hid in the size of the place: but in fact from this very circumstance you are within two or three miles' reach of persons that without it you would be some hundreds apart from. Secondly, London is the only place in which each individual in company is treated according to his value in company, and to that only. In every other part of the kingdom he carries another character about with him, which supersedes the intellectual or social one. It is known in Manchester or Liverpool what every man in the room is worth in land or money; what are his connexions and prospects in life – and this gives a character of servility or arrogance, of mercenariness or impertinence to the whole of provincial intercourse. You laugh not in proportion to a man's wit, but his wealth: you have to consider not what, but whom you contradict. You speak by the pound, and are heard by the rood. In the metropolis there is neither time nor inclination for these remote calculations. Every man depends on the quantity of sense, wit, or good manners he brings into society for the reception he meets with in it. A member of parliament soon finds his level as a commoner: the merchant and manufacturer cannot bring his goods to market here: the great landed proprietor shrinks from being the lord of acres into a pleasant companion or a dull fellow. When a visitor enters or leaves a room, it is not inquired whether he is rich or poor, whether he lives in a garret or a palace, or comes in his own or a hackney-coach, but whether he has a good expression of countenance, with an unaffected manner, and whether he is a man of understanding or a blockhead. These are the circumstances by which you make a favourable impression on the company, and by which they estimate you in the abstract. In the country, they consider whether you have a vote at the next election, or a place in your gift; and measure the capacity of others to instruct or entertain them by the strength of their pockets and their credit with their banker. Personal merit is at a prodigious discount in the provinces. I like the country very well, if I want to enjoy my own company: but London is the only place for equal society, or where a man can say a good thing or express an honest opinion without subjecting himself to being insulted, unless he

first lays his purse on the table to back his pretensions to talent or
independence of spirit. I speak from experience.*

---

*   When I was young, I spent a good deal of my time at Manchester and Liverpool;
and I confess I give the preference to the former. There you were oppressed only
by the aristocracy of wealth; in the latter by the aristocracy of wealth and letters
by turns. You could not help feeling that some of their great men were authors
among merchants and merchants among authors. Their bread was buttered on
both sides, and they had you at a disadvantage either way. The Manchester
cotton-spinners, on the contrary, set up no pretensions beyond their looms, were
hearty good fellows, and took any information or display of ingenuity on other
subjects in good part. I remember well being introduced to a distinguished
patron of art and rising merit at a little distance from Liverpool, and was received
with every mark of attention and politeness, till the conversation turning on
Italian literature, our host remarked that there was nothing in the English
language corresponding to the severity of the Italian ode – except perhaps
Dryden's *Alexander's Feast*, and Pope's *St Cecilia*! I could no longer contain my
desire to display my smattering in criticism, and began to maintain that Pope's
Ode was, as it appeared to me, far from an example of severity in writing. I soon
perceived what I had done, but here am I writing *Table-talks* in consequence.
Alas! I knew as little of the world then as I do now. I never could understand
anything beyond an abstract definition.

On the Aristocracy of Letters

From volume two of *Table-Talk* (1822). Initially an attack on the idle aristocracy of literature, from supercilious scholars to neutered pets of the nobility, this broadens into a passionate critique of social snobbery as the main arbiter of literary merit. 'There is not a more helpless or a more despised animal than a mere author', Hazlitt writes, 'without any extrinsic advantages of birth, breeding or fortune to set him off.' Following the line adopted by Byron, Shelley and Leigh Hunt, he contends that it was hostile reviews from the Tory magazines that shortened the life of the 'Cockney' poet John Keats. Keats, who was a great admirer of Hazlitt's, had died of tuberculosis in 1821, at the age of twenty-five.

Ha! here's three of us are sophisticated: – off, you lendings.[1]

There is such a thing as an aristocracy or privileged order in letters, which has sometimes excited my wonder, and sometimes my spleen. We meet with authors who have never done any thing, but who have a vast reputation for what they could have done. Their names stand high, and are in every body's mouth, but their works are never heard of, or had better remain undiscovered for the sake of their admirers. – *Stat nominis umbra* – their pretensions are lofty and unlimited, as they have nothing to rest upon, or because it is impossible to confront them with the proofs of their deficiency. If you inquire farther, and insist upon some act of authorship to establish the claims of these Epicurean votaries of the Muses, you find that they had a great reputation at Cambridge, that they were senior wranglers or successful prize-essayists, that they visit at [Holland] House,[2] and to support that honour, must be supposed of course to occupy the first rank in the world of letters.* It is

---

* Lord H[olland] had made a diary (in the manner of Boswell) of the conversation held at his house, and read it at the end of a week *pro bono publico*. Sir J[ames] M[ackintosh] made a considerable figure in it, and a celebrated poet none at all, merely answering Yes and No. With this result he was by no means satisfied, and talked incessantly from that day forward. At the end of the week he asked,

possible, however, that they have some manuscript work in hand, which is of too much importance (and the writer has too much at stake in publishing it) hastily to see the light: or perhaps they once had an article in the *Edinburgh Review,* which was much admired at the time, and is kept by them ever since as a kind of diploma and unquestionable testimonial of merit. They are not like Grub-street authors, who write for bread, and are paid by the sheet. Like misers who hoard their wealth, they are supposed to be masters of all the wit and sense they do not impart to the public. 'Continents have most of what they contain,' says a considerable philosopher; and these persons, it must be confessed, have a prodigious command over themselves in the expenditure of light and learning. The Oriental curse – 'O that mine enemy had written a book' – hangs suspended over them. By never committing themselves, they neither give a handle to the malice of the world, nor excite the jealousy of friends; and keep all the reputation they have got, not by discreetly blotting, but by never writing a line. Some one told Sheridan, who was always busy about some new work and never advancing any farther in it, that he would not write because he was afraid of the Author of the *School for Scandal.*[3] So these idle pretenders are afraid of undergoing a comparison with themselves in something they have never done, but have had credit for doing. They do not acquire celebrity, they assume it; and escape detection by never venturing out of their imposing and mysterious *incognito.* They do not let themselves down by every-day work: for them to appear in print is a work of supererogation as much as in lords or kings, and like gentlemen with a large landed estate, they live on their established character, and do nothing (or as little as possible) to increase or lose it. There is not a more deliberate piece of grave imposture going. I know a person of this description who has been employed many years (by implication) on a translation of Thucydides, of which no one ever saw a word, but it does not answer the purpose of bolstering up a factitious reputation the less on that account. The longer it is delayed and kept sacred from the vulgar gaze, the more it swells into imaginary consequence; the labour and care required for a work of this kind being immense: –

with some anxiety and triumph, if his Lordship had continued his diary, expecting himself to shine in 'the first row of the rubric'. To which his Noble Patron answered in the negative, with an intimation that it had not appeared to him worth while. Our poet was thus thrown again into the back ground, and Sir James remained master of the field!

and then there are no faults in an unexecuted translation. The only impeccable writers are those who never wrote. Another is an oracle on subjects of taste and classical erudition, because (he says at least) he reads Cicero once a year to keep up the purity of his Latinity. A third makes the indecency pass for the depth of his researches and for a high gusto in *virtù*, till from his seeing nothing in the finest remains of ancient art, the world by the merest accident find out that there is nothing in him. There is scarcely any thing that a grave face with an impenetrable manner will not accomplish, and whoever is weak enough to impose upon himself, will have wit enough to impose upon the public – particularly if he can make it their interest to be deceived by shallow boasting, and contrives not to hurt their self-love by sterling acquirements. Do you suppose that the understood translation of Thucydides costs its supposed author nothing? A select party of friends and admirers dine with him once a week at a magnificent town-mansion or a more elegant and picturesque retreat in the country. They broach their Horace and their old hock, and sometimes allude with a considerable degree of candour to the defects of works which are brought out by contemporary writers – the ephemeral offspring of haste and necessity!

Among other things, the learned languages are a ready passport to this sort of unmeaning, unanalysed reputation. They presently lift a man up among the celestial constellations, the signs of the Zodiac (as it were) and third heaven of inspiration, from whence he looks down on those who are toiling on in this lower sphere, and earning their bread by the sweat of their brain, at leisure and in scorn. If the graduates in this way condescend to express their thoughts in English, it is understood to be *infra dignitatem* – such light and unaccustomed essays do not fit the ponderous gravity of their pen – they only draw to advantage and with full justice to themselves in the bow of the ancients. Their native-tongue is to them strange, inelegant, unapt, and crude. They 'cannot command it to any utterance of harmony. They have not the skill.' This is true enough; but you must not say so, under a heavy penalty – the displeasure of pedants and blockheads. It would be sacrilege against the privileged classes, the Aristocracy of Letters. What! will you affirm that a profound Latin scholar, a perfect Grecian, cannot write a page of common sense or grammar? Is it not to be presumed, by all the charters of the Universities and the foundations of grammar-schools, that he who can speak a dead language must be *a fortiori* conversant with his own? Surely, the greater implies the less. He who knows every science and every art cannot be ignorant of the most familiar forms of speech. Or if this plea is found not to hold water, then our scholastic bungler is said to be above this vulgar trial of skill, 'something must be excused to want of practice – but did you not observe the elegance of the Latinity, how well that period would become a classical and studied dress?' Thus defects are 'monster'd' into excellences, and they screen their idol, and require you, at your peril, to pay prescriptive homage to false concords and inconsequential criticisms, because the writer of them has the character of the first or second Greek or Latin scholar in the kingdom. If you do not swear to the truth of these spurious credentials, you are ignorant and malicious, a quack and a scribbler – *flagranti delicto!* Thus the man who can merely read and construe some old author is of a class superior to any living one, and, by parity of reasoning, to those old authors themselves: the poet or prose-writer of true and original genius, by the courtesy of custom, 'ducks to the learned fool': or as the author of *Hudibras* has so well stated the same thing,

> – He that is but able to express
> No sense at all in several languages
> Will pass for learneder than he that's known
> To speak the strongest reason in his own.[4]

These preposterous and unfounded claims of mere scholars to precedence in the commonwealth of letters, which they set up so formally themselves and which others so readily bow to, are partly owing to traditional prejudice: – there was a time when learning was the only distinction from ignorance, and when there was no such thing as popular English literature. Again, there is something more palpable and positive in this kind of acquired knowledge, like acquired wealth, which the vulgar easily recognise. That others know the meaning of signs which they are confessedly and altogether ignorant of, is to them both a matter of fact and a subject of endless wonder. The languages are worn like a dress by a man, and distinguish him sooner than his natural figure; and we are, from motives of self-love, inclined to give others credit for the ideas they have borrowed or have come into indirect possession of, rather than for those that originally belong to them and are exclusively their own. The merit in them and the implied inferiority in ourselves is less. Learning is a kind of external appendage or transferable property –

'Twas mine, 'tis his, and may be any man's[5] –

Genius and understanding are a man's self, an integrant part of his personal identity; and the title to these last, as it is the most difficult to be ascertained, is also the most grudgingly acknowledged. Few persons would pretend to deny that Porson had more Greek than they. It was a question of fact which might be put to the immediate proof, and could not be gainsaid. But the meanest frequenter of the Cider-Cellar or the Hole in the Wall would be inclined, in his own conceit, to dispute the palm of wit or sense with him; and indemnify his self-complacency for the admiration paid to living learning by significant hints to friends and casual droppers-in, that the greatest men, when you came to know them, were not without their weak sides as well as others. – Pedants, I will add here, talk to the vulgar as pedagogues talk to school-boys, on an understood principle of condescension and superiority, and therefore make little progress in the knowledge of men or things. While they fancy they are accommodating themselves to, or else assuming airs of importance over, inferior capacities, these inferior capacities are really laughing at them. There can be no true superiority but what arises out of the presupposed ground of equality: there can be no improvement but from the free communication and comparing of ideas. Kings and nobles, for this reason, receive little benefit from society – where all is submission on one side, and condescension on the other. The mind strikes out truth by collision, as steel strikes fire from the flint!

There are whole families who are born classical, and are entered in the heralds' college of reputation by the right of consanguinity. Literature, like nobility, runs in the blood. There is the B[urney] family. There is no end of it or its pretensions. It produces wits, scholars, novelists, musicians, artists in 'numbers numberless'. The name is alone a passport to the Temple of Fame. Those who bear it are free of Parnassus by birth-right. The founder of it[6] was himself an historian and a musician, but more of a courtier and man of the world than either. The secret of his success may perhaps be discovered in the following passage, where, in alluding to three eminent performers on different instruments, he says, 'These three illustrious personages were introduced at the Emperour's court', &c.; speaking of them as if they were foreign ambassadours or princes of the blood, and thus magnifying himself and his profession. This overshadowing manner carries nearly every thing before it, and mystifies a great many. There is nothing like putting the best face upon things, and leaving others to find out the difference. He who could call three musicians 'personages', would himself play a personage through life, and succeed in his leading object. Sir Joshua Reynolds, remarking on this passage, said, 'No one had a greater respect than he had for his profession, but that he should never think of applying to it epithets that were appropriated merely to external rank and distinction.' Madame D['Arblay], it must be owned, had cleverness enough to stock a whole family, and to set up her cousin-germans, male and female, for wits and virtuosos to the third and fourth generation. The rest have done nothing, that I know of, but keep up the name.

The most celebrated author in modern times has written without a name, and has been knighted for anonymous productions.[7] Lord Byron complains that Horace Walpole was not properly appreciated, 'first, because he was a gentleman, and secondly, because he was a nobleman'. His Lordship stands in one, at least, of the predicaments here mentioned, and yet he has had justice, or somewhat more, done him. He towers above his fellows by all the height of the peerage. If the poet lends a grace to the nobleman, the nobleman pays it back to the poet with interest. What a fine addition is ten thousand a year and a title to the flaunting pretensions of a modern rhapsodist! His name so accompanied becomes the mouth well: it is repeated thousands of times, instead of hundreds, because the reader in being familiar with the Poet's works seems to claim acquaintance with the Lord.

> Let but a lord once own the happy lines:
> How the wit brightens, and the style refines![8]

He smiles at the high-flown praise or petty cavils of little men. Does he make a slip in decorum, which Milton declares to be the principal thing? His proud crest and armorial bearings support him: – no bend-sinister slurs his poetical escutcheon! Is he dull, or does he put off some trashy production on the public? It is not charged to his account, as a deficiency which he must make good at the peril of his admirers. His Lordship is not answerable for the negligence or extravagances of his Muse. He 'bears a charmed reputation, which must not yield' like one of vulgar birth. The Noble Bard is for this reason scarcely vulnerable to the critics. The double barrier of his pretensions baffles their puny, timid efforts. Strip off some of his tarnished laurels, and the coronet appears glittering beneath: restore them, and it still shires through with keener lustre. In fact, his Lordship's blaze of reputation culminates from his rank and place in society. He sustains two lofty and imposing characters; and in order to simplify the process of our admiration, and 'leave no rubs or botches in the way', we equalise his pretensions, and take it for granted that he must be as superior to other men in genius as he is in birth. Or, to give a more familiar solution of the enigma, the Poet and the Peer agree to honour each other's acceptances on the bank of Fame, and sometimes cozen the town to some tune between them. – Really, however, and with all his privileges, Lord Byron might as well not have written that strange letter about Pope.[9] I could not afford it, poor as I am. Why does he pronounce, *ex cathedrâ* and robed, that Cowper is no poet? Cowper was a gentleman and of noble family like his critic. He was a teacher of morality as well as a describer of nature, which is more than his Lordship is. His *John Gilpin* will last as long as *Beppo*, and his verses to Mary are not less touching than the *Farewell*. If I had ventured upon such an assertion as this, it would have been worse for me than finding out a borrowed line in the *Pleasures of Hope*.[10]

There is not a more helpless or more despised animal than a mere author, without any extrinsic advantages of birth, breeding, or fortune to set him off. The real ore of talents or learning must be stamped before it will pass current. To be at all looked upon as an author, a man must be something more or less than an author – a rich merchant, a banker, a lord, or a ploughman. He is admired for something foreign to himself, that acts as a bribe to the servility or a set-off to the envy of the community. 'What should such fellows as we do, crawling betwixt heaven and earth'; – 'coining our hearts for drachmas'; now scorched in the sun, now shivering in the breeze, now coming out in our newest gloss and best attire, like swallows in the spring, now 'sent back like hollowmas or shortest day'? The best wits, like the handsomest faces *upon the town*, lead a harassing, precarious life – are taken up for the bud and promise of talent, which they no sooner fulfil than they are thrown aside like an old fashion – are caressed without reason, and insulted with impunity – are subject to all the caprice, the malice, and fulsome advances of that great keeper, the Public – and in the end come to no good, like all those who lavish their favours on mankind at large and look to the gratitude of the world for their reward. Instead of this set of Grub-street authors, the mere *canaille* of letters, this corporation of Mendicity, this ragged regiment of genius suing at the corners of streets, *in forma pauperis*, give me the gentleman and scholar, with a good house over his head and a handsome table 'with wine of Attic taste' to ask his friends to, and where want and sorrow never come. Fill up the sparkling bowl, heap high the dessert with roses crowned, bring out the hot-pressed poem, the vellum manuscripts, the medals, the portfolios, the intaglios – this is the true model of the life of a man of taste and *virtù* – the possessors, not the inventors of these things, are the true benefactors of mankind and ornaments of letters. Look in, and there, amidst silver services and shining chandeliers, you will see the man of genius at his proper post, picking his teeth and mincing an opinion, sheltered by rank, bowing to wealth – a poet framed, glazed, and hung in a striking light: not a straggling weed, torn and trampled on; not a poor *Kit-run-the-street*, but a powdered beau, a sycophant plant, an exotic reared in a glass-case, hermetically sealed,

Free from the Sirian star and the dread thunder-stroke[11] –

whose mealy coat no moth can corrupt nor blight can wither. The poet Keats had not this sort of protection for his person – he lay bare to weather – the serpent stung him, and the poison-tree dropped upon this little western flower: – when the mercenary servile crew approached him, he had no pedigree to show them, no rent-roll to hold out in reversion for their praise: he was not in any great man's train, nor the butt and puppet of a lord – he could only offer them 'the fairest flowers of the season, carnations and streaked gilliflowers', – 'rue for remembrance and pansies for thoughts' – they recked not of his gift, but tore him with hideous shouts and laughter,

Nor could the Muse protect her son![12]

Unless an author has an establishment of his own, or is entered on that of some other person, he will hardly be allowed to write English or to spell his own name. To be well-spoken of, he must enlist under some standard; he must belong to some *coterie*. He must get the *esprit de corps* on his side: he must have literary bail in readiness. Thus they prop one another's ricketty heads at M[urray]'s shop,[13] and a spurious reputation, like false argument, runs in a circle. C[roker] affirms that G[ifford] is sprightly, and

G[ifford] that C[roker] is genteel: D'I[israeli] that J[acob] is wise, and J[acob] that D'I[israeli] is good-natured.[14] A member of Parliament must be answerable that you are not dangerous or dull before you can be of the *entrée*. You must commence toad-eater[15] to have your observations attended to; if you are independent, unconnected, you will be regarded as a poor creature. Your opinion is honest, you will say: then ten to one, it is not profitable. It is at any rate your own. So much the worse; for then it is not the world's. T[ommy] Hill] is a very tolerable barometer in this respect.[16] He knows nothing, hears every thing, and repeats just what he hears; so that you may guess pretty well from this round-faced echo what is said by others! Almost every thing goes by presumption and appearances. 'Did you not think Mr B——'s language very elegant?' – I thought he bowed very low. 'Did you not think him remarkably well-behaved?' – He was unexceptionably dressed. 'But were not Mr C——'s manners quite insinuating?' – He said nothing. 'You will at least allow his friend to be a well-informed man?' – He talked upon all subjects alike. Such would be a pretty faithful interpretation of the tone of what is called *good society*. The surface is every thing: we do not pierce to the core. The setting is more valuable than the jewel. Is it not so in other things as well as letters? Is not an RA[17] by the supposition a greater man in his profession than any one who is not so blazoned? Compared with that unrivalled list, Raphael had been illegitimate, Claude not classical, and Michael Angelo admitted by special favour. What is a physician without a diploma? An alderman without being knighted? An actor whose name does not appear in great letters? All others are counterfeits – men 'of no mark or likelihood'. This was what made the Jackalls of the North so eager to prove that I had been turned out of the *Edinburgh Review*.[18] It was not the merit of the articles which excited their spleen – but their being there. Of the style they knew nothing; for the thought they cared nothing: – all that they knew was that I wrote in that powerful journal, and therefore they asserted that I did not!

We find a class of persons who labour under an obvious natural inaptitude for whatever they aspire to. Their manner of setting about it is a virtual disqualification. The simple affirmation – 'What this man has said, I will do,' – is not always considered as the proper test of capacity. On the contrary, there are people whose bare pretensions are as good or better than the actual performance of others. What I myself have done, for instance, I never find admitted as proof of what I shall be able to do: whereas I observe others who bring as proof of their competence to any task (and are taken at their word) what they have never done, and who gravely assure those who are inclined to trust them that their talents are exactly fitted for some post because they are just the reverse of what they have ever shown them to be. One man has the air of an Editor as much as another has that of a butler or porter in a gentleman's family. ——is the model of this character, with a prodigious look of business, an air of suspicion which passes for sagacity, and an air of deliberation which passes for judgment. If his own talents are no ways prominent, it is inferred he will be more impartial and in earnest in making use of those of others. There is [John Britton],[19] the responsible conductor of several works of taste and erudition, yet (God knows) without an idea in his head relating to any one of them. He is learned by proxy, and successful from sheer imbecility. If he were to get the smallest smattering of the departments which are under his controul, he would betray himself from his desire to shine; but as it is, he leaves others to do all the drudgery for him. He signs his name in the title-page or at the bottom of a vignette, and nobody suspects any mistake. This contractor for useful and ornamental literature once offered me Two Guineas for a *Life and Character of Shakespear*, with an admission to his *conversationis*. I went once. There was a collection of learned lumber, of antiquaries, lexicographers, and other Illustrious Obscure, and I had given up the day for lost, when in dropped Jack T[aylor][20] of the *Sun* – (Who would dare to deny that he was 'the Sun of our table'?) – and I had nothing now to do but hear and laugh. Mr T[aylor] knows most of the good things that have been said in the metropolis for the last thirty years, and is in particular an excellent retailer of the humours and extravagances of his old friend, Peter Pindar. He had recounted a series of them, each rising above the other in a sort of magnificent burlesque and want of literal preciseness, to a medley of laughing and sour faces, when on his proceeding to state a joke of a practical nature by the said Peter, a Mr ——, (I forget the name) objected to the moral of the story, and to the whole texture of Mr T[aylor]'s *facetiæ* – upon which our host, who had till now supposed that all was going on swimmingly, thought it time to interfere and give a turn to the conversation by saying – 'Why yes, Gentlemen, what we have hitherto heard fall from the lips of our friend has been no doubt entertaining and highly agreeable in its way: but perhaps we have had enough of what is altogether delightful and pleasant and light and laughable in conduct. Suppose, therefore, we were to shift the subject, and talk of what is serious and moral and industrious and laudable in character – Let us talk of Mr Tomkins, the Penman!'[21] – This staggered the gravest of us, broke up our dinner-party, and we went up stairs to tea. So much for the didactic vein of one of our principal guides in the embellished walks of modern taste, and master-manufacturers of letters. He had found that gravity had been a never-failing resource when taken at a pinch – for once the joke miscarried – and Mr Tomkins the Penman figures to this day nowhere but in Sir Joshua's picture of him!

To complete the natural Aristocracy of Letters we only want a Royal Society of Authors!

Why Distant Objects Please

From volume two of *Table-Talk* (1822). A beautifully balanced essay, alternately analytical and sentimental, on the romance of distance, touching on sight, sound, taste and time. In the section on sound and memory there is a painful reminiscence of the angel-like voice of Sarah Walker, but the early part of the essay is dominated by older, mellower experiences: the view of the Welsh hills from the essayist's childhood home in Wem, and the trip he made with his father when 'quite a boy' to the Montpelier Tea Gardens at Walworth.

Distant objects please, because, in the first place, they imply an idea of space and magnitude, and because, not being obtruded too close upon the eye, we clothe them with the indistinct and airy colours of fancy. In looking at the misty mountain-tops that bound the horison, the mind is as it were conscious of all the conceivable objects and interests that lie between; we imagine all sorts of adventures in the interim; strain our hopes and wishes to reach the air-drawn circle, or to 'descry new lands, rivers, and mountains', stretching far beyond it: our feelings carried out of themselves lose their grossness and their husk, are rarefied, expanded, melt into softness and brighten into beauty, turning to 'ethereal mould, sky-tinctured'. We drink the air before us, and borrow a more refined existence from objects that hover on the brink of nothing. Where the landscape fades from the dull sight, we fill the thin, viewless space with shapes of unknown good, and tinge the hazy prospect with hopes and wishes and more charming fears.

> But thou, oh Hope! with eyes so fair,
> What was thy delighted measure?
> Still it whisper'd promised pleasure,
> And bade the lovely scenes at distance hail![1]

Whatever is placed beyond the reach of sense and knowledge, whatever is imperfectly discerned, the fancy pieces out at its leisure; and all but the present moment, but the present spot, passion claims for its own, and brooding over it with wings outspread, stamps it with an image of itself. Passion is lord of infinite space, and distant objects please because they border on its confines, and are moulded by its touch. When I was a boy, I lived within sight of a range of lofty hills, whose blue tops blending with the setting sun had often tempted my longing eyes and wandering feet. At last I put my project in execution, and on a nearer approach, instead of glimmering air woven into fantastic shapes, found them huge lumpish heaps of discoloured earth. I learnt from this (in part) to leave 'Yarrow unvisited',[2] and not idly to disturb a dream of good!

Distance of time has much the same effect as distance of place. It is not surprising that fancy colours the prospect of the future as it thinks good, when it even effaces the forms of memory. Time takes out the sting of pain; our sorrows after a certain period have been so often steeped in a medium of thought and passion, that they 'unmould their essence'; and all that remains of our original impressions is what we would wish them to have been. Not only the untried steep ascent before us, but the rude, unsightly masses of our past experience presently resume their power of deception over the eye: the golden cloud soon rests upon their heads, and the purple light of fancy clothes their barren sides! Thus we pass on, while both ends of our existence touch upon Heaven! – There is (so to speak) 'a mighty stream of tendency' to good in the human mind, upon which all objects float and are imperceptibly borne along: and though in the voyage of life we meet with strong rebuffs, with rocks and quicksands, yet there is 'a tide in the affairs of men', a heaving and a restless aspiration of the soul, by means of which, 'with sails and tackle torn', the wreck and scattered fragments of our entire being drift into the port and haven of our desires! In all that relates to the affections, we put the will for the deed: – the instant the pressure of unwelcome circumstances is removed, the mind recoils from their grasp, recovers its elasticity, and re-unites itself to that image of good, which is but a reflection and configuration of its own nature. Seen in the distance, in the long perspective of waning years, the meanest incidents, enlarged and enriched by countless recollections, become interesting; the most painful, broken and softened by time, soothe. How any object, that unexpectedly brings back to us old scenes and associations, startles the mind! What a yearning it creates within us; what a longing to leap the intermediate space! How fondly we cling to, and try to revive the impression of all that we then were!

Such tricks hath strong Imagination![3]

In truth, we impose upon ourselves, and know not what we wish. It is a cunning artifice, a quaint delusion, by which, in pretending to be what we were at a particular moment of time, we would fain be all that we have since been, and have our lives to come over again. It is not the little, glimmering, almost annihilated speck in the distance, that rivets our attention and 'hangs upon the beatings of our hearts': it is the interval that separates us from it, and of which it is the trembling boundary, that excites all this coil and mighty pudder in the breast. Into that great gap in our being 'come thronging soft desires' and infinite regrets. It is the contrast, the change from what we then were, that arms the half-extinguished recollection with its giant-strength, and lifts the fabric of the affections from its shadowy base. In contemplating its utmost verge, we overlook the map of our existence, and re-tread, in apprehension, the journey of life. So it is that in early youth we strain our eager sight after the pursuits of manhood; and, as we are sliding off the stage, strive to gather up the toys and flowers that pleased our thoughtless childhood.

When I was quite a boy, my father used to take me to the Montpelier Tea-gardens at Walworth. Do I go there now? No; the place is deserted, and its borders and its beds o'erturned. Is there, then, nothing that can

Bring back the hour
Of glory in the grass, of splendour in the flower?[4]

Oh! yes. I unlock the casket of memory, and draw back the warders of the brain; and there this scene of my infant wanderings still lives unfaded, or with fresher dyes. A new sense comes upon me, as in a dream; a richer perfume, brighter colours start out; my eyes dazzle; my heart heaves with its new load of bliss, and I am a child again. My sensations are all glossy, spruce, voluptuous, and fine: they wear a candied coat, and are in holiday trim. I see the beds of larkspur with purple eyes; tall holy-oaks, red and yellow; the broad sun-flowers, caked in gold, with bees buzzing round them; wildernesses of pinks, and hot-glowing pionies; poppies run to seed; the sugared lily, and faint mignionette, all ranged in order, and as thick as they can grow; the box-tree borders; the gravel-walks, the painted alcove, the confectionery, the clotted cream: – I think I see them now with sparkling looks; or have they vanished while I have been writing this description of them? No matter; they will return again when I least think of them. All that I have observed since, of flowers and plants, and grass-plots, and of suburb delights, seems, to me, borrowed from 'that first garden of my innocence' – to be slips and scions stolen from that bed of memory. In this manner the darlings of our childhood burnish out in the eye of after-years, and derive their sweetest perfume from the first heartfelt sigh of pleasure breathed upon them,

> – like the sweet south,
> That breathes upon a bank of violets.
> Stealing and giving odour!⁵

If I have pleasure in a flower-garden, I have in a kitchen-garden too, and for the same reason. If I see a row of cabbage-plants or of peas or beans coming up, I immediately think of those which I used so carefully to water of an evening at W[em], when my day's tasks were done, and of the pain with which I saw them droop and hang down their leaves in the morning's sun. Again, I never see a child's kite in the air, but it seems to pull at my heart. It is to me a 'thing of life'. I feel the twinge at my elbow, the flutter and palpitation, with which I used to let go the string of my own, as it rose in the air and towered among the clouds. My little cargo of hopes and fears ascended with it; and as it made a part of my own consciousness then, it does so still, and appears 'like some gay creature of the element', my playmate when life was young, and twin-born with my earliest recollections. I could enlarge on this subject of childish amusements, but Mr Leigh Hunt has treated it so well, in a paper in the *Indicator*, on the productions of the toy-shops of the metropolis, that if I were to insist more on it, I should only pass for an imitator of that ingenious and agreeable writer, and for an indifferent one into the bargain.⁶

Sounds, smells, and sometimes tastes, are remembered longer than visible objects, and serve, perhaps, better for links in the chain of association. The reason seems to be this: they are in their nature intermittent, and comparatively rare; whereas objects of sight are always before us, and, by their continuous succession, drive one another out. The eye is always open; and between any given impression and its recurrence a second time, fifty thousand other impressions have, in all likelihood, been stamped upon the sense and on the brain. The other senses are not so active or vigilant. They are but seldom called into play. The ear, for example, is oftener courted by silence than noise; and the sounds that break that silence sink deeper and more durably into the mind. I have, for this reason, a more present and lively recollection of certain scents, tastes, and sounds than I have of mere visible images, because they are more original, and less worn by frequent repetition. Where there is nothing interposed between any two impressions, whatever the distance of time that parts them, they naturally seem to touch; and the renewed impression recalls the former one in full force, without distraction or competition. The taste of barberries, which have hung out in the snow during the severity of a North American winter, I have in my mouth still, after an interval of thirty years; for I have met with no other taste, in all that time, at all like it.[7] It remains by itself, almost like the impression of a sixth sense. But the colour is mixed up indiscriminately with the colours of many other berries, nor should I be able to distinguish it among them. The smell of a brick-kiln carries the evidence of its own identity with it: neither is it to me (from peculiar associations) unpleasant. The colour of brick-dust, on the contrary, is more common, and easily confounded with other colours. Raphael did not keep it quite distinct from his flesh-colour. I will not say that we have a more perfect recollection of the human voice than of that complex picture, the human face; but I think the sudden hearing of a well-known voice has something in it more affecting and striking than the sudden meeting with the face: perhaps, indeed, this may be because we have a more familiar remembrance of the one than the other, and the voice takes us more by surprise on that account. I am by no means certain (generally speaking) that we have the ideas of the other senses so accurate and well-made out as those of visible form: what I chiefly mean is, that the feelings belonging to the sensations of our other organs, when accidentally recalled, are kept more separate and pure. Musical sounds, probably, owe a good deal of their interest and romantic effect to the principle here spoken of. Were they constant, they would become indifferent, as we may find with respect to disagreeable noises, which we do not hear after a time. I know no situation more pitiable than that of a blind fiddler, who has but one sense left (if we except the sense of snuff-taking*) and who has that stunned or deafened by his own villanous noises. Shakespear says,

How silver-sweet sound lovers' tongues by night!

*   See Wilkie's *Blind Fiddler.*[8]

It has been suggested, in explanation of this passage, that it is because in the day-time lovers are occupied with one another's faces, but that at night they can only distinguish the sound of each other's voices. I know not how this may be: but I have, ere now, heard a voice break so upon the silence,

> To angels' 'twas most like,

and charm the moonlight air with its balmy essence, while the budding leaves trembled to its accents. Would I might have heard it once more whisper peace and hope (as erst when it was mingled with the breath of spring), and with its soft pulsations lift winged fancy to heaven! But it has ceased, or turned where I no more shall hear it! – Hence, also, we see what is the charm of the shepherd's pastoral reed; and why we hear him, as it were, piping to his flock, even in a picture. Our ears are fancy-stung! I remember once strolling along the margin of a stream, skirted with willows and plashy sedges, in one of those low sheltered valleys on Salisbury Plain, where the monks of former ages had planted chapels and built hermits' cells. There was a little parish-church near; but tall elms and quivering alders hid it from my sight, when, all of a sudden, I was startled by the sound of the full organ pealing on the ear, accompanied by rustic voices and the willing quire of village-maids and children. It rose, indeed, 'like an exhalation of rich distilled perfumes'. The dew from a thousand pastures was gathered in its softness; the silence of a thousand years spoke in it. It came upon the heart like the calm beauty of death: fancy caught the sound, and faith mounted on it to the skies. It filled the valley like a mist, and still poured out its endless chaunt, and still it swells upon the ear, and wraps me in a golden trance, drowning the noisy tumult of the world!

There is a curious and interesting discussion, on the comparative distinctness of our visual and other external impressions, in Mr Fearn's *Essay on Consciousness*,[9] with which I shall try to descend from this rhapsody to the ground of common sense and plain reasoning again. After observing, a little before, that 'nothing is more untrue than that sensations of vision do necessarily leave more vivid and durable ideas than those of grosser senses,' he proceeds to give a number of illustrations in support of this position. 'Notwithstanding,' he says, 'the advantages here enumerated in favour of sight, I think there is no doubt that a man will come to forget acquaintance, and many other visible objects, noticed in mature age, before he will in the least forget tastes and smells, of only moderate interest, encountered either in his childhood, or at any time since.

'In the course of voyaging to various distant regions, it has several times happened that I have eaten once or twice of different things that never came in my way before nor since. Some of these have been pleasant, and some scarce better than insipid; but I have no reason to think I have forgot, or much altered the ideas left by those single impulses of taste; though here the memory of them certainly has not been preserved by repetition. It is clear I must have seen, as well as tasted those things; and I am decided that I remember the tastes with more precision than I do the visual sensations.

'I remember having once, and only once, eaten Kangaroo in New Holland; and having once smelled a baker's shop, having a peculiar odour, in the city of Bassorah. Now both these gross ideas remain with me quite as vivid as any visual ideas of those places; and this could not be from repetition, but really from interest in the sensation.

'Twenty-eight years ago, in the island of Jamaica, I partook (perhaps twice) of a certain fruit, of the taste of which I have now a very fresh idea; and I could add other instances of that period.

'I have had repeated proofs of having lost retention of visual objects, at various distances of time, though they had once been familiar. I have not, during thirty years, forgot the delicate, and in itself most trifling sensation, that the palm of my hand used to convey, when I was a boy, trying the different effects of what boys call *light* and *heavy* tops; but I cannot remember within several shades of the brown coat which I left off a week ago. If any man thinks he can do better, let him take an ideal survey of his wardrobe, and then actually refer to it for proof.

'After retention of such ideas, it certainly would be very difficult to persuade me that feeling, taste, and smell can scarce be said to leave ideas, unless indistinct and obscure ones...

'Shew a Londoner correct models of twenty London churches, and, at the same time, a model of each, which differs, in several considerable features, from the truth, and I venture to say he shall not tell you, in any instance, which is the correct one, except by mere chance.

'If he is an architect, he may be much more correct than any ordinary person: and this obviously is, because he has felt an interest in viewing these structures, which an ordinary person does not feel: and here interest is the sole reason of his remembering more correctly than his neighbour.

'I once heard a person quaintly ask another, How many trees there are in St Paul's churchyard? The question itself indicates that many cannot answer it; and this is found to be the case with those who have passed the church an hundred times: whilst the cause is, that every individual in the busy stream which glides past St Paul's is engrossed in various other interests.

'How often does it happen that we enter a well-known apartment, or meet a well-known friend, and receive some vague idea of visible difference, but cannot possibly find out *what* it is; until at length we come to perceive (or perhaps must be told) that some ornament or furniture is removed, altered, or added in the apartment; or that our friend has cut his hair, taken a wig, or has made any of twenty considerable alterations in his appearance. At other times, we have no perception of alteration whatever, though the like has taken place.

'It is, however, certain, that sight, apposited with interest, can retain tolerably exact copies of sensations, especially if not too complex; such as of the human countenance and figure. Yet the voice will convince us, when the countenance will not; and he is reckoned an excellent painter, and no ordinary genius, who can make a tolerable likeness from memory. Nay, more, it is a conspicuous proof of the inaccuracy of visual ideas that it is an effort of consummate art, attained by many years' practice, to take a strict likeness of the human countenance, even when the object is present; and among those cases, where the wilful cheat of flattery has been avoided, we still find in how very few instances the best painters produce a likeness up to the life, though practice and interest join in the attempt.

'I imagine an ordinary person would find it very difficult, supposing he had some knowledge of drawing, to afford, from memory, a tolerable sketch of such a familiar object as his curtain, his carpet, or his dressing-gown, if the pattern of either be at all various or irregular; yet he will instantly tell, with precision, either if his snuff or his wine has not the same character it had yesterday, though both these are compounds.

'Beyond all this I may observe, that a draper, who is in the daily habit of such comparisons, cannot carry in his mind the particular shade of a colour during a second of time; and has no certainty of tolerably matching two simple colours, except by placing the patterns in contact.' *Essay on Consciousness*, p. 303.

I will conclude the subject of this Essay with observing, that a nearer and more familiar acquaintance with persons has a different and more favourable effect than that with places or things. The latter improve by being removed to a distance, for we have no interest in *backbiting* them: the former gain by being brought nearer and more home to us, and thus stripped of artful and ill-natured misrepresentations. Report or imagination very seldom raises any individual so high in our estimation as to disappoint us greatly when we are introduced to him: prejudice and malice constantly exaggerate defects beyond the reality. Ignorance alone makes monsters or bugbears: our actual acquaintances are all very commonplace people. The thing is, that as a matter of hearsay or conjecture, we make abstractions of particular vices, and irritate ourselves against some particular quality or action of the person we dislike: – whereas, individuals are concrete existences, not arbitrary denominations or nicknames; and have innumerable other qualities, good, bad, and indifferent, besides the damning feature with which we fill up the portrait or caricature, in our previous fancies. We can scarcely hate any one that we know. An acute observer complained, that if there was any one to whom he had a particular spite, and a wish to let him see it, the moment he came to sit down with him, his enmity was disarmed by some unforeseen circumstance. If it was a Quarterly Reviewer, he was in other respects like any other man. Suppose, again, your adversary turns out a very ugly man, or wants an eye, you are balked in that way: – he is not what you expected, the object of your abstract hatred and implacable disgust. He may be a very disagreeable person, but he is no longer the same. If you come into a room where a man is, you find, in general, that he has a nose upon his face. 'There's sympathy!' This alone is a diversion to your unqualified contempt. He is stupid, and says nothing, but he seems to have something in him when he laughs. You had conceived of him as a rank Whig or Tory – yet he talks upon other subjects. You knew that he was a virulent party-writer; but you find that the man himself is a tame sort of animal enough. He does not bite. That's something. In short, you can make nothing of it. Even opposite vices balance one another. A man may be pert in company, but he is also dull; so that you cannot, though you try, hate him cordially, merely for the wish to be offensive. He is a knave. Granted. You learn, on a nearer acquaintance, what you did not know before – that he is a fool as well; so you forgive him. On the other hand, he may be a profligate public character, and may make no secret of it; but he gives you a hearty shake by the hand, speaks kindly to servants, and supports an aged father and mother. Politics apart, he is a very honest fellow. You are told that a person has carbuncles on his face; but you have ocular proofs that he is sallow, and pale as a ghost. This does not much mend the matter; but it blunts the edge of the ridicule, and turns your indignation against the inventor of the lie; but he is ——, the editor of a Scotch magazine; so you are just where you were. I am not very fond of anonymous criticism; I want to know who the author can be: but the moment I learn this, I am satisfied. Even —— would do well to come out of his disguise. It is the mask only that we dread and hate: the man may have something human about him![10] The notions, in short, which we entertain of people at a distance, or from partial representations, or from guess-work, are simple, uncompounded ideas, which answer to nothing in reality: those which we derive from experience are mixed modes, the only true, and, in general, the most favourable ones. Instead of naked deformity, or abstract perfection –

Those faultless monsters which the world ne'er saw, –[11]

'the web of our lives is of a mingled yarn, good and ill together: our virtues would be proud, if our faults whipt them not; and our vices would despair, if they were not encouraged by our virtues.'[12] This was truly and finely said long ago, by one who knew the strong and weak points of human nature: but it is what sects, and parties, and those philosophers whose pride and boast it is to classify by nicknames, have yet to learn the meaning of!

On Mr Wordsworth's Excursion

First published in Leigh Hunt's *Examiner*, 2 October 1814,
then republished in the second volume of *The Round Table*
(Edinburgh: Constable, 1817). This is the second of two
connected reviews that Hazlitt contributed on Wordsworth's
philosophical pastoral *The Excursion* (1814). A fervent
admirer of Wordsworth's radical poetic genius since their
historic meeting in 1798, Hazlitt felt bitterly disappointed,
even betrayed, by the Lakelander's later descent into
Toryism. On a less serious note, Hazlitt was also irritated by
the insistently pro-rural and anti-metropolitan bias of his
poems, hence the gloriously extreme contention in this review
that, far from representing the best there is in terms of
philosophical wisdom, simplicity and virtue, 'all country
people hate each other'.

Mr Wordsworth's writings exhibit all the internal power, without
the external form of poetry. He has scarcely any of the pomp and
decoration and scenic effect of poetry: no gorgeous palaces nor
solemn temples awe the imagination; no cities rise 'with glistering
spires and pinnacles adorned'; we meet with no knights pricked
forth on airy steeds; no hair-breadth 'scapes and perilous accidents
by flood or field. Either from the predominant habit of his mind
not requiring the stimulus of outward impressions, or from the
want of an imagination teeming with various forms, he takes the
common every-day events and objects of nature, or rather seeks
those that are the most simple and barren of effect; but he adds to
them a weight of interest from the resources of his own mind,
which makes the most insignificant things serious and even
formidable. All other interests are absorbed in the deeper interest
of his own thoughts, and find the same level. His mind magnifies
the littleness of his subject, and raises its meanness; lends it his
strength, and clothes it with borrowed grandeur. With him, a
molehill, covered with wild thyme, assumes the importance of 'the
great vision of the guarded mount': a puddle is filled with preter-
natural faces, and agitated with the fiercest storms of passion.

The extreme simplicity which some persons have objected to in Mr Wordsworth's poetry, is to be found only in the subject and the style: the sentiments are subtle and profound. In the latter respect, his poetry is as much above the common standard or capacity, as in the other it is below it. His poems bear a distant resemblance to some of Rembrandt's landscapes, who, more than any other painter, created the medium through which he saw nature, and out of the stump of an old tree, a break in the sky, and a bit of water, could produce an effect almost miraculous.

Mr Wordsworth's poems in general are the history of a refined and contemplative mind, conversant only with itself and nature. An intense feeling of the associations of this kind is the peculiar and characteristic feature of all his productions. He has described the love of nature better than any other poet. This sentiment, inly felt in all its force, and sometimes carried to an excess, is the source both of his strength and of his weakness. However we may sympathise with Mr Wordsworth in his attachment to groves and fields, we cannot extend the same admiration to their inhabitants, or to the manners of country life in general. We go along with him, while he is the subject of his own narrative, but we take leave of him when he makes pedlars and ploughmen his heroes and the interpreters of his sentiments. It is, we think, getting into low company, and company, besides, that we do not like. We take Mr Wordsworth himself for a great poet, a fine moralist, and a deep philosopher; but if he insists on introducing us to a friend of his, a parish clerk, or the barber of the village, who is as wise as himself, we must be excused if we draw back with some little want of cordial faith. We are satisfied with the friendship which subsisted between *Parson Adams* and *Joseph Andrews*.[1] The author himself lets out occasional hints that all is not as it should be amongst these northern Arcadians. Though, in general, he professes to soften the harsher features of rustic vice, he has given us one picture of depraved and inveterate selfishness, which we apprehend could only be found among the inhabitants of these boasted mountain districts. The account of one of his heroines concludes as follows:

> A sudden illness seiz'd her in the strength
> Of life's autumnal season. Shall I tell
> How on her bed of death the matron lay,
> To Providence submissive, so she thought;
> But fretted, vexed, and wrought upon – almost

To anger, by the malady that griped
Her prostrate frame with unrelaxing power,
As the fierce eagle fastens on the lamb.
She prayed, she moaned – her husband's sister watched
Her dreary pillow, waited on her needs;
And yet the very sound of that kind foot
Was anguish to her ears! 'And must she rule
Sole mistress of this house when I am gone?
Sit by my fire – possess what I possessed –
Tend what I tended – calling it her own!'
Enough; – I fear too much. Of nobler feeling
Take this example: – One autumnal evening,
While she was yet in prime of health and strength,
I well remember, while I passed her door,
Musing with loitering step, and upward eye
Turned tow'rds the planet Jupiter, that hung
Above the centre of the vale, a voice
Roused me, her voice; – it said, 'That glorious star
In its untroubled element will shine
As now it shines, when we are laid in earth,
And safe from all our sorrows.' She is safe,
And her uncharitable acts, I trust,
And harsh unkindnesses, are all forgiven;
Though, in this vale, remembered with deep awe![2]

We think it is pushing our love of the admiration of natural objects a good deal too far, to make it a set-off against a story like the preceding.

All country people hate each other. They have so little comfort, that they envy their neighbours the smallest pleasure or advantage, and nearly grudge themselves the necessaries of life. From not being accustomed to enjoyment, they become hardened and averse to it – stupid, for want of thought – selfish, for want of society. There is nothing good to be had in the country, or, if there is, they will not let you have it. They had rather injure themselves than oblige any one else. Their common mode of life is a system of wretchedness and self-denial, like what we read of among barbarous tribes. You live out of the world. You cannot get your tea and sugar without sending to the next town for it: you pay double, and have it of the worst quality. The small-beer is sure to be sour – the milk skimmed – the meat bad, or spoiled in the cooking. You cannot do a single thing you like; you cannot walk out or sit at home, or write or read, or think or look as if you did, without being subject to impertinent curiosity. The apothecary annoys you with his complaisance; the parson with his superciliousness. If you are poor, you are despised; if you are rich, you are feared and hated. If you do any one a favour, the whole neighbourhood is up in arms; the clamour is like that of a rookery; and the person himself, it is ten to one, laughs at you for your pains, and takes the first opportunity of showing you that he labours under no uneasy sense of obligation. There is a perpetual round of mischief-making and backbiting for want of any better amusement. There are no shops, no taverns, no theatres, no opera, no concerts, no pictures, no public-buildings, no crowded streets, no noise of coaches, or of courts of law, – neither courtiers nor courtesans, no literary parties, no fashionable routs, no society, no books, or knowledge of books. Vanity and luxury are the civilisers of the world, and sweeteners of human life. Without objects either of pleasure or action, it grows harsh and crabbed: the mind becomes stagnant, the affections callous, and the eye dull. Man left to himself soon degenerates into a very disagreeable person. Ignorance is always bad enough; but rustic ignorance is intolerable. Aristotle has observed, that tragedy purifies the affections by terror and pity. If so, a company of tragedians should be established at the public expence, in every village or hundred, as a better mode of education than either Bell's or Lancaster's. The benefits of knowledge are never so well understood as from seeing the effects of ignorance, in their naked, undisguised state, upon the common country people. Their selfishness and insensibility are perhaps less owing to the hardships and privations, which make them, like people out at sea in a boat, ready to devour one another, than to their having no idea of anything beyond themselves and their immediate sphere of action. They have no knowledge of, and consequently can take no interest in, anything which is not an object of their senses, and of their daily pursuits. They hate all strangers, and have generally a nick-name for the inhabitants of the next village. The two young noblemen in *Guzman d'Alfarache*, who went to visit their mistresses only a league out of Madrid, were set upon by the peasants, who came round them calling out, '*A wolf*'. Those who have no enlarged or liberal ideas, can have no disinterested or generous sentiments. Persons who are in the habit of reading novels and romances, are compelled to take a deep interest in, and to have their affections strongly excited by, fictitious characters and imaginary situations; their thoughts and feelings are constantly carried out of themselves, to persons they never saw, and things that never existed: history enlarges the mind, by familiarising us with the great vicissitudes of human affairs, and the catastrophes of states and kingdoms; the study of morals accustoms us to refer our actions to a general standard of right and wrong; and abstract reasoning, in general, strengthens the love of truth, and produces an inflexibility of principle which cannot stoop to low trick and cunning. Books, in Lord Bacon's phrase, are 'a discipline of humanity'. Country people have none of these advantages, nor any others to supply the place of them. Having no circulating libraries to exhaust their love of the marvellous, they amuse themselves with fancying the disasters and disgraces of their particular acquaintance. Having no hump-backed *Richard* to excite their wonder and abhorrence, they make themselves a bug-bear of their own, out of the first obnoxious person they can lay their hands on. Not having the fictitious distresses and gigantic crimes of poetry to stimulate their imagination and their passions, they vent their whole stock of spleen, malice, and invention, on their friends and next-door neighbours. They get up a little pastoral drama at home, with fancied events, but real characters. All their spare time is spent in manufacturing and propagating the lie for the day, which does its office, and expires. The next day is spent in the same manner. It is thus that they embellish the simplicity of rural life! The common people in civilised countries are a kind of domesticated savages. They have not the wild imagination, the passions, the fierce energies, or dreadful vicissitudes of the savage tribes, nor have they the leisure, the indolent enjoyments and romantic superstitions, which belonged to the pastoral life in milder climates, and more remote periods of society. They are taken out of a state of nature, without being put in possession of the refinements of art. The customs and institutions of society cramp their imaginations without giving them knowledge. If the inhabitants of the mountainous districts described by Mr Wordsworth are less gross and sensual than others, they are more selfish. Their egotism becomes more concentrated, as they are more insulated, and their purposes more inveterate, as they have less competition to struggle with. The weight of matter which surrounds them, crushes the finer sympathies. Their minds become hard and cold, like the rocks which they cultivate. The immensity of their mountains makes the human form appear little and insignificant. Men are seen crawling between Heaven and earth, like insects to their graves. Nor do they regard one another more than flies on a wall. Their physiognomy expresses the materialism of their character, which has only one principle – rigid self-will. They move on with their eyes and foreheads fixed, looking neither to the right nor to the left, with a heavy slouch in their gait, and seeming as if nothing would divert tbem from their path. We do not admire this plodding pertinacity, always directed to the main chance. There is nothing which excites so little sympathy in our minds, as exclusive selfishness. If our theory is wrong, at least it is taken from pretty close observation, and is, we think, confirmed by Mr Wordsworth's own account.

Of the stories contained in the latter part of the volume, we like that of the Whig and Jacobite friends, and of the good knight, Sir Alfred Irthing, the best. The last reminded us of a fine sketch of a similar character in the beautiful poem of *Hart Leap Well*. To conclude, – if the skill with which the poet had chosen his materials had been equal to the power which he has undeniably exerted over them, if the objects (whether persons or things) which he makes use of as the vehicle of his sentiments, had been such as to convey them in all their depth and force, then the production before us might indeed 'have proved a monument', as he himself wishes it, worthy of the author, and of his country. Whether, as it is, this very original and powerful performance may not rather remain like one of those stupendous but half-finished structures, which have been suffered to moulder into decay, because the cost and labour attending them exceeded their use or beauty, we feel that it would be presumptuous in us to determine.

On Londoners and Country People

First published in the *New Monthly Magazine*, August 1823, then republished in volume one of *The Plain Speaker*, 2 vols (London: Colburn, 1826). Since October 1817, with the commencement of the notorious 'Cockney School of Poetry' articles in *Blackwood's Magazine*, Hazlitt had been regularly stigmatised by his political and literary enemies as a vulgar Cockney upstart. Certainly, there was a class element in this insult, but it is interesting to reflect that, in the early nineteenth century, the word 'Cockney' did not, primarily, refer to the London working class. It was only much later, in the second half of the 1800s, that its meaning became fixed in that direction. Instead, it drew on a satirical tradition which went back to Shakespeare's time, of the 'Cockney' as a metropolitan miscreant, a kind of misfit, a pampered and effeminate child of the city.

In 'On Londoners and Country People' Hazlitt opens with a brilliant and highly entertaining critique of modern metropolitan psychology, and its extraordinary tendency towards vanity and false consciousness. But, as in 'On Coffee-House Politicians', the essay soon softens as it grows more personal, and ends up by redescribing many of its prejudices in more positive terms. The conclusion represents a surprising, but utterly convincing, *volte-face*, in which the caricature of the pert, fantasy-struck Cockney is replaced by that of the proud, liberty-loving Londoner, and the peculiar abstraction of London life is made responsible for its underlying tone of humane and democratic feeling.

I do not agree with Mr *Blackwood* in his definition of the word *Cockney*.[1] He means by it a person who has happened at any time to live in London, and who is not a Tory – I mean by it a person who has never lived out of London, and who has got all his ideas from it.

The true Cockney has never travelled beyond the purlieus of the Metropolis, either in the body or the spirit. Primrose-hill is the

Ultima Thule[2] of his most romantic desires; Greenwich Park stands him instead of the Vales of Arcady. Time and space are lost to him. He is confined to one spot, and to the present moment. He sees every thing near, superficial, little, in hasty succession. The world turns round, and his head with it, like a roundabout at a fair, till he becomes stunned and giddy with the motion. Figures glide by as in a *camera obscura*. There is a glare, a perpetual hubbub, a noise, a crowd about him; he sees and hears a vast number of things, and knows nothing. He is pert, raw, ignorant, conceited, ridiculous, shallow, contemptible. His senses keep him alive; and he knows, inquires, and cares for nothing farther. He meets the Lord Mayor's coach, and without ceremony treats himself to an imaginary ride in it. He notices the people going to court or to a city-feast, and is quite satisfied with the show. He takes the wall of a Lord, and fancies himself as good as he. He sees an infinite quantity of people pass along the street, and thinks there is no such thing as life or a knowledge of character to be found out of London. 'Beyond Hyde Park all is a desert to him.' He despises the country, because he is ignorant of it, and the town, because he is familiar with it. He is as well acquainted with St Paul's as if he had built it, and talks of Westminster Abbey and Poets' Corner with great indifference. The King, the House of Lords and Commons are his very good friends. He knows the members for Westminster or the City by sight, and bows to the Sheriffs or the Sheriffs' men. He is hand and glove with the Chairman of some Committee. He is, in short, a great man by proxy, and comes so often in contact with fine persons and things, that he rubs off a little of the gilding, and is surcharged with a sort of second-hand, vapid, tingling, troublesome self-importance. His personal vanity is thus continually flattered and perked up into ridiculous self-complacency, while his imagination is jaded and impaired by daily misuse. Every thing is vulgarised in his mind. Nothing dwells long enough on it to produce an interest; nothing is contemplated sufficiently at a distance to excite curiosity or wonder. *Your true Cockney is your only true leveller.* Let him be as low as he will, he fancies he is as good as any body else. He has no respect for himself, and still less (if possible) for you. He cares little about his own advantages, if he can only make a jest at yours. Every feeling comes to him through a medium of levity and impertinence; nor does he like to have this habit of mind disturbed by being brought into collision with any thing serious or respectable. He despairs (in such a crowd of competitors) of distinguishing himself, but laughs heartily at the idea of being able to trip up the heels of other people's pretensions. A Cockney feels no gratitude. This is a first principle with him. He regards any obligation you confer upon him as a species of imposition, a ludicrous assumption of fancied superiority. He talks about everything, for he has heard something about it; and understanding nothing of the matter, concludes he has as good a right as you. He is a politician; for he has seen the Parliament House: he is a critic; because he knows the principal actors by sight – has a taste for music, because he belongs to a glee-club at the West End, and is gallant, in virtue of sometimes frequenting the lobbies at half-price. A mere Londoner, in fact, from the opportunities he has of knowing something of a number of objects (and those striking ones) fancies himself a sort of privileged person, remains satisfied with the assumption of merits, so much the more unquestionable as they are not his own; and from being dazzled with noise, show, and appearances, is less capable of giving a real opinion, or entering into any subject than the meanest peasant. There are greater lawyers, orators, painters, philosophers, poets, players in London, than in any other part of the United Kingdom: he is a Londoner, and therefore it would be strange if he did not know more of law, eloquence, art, philosophy, poetry, acting, than any one without his local advantages, and who is merely from the country. This is a *non sequitur*; and it constantly appears so when put to the test.

A real Cockney is the poorest creature in the world, the most literal, the most mechanical, and yet he too lives in a world of romance – a fairy-land of his own. He is a citizen of London; and this abstraction leads his imagination the finest dance in the world. London is the first city on the habitable globe; and therefore he must be superior to every one who lives out of it. There are more people in London than any where else; and though a dwarf in stature, his person swells out and expands into *ideal* importance and borrowed magnitude. He resides in a garret or in a two pair of stairs' back room; yet he talks of the magnificence of London, and gives himself airs of consequence upon it, as if all the houses in Portman or in Grosvenor Square were his by right or in reversion. 'He is owner of all he surveys.' The Monument, the Tower of London, St James's Palace, the Mansion House, White-Hall, are part and parcel of his being. Let us suppose him to be a lawyer's clerk at half-a guinea a week: but he knows the Inns of Court, the Temple Gardens, and Gray's Inn Passage, sees the lawyers in their wigs walking up and down Chancery Lane, and has advanced within half-a-dozen yards of the Chancellor's chair: – who can doubt that he understands (by implication) every point of law (however intricate) better than the most expert country practitioner? He is a shopman, and nailed all day behind the counter: but he sees hundreds and thousands of gay, well-dressed people pass – an endless phantasmagoria – and enjoys their liberty and gaudy fluttering pride. He is a footman – but he rides behind beauty, through a crowd of carriages, and visits a thousand shops. Is he a tailor – that last infirmity of human nature? The stigma on his profession is lost in the elegance of the patterns he provides, and of the persons he adorns; and he is something very different from a mere country botcher. Nay, the very scavenger and nightman thinks the dirt in the street has something precious in it, and his employment is solemn, silent, sacred, peculiar to London! A barker in Monmouth Street, a slop-seller in Radcliffe Highway, a tapster at a night-cellar, a beggar in St Giles's, a drab in Fleet-Ditch, live in the eyes of millions, and eke out a dreary, wretched, scanty, or loathsome existence from the gorgeous, busy, glowing scene around them.[3] It is a common saying among such persons that 'they had rather be hanged in London than die a natural death out of it any where else' – such is the force of habit and imagination. Even the eye of childhood is dazzled and delighted with the polished splendour of the jewellers' shops; the neatness of the turnery ware, the festoons of artificial flowers, the confectionery, the chemists' shops, the lamps, the horses, the carriages, the sedan-chairs: to this was formerly added a set of traditional associations – Whittington and his Cat, Guy Faux and the Gunpowder Treason, the Fire and the Plague of London, and the Heads of the Scotch Rebels that were stuck on Temple Bar in 1745. These have vanished, and in their stead the curious and romantic eye must be content to pore in Pennant for the site of old London-Wall, or to peruse the sentimental mile-stone that marks the distance to the place 'where Hickes's Hall formerly stood'!

The *Cockney* lives in a go-cart of local prejudices and positive illusions; and when he is turned out of it, he hardly knows how to stand or move. He ventures through Hyde Park Corner, as a cat crosses a gutter. The trees pass by the coach very oddly. The country has a strange blank appearance. It is not lined with houses all the way, like London. He comes to places he never saw or heard of. He finds the world is bigger than he thought for. He might have dropped from the moon, for any thing he knows of the matter. He is mightily disposed to laugh, but is half afraid of making some blunder. Between sheepishness and conceit, he is in a very ludicrous situation. He finds that the people walk on two legs, and wonders to hear them talk a dialect so different from his own. He perceives London fashions have got down into the country before him, and that some of the better sort are dressed as well as he is. A drove of pigs or cattle stopping the road is a very troublesome interruption. A crow in a field, a magpie in a hedge, are to him very odd animals – he can't tell what to make of them, or how they live. He does not altogether like the accommodations at the inns – it is not what he has been used to in town. He begins to be communicative – says he was 'born within the sound of Bow-bell', and attempts some jokes, at which nobody laughs. He asks the coachman a question, to which he receives no answer. All this is to him very unaccountable and unexpected. He arrives at his journey's end; and instead of being the great man he anticipated among his friends and country relations, finds that they are barely civil to him, or make a butt of him; have topics of their own which he is as completely ignorant of as they are indifferent to what he says, so that he is glad to get back to London again, where he meets with his favourite indulgences and associates, and fancies the whole world is occupied with what he hears and sees.

A Cockney loves a tea-garden in summer, as he loves the play or the Cider-Cellar in winter – where he sweetens the air with the fumes of tobacco, and makes it echo to the sound of his own voice. This kind of suburban retreat is a most agreeable relief to the close and confined air of a city life. The imagination, long pent up behind a counter or between brick walls, with noisome smells, and dingy objects, cannot bear at once to launch into the boundless expanse of the country, but 'shorter excursions tries,' coveting something between the two, and finding it at White-conduit House, or the Rosemary Branch, or Bagnigge Wells.[4] The landlady is seen at a bow-window in near perspective, with punch-bowls and lemons disposed orderly around – the lime-trees or poplars wave overhead to 'catch the breezy air', through which, typical of the huge dense cloud that hangs over the metropolis, curls up the thin, blue, odoriferous vapour of Virginia or Oronooko – the benches are ranged in rows, the fields and hedge-rows spread out their verdure; Hampstead and Highgate are seen in the back-ground, and contain the imagination within gentle limits – here the holiday people are playing ball; here they are playing bowls – here they are quaffing ale, there sipping tea – here the loud wager is heard, there the political debate. In a sequestered nook a slender youth with purple face and drooping head, nodding over a glass of gin toddy, breathes in tender accents – 'There's nought so sweet on earth as Love's young dream'; while 'Rosy Ann' takes its turn, and 'Scots wha hae wi' Wallace bled' is thundered forth in accents that might wake the dead. In another part sit carpers and critics, who dispute the score of the reckoning or the game, or cavil at the taste and execution of the *would-be* Brahams and Durusets.[5] Of this latter class was Dr Goodman, a man of other times – I mean of those of Smollett and Defoe – who was curious in opinion, obstinate in the wrong, great in little things, and inveterate in petty warfare. I vow he held me an argument once 'an hour by St Dunstan's clock', while I held an umbrella over his head (the friendly protection of which he was unwilling to quit to walk in the rain to Camberwell) to prove to me that Richard Pinch[6] was neither a fives-player nor a pleasing singer. 'Sir,' said he, 'I deny that Mr Pinch plays the game. He is a cunning player, but not a good one. I grant his tricks, his little mean dirty ways, but he is not a manly antagonist. He has no hit, and no left-hand. How then can he set up for a superior player? And then as to his always striking the ball against the side-wings at Copenhagen-house, Cavanagh, sir, used to say, "The wall was made to hit at!" I have no patience with such pitiful shifts and advantages. They are an insult upon so fine and athletic a game! And as to his setting up for a singer, it's quite ridiculous. You know, Mr H[azlitt], that to be a really excellent singer, a man must lay claim to one of two things; in the first place, sir, he must have a naturally fine ear for music, or secondly, an early education, exclusively devoted to that study. But no one ever suspected Mr Pinch of refined sensibility; and his education, as we all know, has been a little at large. Then again, why should he of all other things be always singing "Rosy Ann", and "Scots wha hae wi' Wallace bled", till one is sick of hearing them? It's preposterous, and I mean to tell him so. You know, I'm sure, without my hinting it, that in the first of these admired songs, the sentiment is voluptuous and tender, and in the last patriotic. Now Pinch's romance never wandered from behind his counter, and his patriotism lies in his breeches' pocket. Sir, the utmost he should aspire to would be to play upon the Jews' harp!' This story of the Jews' harp tickled some of Pinch's friends, who gave him various hints of it, which nearly

drove him mad, till he discovered what it was; for though no jest
or sarcasm ever had the least effect upon him, yet he cannot bear
to think that there should be any joke of this kind about him, and
he not in the secret: it makes against that *knowing* character which
he so much affects. Pinch is in one respect a complete specimen of
a *Cockney*. He never has any thing to say, and yet is never at a loss
for an answer. That is, his pertness keeps exact pace with his
dulness. His friend, the Doctor, used to complain of this in good
set terms. – 'You can never make any thing of Mr Pinch,' he would
say. 'Apply the most cutting remark to him, and his only answer
is, "*The same to you, sir.*" If Shakespear were to rise from the dead
to confute him, I firmly believe it would be to no purpose. I assure
you, I have found it so. I once thought indeed I had him at a
disadvantage, but I was mistaken. You shall hear, sir. I had been
reading the following sentiment in a modern play – "The Road to
Ruin", by the late Mr Holcroft – "For how should the soul of
Socrates inhabit the body of a stocking-weaver?" This was pat to
the point (you know our friend is a hosier and haberdasher) I came
full with it to keep an appointment I had with Pinch, began a game,
quarrelled with him in the middle of it on purpose, went up stairs
to dress, and as I was washing my hands in the slop-basin
(watching my opportunity) turned coolly round and said, "It's
impossible there should be any sympathy between you and me,
Mr Pinch: for as the poet says, how should the soul of Socrates
inhabit the body of a stocking-weaver?" "Ay," says he, "does the
poet say so? *then the same to you sir!*" I was confounded, I gave up
the attempt to conquer him in wit or argument. He would pose the
Devil, sir, by his "*The same to you, sir.*" We had another joke against
Richard Pinch, to which the Doctor was not a party, which was,
that being asked after the respectability of the Hole in the Wall, at
the time that Randall took it, he answered quite unconsciously,
'Oh! it's a very genteel place, I go there myself sometimes!' Dr
Goodman was descended by the mother's side from the poet Jago,
was a private gentleman in town, and a medical dilettante in the
country, dividing his time equally between business and pleasure;
had an inexhaustible flow of words, and an imperturbable vanity,
and held 'stout notions on the metaphysical score'. He maintained
the free agency of man, with the spirit of a martyr and the gaiety
of a man of wit and pleasure about town – told me he had a curious
tract on that subject by A.C. (Anthony Collins)[7] which he carefully
locked up in his box, lest any one should see it but himself, to the

detriment of their character and morals, and put it to me whether it was not hard, on the principles of *philosophical necessity*, 'for a man to come to be hanged? To which I replied, 'I thought it hard on any terms!' A knavish *marker*,[8] who had listened to the dispute, laughed at this retort, and seemed to assent to the truth of it, supposing it might one day be his own case.

Mr Smith and the Brangtons, in *Evelina*,[9] are the finest possible examples of the spirit of *Cockneyism*. I once knew a linen-draper in the City, who owned to me he did not quite like this part of Miss Burney's novel. He said, 'I myself lodge in a first floor, where there are young ladies in the house: they sometimes have company, and if I am out, they ask me to lend them the use of my apartment, which I readily do out of politeness, or if it is an agreeable party, I perhaps join them. All this is so like what passes in the novel, that I fancy myself a sort of second Mr Smith, and am not quite easy at it!' This was mentioned to the fair Authoress, and she was delighted to find that her characters were so true, that an actual person fancied himself to be one of them. The resemblance, however, was only in the externals; and the real modesty of the individual stumbled on the likeness to a city coxcomb!

It is curious to what a degree persons, brought up in certain occupations in a great city, are shut up from a knowledge of the world, and carry their simplicity to a pitch of unheard-of extravagance. London is the only place in which the child grows completely up into the man. I have known characters of this kind, which, in the way of childish ignorance and self-pleasing delusion, exceeded any thing to be met with in Shakespear or Ben Jonson, or the old comedy. For instance, the following may be taken as a true sketch. Imagine a person with a florid, shining complexion like a plough-boy, large staring teeth, a merry eye, his hair stuck into the fashion with curling-irons and pomatum, a slender figure, and a decent suit of black – add to which the thoughtlessness of the school-boy, the forwardness of the thriving tradesman, and the plenary consciousness of the citizen of London – and you have Mr Dunster before you, the fishmonger in the Poultry. You shall hear how he chirps over his cups, and exults in his private opinions. 'I'll play no more with you,' I said, 'Mr Dunster – you are five points in the game better than I am.' I had just lost three half-crown rubbers at cribbage to him, which loss of mine he presently thrust into a canvas pouch (not a silk purse) out of which he had produced just before, first a few halfpence, then half a dozen pieces of silver,

then a handfull of guineas, and lastly, lying *perdu* at the bottom, a
fifty pound Bank-Note. 'I'll tell you what,' I said, 'I should like to
play you a game at marbles' – this was at a sort of Christmas party
or Twelfth Night merry-making. 'Marbles!' said Dunster, catching
up the sound, and his eye brightening with childish glee, 'What!
you mean *ring-taw*?'[10] 'Yes.' 'I should beat you at it, to a certainty.
I was one of the best in our school (it was at Clapham, sir, the Rev.
Mr Denman's, at Clapham, was the place where I was brought up)
though there were two others there better than me. They were the
best that ever were. I'll tell you, sir, I'll give you an idea. There was
a water-butt or cistern, sir, at our school, that turned with a cock.
Now suppose that brass-ring that the window-curtain is fastened
to, to be the cock, and that these boys were standing where we are,
about twenty feet off – well, sir, I'll tell you what I have seen them
do. One of them had a favourite taw (or *alley* we used to call them)
he'd take aim at the cock of the cistern with this marble, as I may
do now. Well, sir, will you believe it? such was his strength of
knuckle and certainty of aim, he'd hit it, turn it, let the water out,
and then, sir, when the water had run out as much as it was wanted,
the other boy (he'd just the same strength of knuckle, and the same
certainty of eye) he'd aim at it too, be sure to hit it, turn it round,
and stop the water from running out. Yes, what I tell you is very
remarkable, but it's true. One of these boys was named Cock, and
t' other Butler.' 'They might have been named Spigot and Fawcett,
my dear sir, from your account of them.' 'I should not mind playing
you at fives neither, though I'm out of practice. I think I should beat
you in a week: I was a real good one at that. A pretty game, sir! I
had the finest ball, that I suppose ever was seen. Made it myself,
I'll tell you how sir. You see, I put a piece of cork at the bottom,
then I wound some fine worsted yarn round it, then I had to bind
it round with some packthread, and then sew the case on. You'd
hardly believe it, but I was the envy of the whole school for that
ball. They all wanted to get it from me, but lord, sir, I would let
none of them come near it. I kept it in my waistcoat pocket all day,
and at night I used to take it to bed with me and put it under my
pillow. I couldn't sleep easy without it.'

The same idle vein might be found in the country, but I doubt
whether it would find a tongue to give it utterance. Cockneyism is
a ground of native shallowness mounted with pertness and
conceit. Yet with all this simplicity and extravagance in dilating on
his favourite topics, Dunster is a man of spirit, of attention to

business, knows how to make out and get in his bills, and is far from being hen-pecked. One thing is certain, that such a man must be a true Englishman and a loyal subject. He has a slight tinge of letters, with shame I confess it – has in his possession a volume of the *European Magazine* for the year 1761, and is an humble admirer of *Tristram Shandy* (particularly the story of the King of Bohemia and his Seven Castles, which is something in his own endless manner) and of *Gil Blas* of Santillane. Over these (the last thing before he goes to bed at night) he smokes a pipe, and meditates for an hour. After all, what is there in these harmless half-lies, these fantastic exaggerations, but a literal, prosaic, *Cockney* translation of the admired lines in Gray's *Ode to Eton College*:

> What idle progeny succeed
> To chase the rolling circle's speed
> Or urge the flying ball?

A man shut up all his life in his shop, without any thing to interest him from one year's end to another but the cares and details of business; with scarcely any intercourse with books or opportunities for society, distracted with the buzz and glare and noise about him, turns for relief to the retrospect of his childish years; and there, through the long vista, at one bright loop-hole, leading out of the thorny mazes of the world into the clear morning light, he sees the idle fancies and gay amusements of his boyhood dancing like motes in the sunshine. Shall we blame or should we laugh at him, if his eye glistens, and his tongue grows wanton in their praise?

None but a Scotchman would – that pragmatical sort of personage, who thinks it a folly ever to have been young, and who instead of dallying with the frail past, bends his brows upon the future, and looks only to the *main-chance*. Forgive me, dear Dunster, if I have drawn a sketch of some of thy venial foibles, and delivered thee into the hands of these Cockneys of the North,[11] who will fall upon thee and devour thee, like so many cannibals, without a grain of salt!

If familiarity in cities breeds contempt, ignorance in the country breeds aversion and dislike. People come too much in contact in town: in other places they live too much apart, to unite cordially and easily. Our feelings, in the former case, are dissipated and exhausted by being called into constant and vain activity; in the latter they rust and grow dead for want of use. If there is an air of levity and indifference in London manners, there is a harshness, a moroseness, and disagreeable restraint in those of the country. We have little disposition to sympathy, when we have few persons to sympathise with: we lose the relish and capacity for social enjoyment, the seldomer we meet. A habit of sullenness, coldness, and misanthropy grows upon us. If we look for hospitality and a cheerful welcome in country places, it must be in those where the arrival of a stranger is an event, the recurrence of which need not be greatly apprehended, or it must be on rare occasions, on 'some high festival of once a year'. Then indeed the stream of hospitality, so long dammed up, may flow without stint for a short season; or a stranger may be expected with the same sort of eager impatience as a caravan of wild beasts, or any other natural curiosity, that excites our wonder and fills up the craving of the mind after novelty. By degrees, however, even this last principle loses its effect: books, newspapers, whatever carries us out of ourselves into a world of which we see and know nothing, becomes distasteful, repulsive; and we turn away with indifference or disgust from every thing that disturbs our lethargic animal existence, or takes off our attention from our petty, local interests and pursuits. Man, left long to himself, is no better than a mere clod; or his activity, for want of some other vent, preys upon himself, or is directed to splenetic, peevish dislikes, or vexatious, harassing persecution of others. I once drew a picture of a country-life: it was a portrait of a particular place, caricature if you will, but with certain allowances, I fear it was too like in the individual instance, and that it would hold too generally true. See *Round Table*, vol. II, p. 116.[12]

If these then are the faults and vices of the inhabitants of town or of the country, where should a man go to live, so as to escape from them? I answer, that in the country we have the society of the groves, the fields, the brooks, and in London a man may keep to himself, or chuse his company as he pleases.

It appears to me that there is an amiable mixture of these two opposite characters in a person who chances to have passed his youth in London, and who has retired into the country for the rest of his life. We may find in such a one a social polish, a pastoral simplicity. He rusticates agreeably, and vegetates with a degree of sentiment. He comes to the next post-town to see for letters, watches the coaches as they pass, and eyes the passengers with a look of familiar curiosity thinking that he too was a gay fellow in his time. He turns his horse's head down the narrow lane that leads homewards, puts on an old coat to save his wardrobe, and fills his glass nearer to the brim. As he lifts the purple juice to his lips and to his eye, and in the dim solitude that hems him round, thinks of the glowing line –

This bottle's the sun of our table[13] –

another sun rises upon his imagination; the sun of his youth, the blaze of vanity, the glitter of the metropolis, 'glares round his soul, and mocks his closing eye-lids.' The distant roar of coaches in his ears – the pit stares upon him with a thousand eyes – Mrs Siddons, Bannister, King,[14] are before him – he starts as from a dream, and swears he will to London; but the expense, the length of way deters him, and he rises the next morning to trace the footsteps of the hare that has brushed the dew-drops from the lawn, or to attend a meeting of Magistrates! Mr Justice Shallow answered in some sort to this description of a retired Cockney and indigenous country-gentleman. He 'knew the Inns of Court, where they would talk of mad Shallow yet, and where the bona robas were, and had them at commandment: aye, and had heard the chimes at midnight!'[15]

It is a strange state of society (such as that in London) where a man does not know his next-door neighbour, and where the feelings (one would think) must recoil upon themselves, and either fester or become obtuse. Mr Wordsworth, in the preface to his poem of the 'Excursion,' represents men in cities as so many wild beasts or evil spirits, shut up in cells of ignorance, without natural affections, and barricadoed down in sensuality and selfishness.[16] The nerve of humanity is bound up, according to him, the circulation of the blood stagnates. And it would be so, if men were merely cut off from intercourse with their immediate neighbours, and did not meet together generally and more at large. But man in London becomes, as Mr Burke has it, a sort of 'public creature'. He lives in the eye of the world, and the world in his. If he witnesses less of the details of private life, he has better opportunities of observing its larger masses and varied movements. He sees the stream of human life pouring along the streets – its comforts and embellishments piled up in the shops – the houses are proofs of the industry, the public buildings of the art and magnificence of man; while the public amusements and places of resort are a centre and support for social feeling. A playhouse alone is a school of humanity, where all eyes are fixed on the same gay or solemn scene, where smiles or tears are spread from face to face, and where a thousand hearts beat in unison! Look at the company in a country-theatre (in comparison) and see the coldness, the sullenness, the want of sympathy, and the way in which they turn round to scan and scrutinise one another. In London there is a *public*; and each man is part of it. We are gregarious, and affect the kind. We have a sort of abstract existence; and a community of ideas and knowledge (rather than local proximity) is the bond of society and good-fellowship. This is one great cause of the tone of political feeling in large and populous cities. There is here a visible body-politic, a type and image of that huge Leviathan the State. We comprehend that vast denomination, the *People*, of which we see a tenth part daily moving before us; and by having our imaginations emancipated from petty interests and personal dependence, we learn to venerate ourselves as men, and to respect the rights of human nature. Therefore it is that the citizens and freemen of London and Westminster are patriots by prescription, philosophers and politicians by the right of their birth-place. In the country, men are no better than a herd of cattle or scattered deer. They have no idea but of individuals, none of rights or principles – and a king, as the greatest individual, is the highest idea they can form. He is 'a species alone', and as superior to any single peasant as the latter is to the peasant's dog, or to a crow flying over his head. In London the king is but as one to a million (numerically speaking), is seldom seen, and then distinguished only from others by the superior graces of his person. A country 'squire or a lord of the manor is a greater man in his village or hundred!

Brummelliana

First published in the *London Weekly Review*, 2 February 1828. Before his catastrophic falling-out with the Prince Regent in 1815, the famous dandy George Bryan 'Beau' Brummell (1778–1840) was for many years a leading figure in English high society, reknowned as much for the readiness of his repartee as for his fanatically fastidious dress-sense. Given Hazlitt's absolute horror of affectation and thoroughgoing anti-aristocratic bias, it is at first sight surprising that he should have chosen to celebrate such a figure. But reading between the lines it is clear that Hazlitt saw something surreptitiously subversive, even revolutionary, in the non-aristocratic Brummell's impudent way with the nobility.

We look upon Beau Brummell as the greatest of small wits. Indeed, he may in this respect be considered, as Cowley says of Pindar, as 'a species alone', and as forming a class by himself. He has arrived at the very *minimum* of wit, and reduced it, 'by happiness or pains', to an almost invisible point. All his *bons-mots* turn upon a single circumstance, the exaggerating of the merest trifles into matters of importance, or treating everything else with the utmost *nonchalance* and indifference, as if whatever pretended to pass beyond those limits was a *bore*, and disturbed the serene air of high life. We have heard of

A sound so fine,
That nothing lived 'twixt it and silence.[1]

So we may say of Mr Brummell's jests, that they are of a meaning so attenuated that 'nothing lives 'twixt them and nonsense':– they hover on the very brink of vacancy, and are in their shadowy composition next of kin to nonentities. It is impossible for anyone to go beyond him without falling flat into insignificance and insipidity: he has touched the *ne plus ultra* that divides the dandy from the dunce. But what a fine eye to discriminate: what a sure hand to hit this last and thinnest of all intellectual partitions! *Exempli gratiâ* – for in so new a species, the theory is unintelligible without furnishing the proofs:–

Thus, in the question addressed to a noble person (which we quoted the other day), 'Do you call that *thing* a coat?' a distinction is taken as nice as it is startling. It seems all at once a vulgar prejudice to suppose that a coat is a coat, the commonest of all common things, – it is here lifted into an ineffable essence, so that a coat is no longer a *thing*; or that it would take infinite gradations of fashion, taste, and refinement, for a *thing* to aspire to the undefined privileges, and mysterious attributes of a coat. Finer 'fooling' than this cannot be imagined. What a cut upon the Duke! The beau becomes an emperor among such insects!

The first anecdote in which Mr Brummell's wit dawned upon us – and it really rises with almost every new instance – was the following: A friend one day called upon him, and found him confined to his room from a lameness in one foot, upon which he expressed his concern at the accident. 'I am sorry for it too,' answered Brummell very gravely, 'particularly as it's *my favourite leg*!' Is not this as if a man of fashion had nothing else to do than to sit and think of which of his legs he liked best; and in the plenitude of his satisfactions, and the absence of all real wants, to pamper this fanciful distinction into a serious sort of *pet* preference? Upon the whole, among so many beauties – *ubi tot nitent*, I am inclined to give my suffrage in favour of this, as the most classical of all our contemporary's *jeux d'esprit* – there is an Horatian ease and elegance about it – a slippered negligence, a cushioned effeminacy – it would take years of careless study and languid enjoyment to strike out so quaint and ingenious a conceit –

> A subtler web Arachne cannot spin;
> Nor the fine nets which oft we woven see
> Of scorched dew, do not in the air more lightly flee![2]

It is truly the art of making something out of nothing.

We shall not go deeply into the common story of Mr Brummell's asking his servant, as he was going out for the evening, 'Where do I dine to-day, John?' This is little more than the common cant of a multiplicity of engagements, so as to make it impossible to bear them all in mind, and of an utter disinclination to all attention to one's own affairs; but the following is brilliant and original. Sitting one day at table between two other persons, Mr Brummell said to his servant, who stood behind his chair – 'John!' 'Yes, sir.' 'Who is this at my right hand?' 'If you please, sir, it's the Marquis of

Headfort.' 'And who is this at my left hand?' 'It's my Lord Yarmouth.' 'Oh, very well!' and the Beau then proceeded to address himself to the persons who were thus announced to him. Now, this is surely superb, and 'high fantastical'. No, the smallest fold of that nicely adjusted cravat was not to be deranged, the least deviation from that select posture was not to be supposed possible. Had his head been fastened in a vice, it could not have been more immovably fixed than by the 'great idea in his mind', of how a coxcomb should sit: the air of fashion and affectation 'bound him with Styx nine times round him'; and the Beau preserved the perfection of an attitude – like a piece of incomprehensible *still-life*, – the whole of dinner-time. The *ideal* is everything, even in frivolity and folly.

It is not one of the least characteristic of our hero's answers to a lady, who asked him if he never tasted vegetables – 'Madam, I once ate a pea!' This was reducing the quantity of offensive grossness to the smallest assignable fraction: anything beyond *that* his imagination was oppressed with; and even this he seemed to confess to, with a kind of remorse, and to hasten from the subject with a certain monosyllabic brevity of style.

I do not like the mere impudence (Mr Theodore Hook,[3] with his extempore dullness, might do the same thing) of forcing himself into a lady's rout, who had not invited him to her parties, and the gabble about Hopkinses and Tomkinses; but there is something piquant enough in his answer to a city-fashionable, who asked him if he would dine with him on a certain day – 'Yes, if you won't mention it to anyone'; and in an altercation with the same person afterwards about obligations, the assumption of superiority implied in the appeal – 'Do you count my having *borrowed* a thousand pounds of you for nothing?' soars immediately above commonplace.

On one occasion, Mr Brummell falling ill, accounted for it by saying, 'They put me to bed to a damp —— !' From what slight causes direst issues spring! So sensitive and apprehensive a constitution makes one sympathise with its delicate possessor, as much as if he had been shut up in the steam of a laundry, or 'his lodging had been on the cold ground'. Mr Brummell having been interrogated as to the choice of his present place of residence (Calais) as somewhat dull replied, 'He thought it hard if a gentleman could not pass his time agreeably between London and Paris.'[4]

Some of Brummell's *bons-mots* have been attributed to Sir Lumley Skeffington,[5] who is even said to have been the first in this minute and tender walk of wit. It is, for instance, reported of him that, being at table and talking of daisies, he should turn round to his valet, and say with sentimental *naïveté* and trivial fondness – 'On what day of the month did I first see a daisy, Matthew?' 'On the 1st of February, sir.' There is here a kindred vein; but whoever was the inventor, Brummell has borne away the prize, as Pope eclipsed his master Dryden, and Titian surpassed Giorgione's fame. In fine, it was said, with equal truth and spirit by one of the parties concerned, that 'the year 1815 was fatal to three great men – Byron, Buonaparte, and Brummell!'

On Fashion

First published in *The Edinburgh Magazine*, September 1818, then reprinted by Hazlitt's son in the posthumously published *Sketches and Essays* (London: John Templeman, 1839). Not all left-wing thinkers have been sniffy about fashion. The twentieth-century Marxist critic Walter Benjamin saw a utopian element in it, a revolutionary tendency towards novelty and improvement. To Hazlitt, however, fashion would always be about unmeaning and arbitrary distinctions, a mere tool for maintaining the artificial superiority of the ruling classes.

'Born of nothing, begot of nothing.'

His garment neither was of silk nor say,
But painted plumes in goodly order dight,
Like as the sun-burnt Indians do array
Their tawny bodies in their proudest plight:
As those same plumes, so seem'd he vain and light,
That by his gait might easily appear
For still he far'd as dancing in delight
And in his hands a windy fan did bear,
That in the idle air he mov'd still here and there.[1]

Fashion is an odd jumble of contradictions, of sympathies and antipathies. It exists only by its being participated among a certain number of persons, and its essence is destroyed by being communicated to a greater number. It is a continual struggle between 'the great vulgar and the small' to get the start of or keep up with each other in the race of appearances, by an adoption on the part of the one of such external and fantastic symbols as strike the attention and excite the envy or admiration of the beholder, and which are no sooner made known and exposed to public view for this purpose, than they are successfully copied by the multitude, the slavish herd of imitators, who do not wish to be behind-hand with their betters in outward show and pretensions, and which then sink, without any farther notice, into disrepute and contempt. Thus fashion lives only in a perpetual round of giddy innovation and restless vanity. To be old-fashioned is the greatest crime a coat or a hat can be guilty of. To look like nobody else is a sufficiently mortifying reflection; to be in danger of being mistaken for one of the rabble is worse. Fashion constantly begins and ends in the two things it abhors most, singularity and vulgarity. It is the perpetual setting up and disowning a certain standard of taste, elegance, and refinement, which has no other foundation or authority than that it is the prevailing distinction of the moment, which was yesterday ridiculous from its being new, and to-morrow will be odious from its being common. It is one of the most slight and insignificant of all things. It cannot be lasting, for it depends on the constant change and shifting of its own harlequin disguises; it cannot be sterling, for, if it were, it could not depend on the breath of caprice; it must be superficial, to produce its immediate effect on the gaping crowd; and frivolous, to admit of its being assumed at pleasure by the numbers of those who affect, by being in the fashion, to be distinguished from the rest of the world. It is not any thing in itself, nor the sign of any thing but the folly and vanity of those who rely upon it as their greatest pride and ornament. It takes the firmest hold of the most flimsy and narrow minds, of those whose emptiness conceives of nothing excellent but what is thought so by others, and whose self-conceit makes them willing to confine the opinion of all excellence to themselves and those like them. That which is true or beautiful in itself, is not the less so for standing alone. That which is good for any thing, is the better for being more widely diffused. But fashion is the abortive issue of vain ostentation and exclusive egotism: it is haughty, trifling, affected, servile, despotic, mean, and ambitious, precise and fantastical, all in a breath – tied to no rule, and bound to conform to every whim of the minute. 'The fashion of an hour old mocks the wearer.' It is a sublimated essence of levity, caprice, vanity, extravagance, idleness, and selfishness. It thinks of nothing but not being contaminated by vulgar use, and winds and doubles like a hare, and betakes itself to the most paltry shifts to avoid being overtaken by the common hunt that are always in full chase after it. It contrives to keep up its fastidious pretensions, not by the difficulty of the attainment, but by the rapidity and evanescent nature of the changes. It is a sort of conventional badge, or understood passport into select circles, which must still be varying (like the water-mark in banknotes) not to be counterfeited by those without the pale of fashionable society; for to make the test of admission to all the privileges of that refined and volatile atmosphere depend on any real merit or extraordinary accomplishment, would exclude too many of the pert, the dull, the ignorant, too many shallow, upstart, and self-admiring pretenders, to enable the few that passed muster to keep one another in any tolerable countenance. If it were the fashion, for instance, to be distinguished for virtue, it would be difficult to set or follow the example; but then this would confine the pretension to a small number (not the most fashionable part of the community), and would carry a very singular air with it. Or if excellence in any art or science were made the standard of fashion, this would also effectually prevent vulgar imitation, but then it would equally prevent fashionable impertinence. There would be an obscure circle of *virtù* as well as virtue, drawn within the established circle of fashion, a little province of a mighty empire; – the example of honesty would spread slowly, and learning would still have to boast of a respectable minority. But of what use would such uncourtly and out-of-the-way accomplishments be to the great and noble, the rich and the fair, without any of the *éclat*, the noise and nonsense which belong to that which is followed and admired by all the world alike? The real and solid will never do for the current coin, the common wear and tear of foppery and fashion. It must be the meretricious, the showy, the outwardly fine, and intrinsically worthless – that which lies within the reach of the most indolent affectation, that which can be put on or off at the suggestion of the most wilful caprice, and for which, through all its fluctuations, no mortal reason can be given, but that it is the newest absurdity in vogue! The shape of a head-dress, whether flat or piled (curl on curl) several stories high by the help of pins and pomatum, the size of a pair of paste buckles, the quantity of gold-lace on an embroidered waistcoat, the mode of taking a pinch of snuff, or of pulling out a pocket handkerchief, the lisping and affected pronunciation of certain words, the saying *Me'm* for *Madam*, Lord Foppington's[2] *Tam* and *'Paun honour*, with a regular set of visiting phrases and insipid sentiments ready sorted for the day, were what formerly distinguished the mob of fine gentlemen and ladies from the mob of their inferiors. These marks and appendages of gentility had their day, and were then discarded for others equally peremptory and unequivocal. But in all this chopping and changing, it is generally one folly that drives out another; one trifle that by its specific levity acquires a momentary and surprising ascendancy over the last. There is no striking deformity of appearance or behaviour that has not been made 'the sign of an inward and invisible grace'. Accidental imperfections are laid hold of to hide real defects. Paint, patches, and powder, were at one time synonymous with health, cleanliness, and beauty. Obscenity, irreligion, small oaths, tippling, gaming, effeminacy in the one sex and Amazon airs in the other, any thing is the fashion while it lasts. In the reign of Charles II, the profession and practice of every species of extravagance and debauchery were looked upon as the indispensable marks of an accomplished cavalier. Since that period the court has reformed, and has had rather a rustic air. Our belles formerly overloaded themselves with dress: of late years, they have affected to go almost naked, – 'and are, when unadorned, adorned the most'. The women having left off stays, the men have taken to wear them, if we are to believe the authentic Memoirs of the Fudge Family.[3] The Niobe head is at present buried in the *poke* bonnet, and the French milliners and *marchands des modes* have proved themselves an overmatch for the Greek sculptors, in matters of taste and costume.

A very striking change has, however, taken place in dress of late years, and some progress has been made in taste and elegance, from the very circumstance, that, as fashion has extended its empire in that direction, it has lost its power. While fashion in dress included what was costly, it was confined to the wealthier classes: even this was an encroachment on the privileges of rank and birth, which for a long time were the only things that commanded or pretended to command respect, and we find Shakespear complaining that 'the city madam bears the cost of princes on unworthy shoulders'; but, when the appearing in the top of the mode no longer depended on the power of purchasing certain expensive articles of dress, or the right of wearing them, the rest was so obvious and easy, that any one who chose might cut as coxcombical a figure as the best. It became a matter of mere affectation on the one side, and gradually ceased to be made a matter of aristocratic assumption on the other. 'In the grand carnival of this our age', among other changes this is not the least remarkable, that the monstrous pretensions to distinctions in dress have dwindled away by tacit consent, and the simplest and most graceful have been in the same request with all classes. In this respect, as well as some others, 'the age is grown so picked, the peasant's toe comes so near the courtier's heel, it galls his kibe'; a lord is hardly to be distinguished in the street from an attorney's clerk; and a plume of feathers is no longer mistaken for the highest distinction in the land! The ideas of natural equality and the Manchester steam-engines together have, like a double battery, levelled the high towers and artificial structures of fashion in dress, and a white muslin gown is now the common costume of the mistress and the maid, instead of their wearing, as heretofore, rich silks and satins or coarse linsey-wolsey.[4] It would be ridiculous (on a similar principle) for the courtier to take the wall of the citizen, without having a sword by his side to maintain his right of precedence; and, from the stricter notions that have prevailed of a man's personal merit and identity, a cane dangling from his arm is the greatest extension of his figure that can be allowed to the modern *petit-maître*.

What shews the worthlessness of mere fashion is, to see how easily this vain and boasted distinction is assumed, when the restraints of decency or circumstances are once removed, by the most uninformed and commonest of the people. I know an undertaker that is the greatest prig in the streets of London, and an Aldermanbury haberdasher, that has the most military strut of any lounger in Bond-street or St James's. We may, at any time, raise a regiment of fops from the same number of fools, who have vanity enough to be intoxicated with the smartness of their appearance, and not sense enough to be ashamed of themselves. Every one remembers the story in *Peregrine Pickle*, of the strolling gipsy that he picked up in spite, had well scoured, and introduced her into genteel company, where she met with great applause, till she got into a passion by seeing a fine lady cheat at cards, rapped out a volley of oaths, and let nature get the better of art.[5] Dress is the great secret of address. Clothes and confidence will set anybody up in the trade of modish accomplishment. Look at the two classes of well-dressed females whom we see at the play-house, in the boxes. Both are equally dressed in the height of the fashion, both are *rouged*, and wear their neck and arms bare, – both have the same conscious, haughty, theatrical air; – the same toss of the head, the same stoop in the shoulders, with all the grace that arises from a perfect freedom from embarrassment, and all the fascination that arises from a systematic disdain of formal prudery, – the same pretence and jargon of fashionable conversation, – the same mimicry of tones and phrases, – the same 'lisping, and ambling, and painting, and nicknaming of Heaven's creatures'; the same every thing but real propriety of behaviour, and real refinement of sentiment. In all the externals, they are as like as the reflection in the looking-glass. The only difference between the woman of fashion and the woman of pleasure is, that the one *is* what the other only *seems to be*; and yet, the victims of dissipation who thus rival and almost outshine women of the first quality in all the blaze, and pride, and glitter of show and fashion, are, in general, no better than a set of raw, uneducated, inexperienced country girls, or awkward, coarse-fisted servant maids, who require no other apprenticeship or qualification to be on a level with persons of the highest distinction in society, in all the brilliancy and elegance of outward appearance, than that they have forfeited its common privileges, and every title to respect in reality. The truth is, that real virtue, beauty, or understanding, are the same, whether 'in a high or low degree'; and the airs and graces of pretended superiority over these which the highest classes give themselves, from mere frivolous and external accomplishments, are easily imitated, with provoking success, by the lowest, whenever they *dare*.

The two nearest things in the world are gentility and vulgarity –

And thin partitions do their bounds divide.[6]

Where there is much affectation of the one, we may be always sure of meeting with a double share of the other. Those who are conscious to themselves of any real superiority or refinement, are not particularly jealous of the adventitious marks of it. Miss Burney's novels all turn upon this slender distinction. It is the only thing that can be said against them. It is hard to say which she has made out to be the worst; low people always aping gentility, or people in high life always avoiding vulgarity. Mr Smith and the Brangtons were everlastingly trying to do as their fashionable acquaintances did, and these again were always endeavouring *not* to do and say what Mr Smith and the Brangtons did or said.[7] What an instructive game at cross-purposes! 'Kings are naturally lovers of low company', according to the observation of Mr Burke; because their rank cannot be called into question by it, and they can only hope to find, in the opposite extreme of natural and artificial inequality, any thing to confirm them in the belief, that their personal pretensions at all answer to the ostensible superiority to which they are raised. By associating only with the worst and weakest, they persuade themselves that they are the best and wisest of mankind.

On the Want of Money

First published in *The Monthly Magazine*, January 1827,
then reprinted by Hazlitt's son in *Literary Remains of the
late William Hazlitt*, 2 vols (London: Saunders and Otley,
1836). An incurably improvident man, Hazlitt suffered from
intermittent financial difficulties throughout his life. Even
after 1820, when the income he was earning from his writings
was quite considerable, he still found himself regularly in
debt. Substantially culled from personal experience, with
some hilarious anecdotes of Sheridan thrown in for good
measure, this delightfully digressive essay is in many ways a
meditation on bohemianism, that is, on the want of money as
a spur to the imagination. But like many an evasive debtor, it
is forced to confront the reality principle in the end. 'Literally
and truly, one cannot get on well in the world without
money,' Hazlitt writes; 'to be in want of money is to pass
through life with little credit or pleasure. It is to live out of the
world, or to be despised if you come into it.'

It is hard to be without money. To get on without it is like travelling
in a foreign country without a passport – you are stopped,
suspected, and made ridiculous at every turn, besides being
subjected to the most serious inconveniences. The want of money
I here allude to is not altogether that which arises from absolute
poverty – for where there is a downright absence of the common
necessaries of life, this must be remedied by incessant hard labour,
and the least we can receive in return is a supply of our daily wants
– but that uncertain, casual, precarious mode of existence, in which
the temptation to spend remains after the means are exhausted, the
want of money joined with the hope and possibility of getting it,
the intermediate state of difficulty and suspense between the
last guinea or shilling and the next that we may have the good luck
to encounter. This gap, this unwelcome interval constantly
recurring, however shabbily got over, is really full of many
anxieties, misgivings, mortifications, meannesses, and deplorable
embarrassments of every description. I may attempt (this essay is

not a fanciful speculation) to enlarge upon a few of them.

It is hard to go without one's dinner through sheer distress, but harder still to go without one's breakfast. Upon the strength of that first and aboriginal meal, one may muster courage to face the difficulties before one, and to dare the worst: but to be roused out of one's warm bed, and perhaps a profound oblivion of care, with golden dreams (for poverty does not prevent golden dreams), and told there is nothing for breakfast, is cold comfort for which one's half-strung nerves are not prepared, and throws a damp upon the prospects of the day. It is a bad beginning. A man without a breakfast is a poor creature, unfit to go in search of one, to meet the frown of the world, or to borrow a shilling of a friend. He may beg at the corner of a street – nothing is too mean for the tone of his feelings – robbing on the highway is out of the question, as requiring too much courage, and some opinion of a man's self. It is, indeed, as old Fuller, or some worthy of that age, expresses it, 'the heaviest stone which melancholy can throw at a man', to learn, the first thing after he rises in the morning, or even to be dunned with it in bed, that there is no loaf, tea, or butter in the house, and that the baker, the grocer, and butterman have refused to give any farther credit. This is taking one sadly at a disadvantage. It is striking at one's spirit and resolution in their very source, – the stomach – it is attacking one on the side of hunger and mortification at once; it is casting one into the very mire of humility and Slough of Despond. The worst is, to know what face to put upon the matter, what excuse to make to the servants, what answer to send to the tradespeople; whether to laugh it off, or be grave, or angry, or indifferent; in short, to know how to parry off an evil which you cannot help. What a luxury, what a God's-send in such a dilemma, to find a half-crown which had slipped through a hole in the lining of your waistcoat, a crumpled bank-note in your breeches-pocket, or a guinea clinking in the bottom of your trunk, which had been thoughtlessly left there out of a former heap! Vain hope! Unfounded illusion! The experienced in such matters know better, and laugh in their sleeves at so improbable a suggestion. Not a corner, not a cranny, not a pocket, not a drawer has been left unrummaged, or has not been subjected over and over again to more than the strictness of a custom-house scrutiny. Not the slightest rustle of a piece of bank-paper, not the gentlest pressure of a piece of hard metal, but would have given notice of its hiding-place with electrical rapidity, long before, in such circumstances.

All the variety of pecuniary resources which form a legal tender on the current coin of the realm, are assuredly drained, exhausted to the last farthing before this time. But is there nothing in the house that one can turn to account? Is there not an old family-watch, or piece of plate, or a ring, or some worthless trinket that one could part with? nothing belonging to one's-self or a friend, that one could raise the wind upon, till something better turns up? At this moment an old clothes-man passes, and his deep, harsh tones sound like an intended insult to one's distress, and banish the thought of applying for his assistance, as one's eye glances furtively at an old hat or a great coat, hung up behind a closet-door. Humiliating contemplations! Miserable uncertainty! One hesitates, and the opportunity is gone by; for without one's breakfast, one has not the resolution to do any thing! – The late Mr Sheridan was often reduced to this unpleasant predicament.[1] Possibly he had little appetite for breakfast himself; but the servants complained bitterly on this head, and said that Mrs Sheridan was sometimes kept waiting for a couple of hours, while they had to hunt through the neighbourhood, and beat up for coffee, eggs, and French rolls. The same perplexity in this instance appears to have extended to the providing for the dinner; for so sharp-set were they, that to cut short a debate with a butcher's apprentice about leaving a leg of mutton without the money, the cook clapped it into the pot: the butcher's boy, probably used to such encounters, with equal coolness took it out again, and marched off with it in his tray in triumph. It required a man to be the author of *The School for Scandal*, to run the gauntlet of such disagreeable occurrences every hour of the day. There was one comfort, however, that poor Sheridan had: he did not foresee that Mr Moore would write his *Life*!*

---

* Taylor, of the Opera-House, used to say of Sheridan, that he could not pull off his hat to him in the street without its costing him fifty pounds; and if he stopped to speak to him, it was a hundred. No one could be a stronger instance than he was of what is called *living from hand to mouth*. He was always in want of money, though he received vast sums which he must have disbursed; and yet nobody can tell what became of them, for he paid nobody. He spent his wife's fortune (sixteen hundred pounds) in a six weeks' jaunt to Bath, and returned to town as poor as a rat. Whenever he and his son were invited out into the country; they always went in two post-chaises and four; he in one, and his son Tom following in another. This is the secret of those who live in a round of extravagance, and are at the same time always in debt and difficulty – they throw away all the ready money they get upon any new-fangled whim or project that comes in their way,

The going without a dinner is another of the miseries of wanting
money, though one can bear up against this calamity better than
the former, which really 'blights the tender blossom and promise

and never think of paying off old scores, which of course, accumulate to a
dreadful amount. 'Such gain the cap of him who makes them fine, yet keeps his
book uncrossed.' Sheridan once wanted to take Mrs Sheridan a very handsome
dress down into the country, and went to Barber and Nunn's to order it, saying
he must have it by such a day, but promising they should have ready money.
Mrs Barber (I think it was) made answer that the time was short, but that ready
money was a very charming thing, and that he should have it. Accordingly, at
the time appointed she brought the dress, which came to five-and-twenty
pounds, and it was sent in to Mr Sheridan: who sent out a Mr Grimm (one of his
jackalls) to say he admired it exceedingly, and that he was sure Mrs Sheridan
would be delighted with it, but he was sorry to have nothing under a hundred
pound bank-note in the house. She said she had come provided for such an
accident, and could give change for a hundred, two hundred, or five hundred
pound note, if it were necessary. Grimm then went back to his principal for
farther instructions: who made an excuse that he had no stamped receipt by him.
For this, Mrs B. said, she was also provided; she had brought one in her pocket.
At each message, she could hear them laughing heartily in the next room at the
idea of having met with their match for once; and presently after, Sheridan came
out in high good-humour, and paid her the amount of her bill, in ten, five, and
one pounds. Once when a creditor brought him a bill for payment, which had
often been presented before, and the man complained of its soiled and tattered
state, and said he was quite ashamed to see it, 'I'll tell you what I'd advise you
to do with it, my friend,' said Sheridan, 'take it home, and write it upon
parchment!' He once mounted a horse which a horse-dealer was shewing off near
a coffee-house at the bottom of St James's-street, rode it to Tattersall's, and sold
it, and walked quietly back to the spot from which he set out. The owner was
furious, swore he would be the death of him; and, in a quarter of an hour
afterwards they were seen sitting together over a bottle of wine in the coffee-
house, the horse-jockey with the tears running down his face at Sheridan's jokes,
and almost ready to hug him as an honest fellow. Sheridan's house and lobby
were beset with duns every morning, who were told that Mr Sheridan was not
yet up, and shewn into the several rooms on each side of the entrance. As soon
as he had breakfasted, he asked, 'Are those doors all shut, John?' and, being
assured they were, marched out very deliberately between them, to the
astonishment of his self-invited guests, who soon found the bird was flown. I
have heard one of his old City friends declare, that such was the effect of his
frank, cordial manner, and insinuating eloquence, that he was always afraid to
go to ask him for a debt of long standing, lest he should borrow twice as much.
A play had been put off one night, or a favourite actor did not appear, and the
audience demanded to have their money back again; but when they came to the
door, they were told by the check-takers there was none for them, for that Mr
Sheridan had been in the mean time, and had carried off all the money in the
till. He used often to get the old cobbler who kept a stall under the ruins of Drury
Lane to broil a beef-steak for him, and take their dinner together. On the night
that Drury Lane was burnt down, Sheridan was in the House of Commons,

of the day.' With one good meal, one may hold a parley with hunger and moralise upon temperance. One has time to turn one's-self and look about one – to 'screw one's courage to the sticking-place', to graduate the scale of disappointment, and stave off appetite till supper-time. You gain time, and time in this weather-cock world is everything. You may dine at two, or at six, or seven – as most convenient. You may in the meanwhile receive an invitation to dinner, or some one (not knowing how you are circumstanced) may send you a present of a haunch of venison or a brace of pheasants from the country, or a distant relation may die and leave you a legacy, or a patron may call and overwhelm you with his smiles and bounty,

As kind as kings upon their coronation-day;[2]

or there is no saying what may happen. One may wait for dinner – breakfast admits of no delay, of no interval interposed between that and our first waking thoughts.* Besides, there are shifts and

making a speech, though he could hardly stand without leaning his hands on the table, and it was with some difficulty he was forced away, urging the plea, 'What signified the concerns of a private individual compared to the good of the state?' When he got to Covent-Garden, he went into the Piazza Coffee-house, to steady himself with another bottle, and then strolled out to the end of the Piazza to look at the progress of the fire. Here he was accosted by Charles Kemble and Fawcett, who complimented him on the calmness with which he seemed to regard so great a loss. He declined this praise, and said – 'Gentlemen, there are but three things in human life that in my opinion ought to disturb a wise man's patience. The first of these is bodily pain, and that (whatever the ancient stoics may have said to the contrary) is too much for any man to bear without flinching: this I have felt severely, and I know it to be the case. The second is the loss of a friend whom you have dearly loved, that gentlemen, is a great evil: this I have also felt, and I know it to be too much for any man's fortitude. And the third is the consciousness of having done an unjust action. That, gentlemen, is a great evil, a very great evil, too much for any man to endure the reflection of; but that' (laying his hand upon his heart,) 'but that, thank God, I have never felt!' I have been told that these were nearly the very words, except that he appealed to the *mens conscia recti* very emphatically three or four times over, by an excellent authority, Mr Mathews the player, who was on the spot at the time, a gentleman whom the public admire deservedly, but with whose real talents and nice discrimination of character his friends only are acquainted. Sheridan's reply to the watchman who had picked him up in the street, and who wanted to know who he was, 'I am Mr Wilberforce!'[3] – is well known, and shews that, however frequently he might be at a loss for money he never wanted wit!

* In Scotland, it seems, the draught of ale or whiskey with which you commence the day, is emphatically called 'taking your *morning*'.

devices, shabby and mortifying enough, but still available in case of need. How many expedients are there in this great city (London), time out of mind and times without number, resorted to by the dilapidated and thrifty speculator, to get through this grand difficulty without utter failure! One may dive into a cellar, and dine on boiled beef and carrots for tenpence, with the knives and forks chained to the table, and jostled by greasy elbows that seem to make such a precaution not unnecessary (hunger is proof against indignity!) – or one may contrive to part with a superfluous article of wearing apparel, and carry home a mutton-chop and cook it in a garret; or one may drop in at a friend's at the dinner-hour, and be asked to stay or not; or one may walk out and take a turn in the Park, about the time, and return home to tea, so as at least to avoid the sting of the evil – the appearance of not having dined. You then have the laugh on your side, having deceived the gossips, and can submit to the want of a sumptuous repast without murmuring, having saved your pride, and made a virtue of necessity. I say all this may he done by a man without a family (for what business has a man without money with one? – See *English Malthus and Scotch Macculloch*)[4] – and it is only my intention here to bring forward such instances of the want of money as are tolerable both in theory and practice. I once lived on coffee (as an experiment) for a fortnight together, while I was finishing the copy of a half-length portrait of a Manchester manufacturer, who had died worth a plum. I rather slurred over the coat, which was a reddish brown, 'of formal cut', to receive my five guineas, with which I went to market myself, and dined on sausages and mashed potatoes, and while they were getting ready, and I could hear them hissing in the pan, read a volume of *Gil Blas*, containing the account of the fair Aurora.[5] This was in the days of my youth. Gentle reader, do not smile! Neither Monsieur de Very, nor Louis XVIII, over an oyster-pâté, nor Apicius himself, ever understood the meaning of the word luxury, better than I did at that moment! If the want of money has its drawbacks and disadvantages, it is not without its contrasts and counterbalancing effects, for which I fear nothing else can make us amends. Amelia's *hashed mutton* is immortal;[6] and there is something amusing, though carried to excess and caricature (which is very unusual with the author), in the contrivances of old Caleb, in 'The Bride of Lammermuir', for raising the wind at breakfast, dinner, and supper-time.[7] I recollect a ludicrous instance of a disappointment in a dinner which happened to a person of my acquaintance some years ago. He was not only poor but a very poor creature, as will be imagined. His wife had laid by fourpence (their whole remaining stock) to pay for the baking of a shoulder of mutton and potatoes, which they had in the house, and on her return home from some errand, she found he had expended it in purchasing a new string for a guitar. On this occasion a witty friend quoted the lines from Milton:

> And ever against *eating* cares,
> wrap me in soft Lydian airs![8]

Defoe, in his *Life of Colonel Jack*, gives a striking picture of his young beggarly hero sitting with his companion for the first time in his life at a three-penny ordinary, and the delight with which he relished the hot smoking soup, and the airs with which he called about him – 'and every time,' he says, 'we called for bread, or beer, or whatever it might be, the waiter answered, "coming, gentlemen, coming"; and this delighted me more than all the rest!' It was about this time, as the same pithy author expresses it, 'the Colonel took upon him to wear a shirt!' Nothing can be finer than the whole of the feeling conveyed in the commencement of this novel, about wealth and finery from the immediate contrast of privation and poverty. One would think it a labour, like the Tower of Babel, to build up a beau and a fine gentleman about town. The little vagabond's admiration of the old man at the banking-house, who sits surrounded by heaps of gold as if it were a dream or poetic vision, and his own eager anxious visits, day by day, to the hoard he had deposited in the hollow tree, are in the very foremost style of truth and nature. See the same intense feeling expressed in Luke's address to his riches in the *City Madam*,[9] and in the extraordinary raptures of the 'Spanish Rogue' in contemplating and hugging his ingots of pure gold and Spanish pieces of eight: to which Mr Lamb has referred[10] in excuse for the rhapsodies of some of our elder poets on this subject, which to our present more refined and tamer apprehensions sound like blasphemy.* In earlier times, before the diffusion of luxury, of knowledge, and other sources of enjoyment had become common, and acted as a diversion to the cravings of avarice, the passionate admiration, the idolatry, the hunger and thirst of wealth and all its precious

---

* Shylock's lamentation over the loss of 'his daughter and his ducats', is another case in point.

symbols, was a kind of madness or hallucination, and Mammon
was truly worshipped as a god!

It is among the miseries of the want of money, not to be able to
pay your reckoning at an inn – or, if you have just enough to do that,
to have nothing left for the waiter; – to be stopped at a turnpike gate,
and forced to turn back; – not to venture to call a hackney-coach in
a shower of rain – (when you have only one shilling left yourself, it
is a *bore* to have it taken out of your pocket by a friend, who comes
into your house eating peaches on a hot summer's day, and desiring
you to pay for the coach in which he visits you); – not to be able to
purchase a lottery-ticket, by which you might make your fortune,
and get out of all your difficulties; – or to find a letter lying for you
at a country post-office, and not to have money in your pocket to
free it, and be obliged to return for it the next day.[11] The letter so
unseasonably withheld may be supposed to contain money, and in
this case there is a foretaste, a sort of actual possession taken
through the thin folds of the paper and the wax, which in some
measure indemnifies us for the delay: the bank-note, the post-bill
seems to smile upon us, and shake hands through its prison bars; –
or it may be a love-letter, and then the tantalisation is at its height:
to be deprived in this manner of the only consolation that can make
us amends for the want of money, by this very want – to fancy you
can see the name – to try to get a peep at the hand-writing – to touch
the seal, and yet not dare to break it open – is provoking indeed –
the climax of amorous and gentlemanly distress. Players are
sometimes reduced to great extremity, by the seizure of their scenes
and dresses, or (what is called) *the property of the theatre*, which
hinders them from acting; as authors are prevented from finishing
a work, for want of money to buy the books necessary to be
consulted on some material point or circumstance, in the progress
of it. There is a set of poor devils, who live upon a printed *prospectus*
of a work that never will be written, for which they solicit your name
and half-a-crown. Decayed actresses take an annual benefit at one
of the theatres; there are patriots who live upon periodical
subscriptions, and critics who go about the country lecturing on
poetry. I confess I envy none of these; but there are persons who,
provided they can live, care not how they live – who are fond of
display, even when it implies exposure; who court notoriety under
every shape, and embrace the public with demonstrations of
wantonness. There are genteel beggars, who send up a well-penned
epistle requesting the loan of a shilling. Your snug bachelors and

retired old-maids pretend they can distinguish the knock of one of these at their door. I scarce know which I dislike the most – the patronage that affects to bring premature genius into notice, or that extends its piecemeal, formal charity towards it in its decline. I hate your Literary Funds, and Funds for Decayed Artists – they are corporations for the encouragement of meanness, pretence, and insolence. Of all people, I cannot tell how it is, but players appear to me the best able to do without money. They are a privileged class. If not exempt from the common calls of necessity and business, they are enabled 'by their so potent art' to soar above them. As they make imaginary ills their own, real ones become imaginary, sit light upon them, and are thrown off with comparatively little trouble. Their life is theatrical – its various accidents are the shifting scenes of a play – rags and finery, tears and laughter, a mock-dinner or a real one, a crown of jewels or of straw, are to them nearly the same. I am sorry I cannot carry on this reasoning to actors who are past their prime. The gilding of their profession is then worn off, and shews the false metal beneath; vanity and hope (the props of their existence) have had their day; their former gaiety and carelessness serve as a foil to their present discouragements; and want and infirmities press upon them at once. 'We know what we are,' as Ophelia says, 'but we know not what we shall be.' A workhouse seems the last resort of poverty and distress – a *parish-pauper is* another name for all that is mean and to be deprecated in human existence. But that name is but an abstraction, an average term – 'within that lowest deep, a lower deep may open to receive us'. I heard not long ago of a poor man, who had been for many years a respectable tradesman in London, and who was compelled to take shelter in one of those receptacles of age and wretchedness, and who said he could be contented with it – he had his regular meals, a nook in the chimney, and a coat to his back – but he was forced to lie three in a bed, and one of the three was out of his mind and crazy, and his great delight was, when the others fell asleep, to tweak their noses, and flourish his night-cap over their heads, so that they were obliged to lie awake, and hold him down between them. One should be quite mad to bear this. To what a point of insignificance may not human life dwindle! To what fine, agonising threads will it not cling! Yet this man had been a lover in his youth, in a humble way, and still begins his letters to an old-maid (his former flame), who sometimes comforts him by listening to his complaints, and treating him to a dish of weak tea, 'My dear Miss Nancy!'

Another of the greatest miseries of a want of money, is the tap of a dun[12] at your door, or the previous silence when you expect it – the uneasy sense of shame at the approach of your tormentor; the wish to meet, and yet to shun the encounter; the disposition to bully; the fear of irritating; the real and the sham excuses; the submission to impertinence; the assurances of a speedy supply; the disingenuousness you practise on him and on yourself; the degradation in the eyes of others and your own. Oh! it is wretched to have to confront a just and oft-repeated demand, and to be without the means to satisfy it; to deceive the confidence that has been placed in you; to forfeit your credit; to be placed at the power of another, to be indebted to his lenity; to stand convicted of having played the knave or the fool; and to have no way left to escape contempt, but by incurring pity. The suddenly meeting a creditor on turning the corner of a street, whom you have been trying to avoid for months, and had been persuaded you were several hundred miles off, discomposes the features and shatters the nerves for some time. It is also a serious annoyance to be unable to repay a loan to a friend, who is in want of it – nor is it very pleasant to be so hard-run, as to be induced to request the repayment. It is difficult to decide the preference between debts of honour and legal demands; both are bad enough, and almost a fair excuse for driving any one into the hands of money-lenders – to whom an application, if successful, is accompanied with a sense of being in the vulture's gripe – a reflection akin to that of those who formerly sold themselves to the devil – or, if unsuccessful, is rendered doubly galling by the smooth, civil leer of cool contempt with which you are dismissed, as if they had escaped from your clutches – not you from theirs. If any thing can be added to the mortification and distress arising from straitened circumstances, it is when vanity comes in to barb the dart of poverty – when you have a picture on which you had calculated, rejected from an Exhibition, or a manuscript returned on your hands, or a tragedy damned, at the very instant when your cash and credit are at the lowest ebb. This forlorn and helpless feeling has reached its *acme* in the prison-scene in Hogarth's *Rake's Progress*, where his unfortunate hero has just dropped the Manager's letter from his hands, with the laconic answer written in it: – 'Your play has been read, and won't do.'*

---

*   It is provoking enough, and makes one look like a fool, to receive a printed notice of a blank in the last lottery, with a postscript hoping for your future favours.

To feel poverty is bad; but to feel it with the additional sense of our incapacity to shake it off, and that we have not merit enough to retrieve our circumstances – and, instead of being held up to admiration, are exposed to persecution and insult – is the last stage of human infirmity. My friend, Mr Leigh Hunt (no one is better qualified than he to judge), thinks that the most pathetic story in the world is that of Smollett's fine gentleman and lady in gaol, who have been roughly handled by the mob for some paltry attempt at raising the wind,[13] and she exclaims in extenuation of the pitiful figure he cuts, 'Ah! he was a fine fellow once!'

It is justly remarked by the poet, that poverty has no greater inconvenience attached to it than that of making men ridiculous. It not only has this disadvantage with respect to ourselves, but it often shews us others in a very contemptible point of view. People are not soured by misfortune, but by the reception they meet with in it. When we do not want assistance, every one is ready to obtrude it on us, as if it were advice. If we do, they shun us instantly. They anticipate the increased demand on their sympathy or bounty, and escape from it as from a falling house. It is a mistake, however, that we court the society of the rich and prosperous, merely with a view to what we can get from them. We do so, because there is something in external rank and splendour that gratifies and imposes on the imagination; just as we prefer the company of those who are in good health and spirits to that of the sickly and hypochondriacal, or as we would rather converse with a beautiful woman than with an ugly one. I never knew but one man who would lend his money freely and fearlessly in spite of circumstances (if you were likely to pay him, he grew peevish, and would pick a quarrel with you). I can only account for this from a certain sanguine buoyancy and magnificence of spirit, not deterred by distant consequences, or damped by untoward appearances. I have been told by those, who shared of the same bounty, that it was not owing to generosity, but ostentation – if so, he kept his ostentation a secret from me, for I never received a hint or a look from which I could infer that I was not the lender, and he the person obliged. Neither was I expected to keep in the background or play an under-part. On the contrary, I was encouraged to do my best; my dormant faculties roused, the ease of my circumstances was on condition of the freedom and independence of my mind, my lucky hits were applauded, and I was paid to shine. I am not ashamed of such patronage as this, nor do I regret any circumstance relating to it but its termination. People endure existence even in Paris: the rows of chairs on the Boulevards are gay with smiles and dress: the saloons, they say, are brilliant; at the theatre there is Mademoiselle Mars – what is all this to me? After a certain period, we live only in the past. Give me back one single evening at Boxhill, after a stroll in the deep-empurpled woods, before Buonaparte was yet beaten, 'with wine of attic taste', when wit, beauty, friendship presided at the board! Oh no! Neither the time nor friends that are fled, can be recalled! – Poverty is the test of sincerity, the touchstone of civility. Even abroad, they treat you scurvily if your remittances do not arrive regularly, and though you have hitherto lived like a *Milord Anglais.* The want of money loses us friends not worth the keeping, mistresses who are naturally jilts or coquets; it cuts us out of society, to which dress and equipage are the only introduction; and deprives us of a number of luxuries and advantages of which the only good is, that they can only belong to the possessors of a large fortune. Many people are wretched because they have not money to buy a fine horse, or to hire a fine house, or to keep a carriage, or to purchase a diamond necklace, or to go to a race-ball, or to give their servants new liveries. I cannot myself enter into all this. If I can *live to think, and think to live,* I am satisfied. Some want to possess pictures, others to collect libraries. All I wish is, sometimes, to see the one and read the other. Gray was mortified because he had not a hundred pounds to bid for a curious library; and the Duchess of —— has immortalised herself by her liberality on that occasion, and by the handsome compliment she addressed to the poet, that 'if it afforded him any satisfaction, she had been more than paid, by her pleasure in reading the *Elegy in a Country Church-yard'.*

Literally and truly, one cannot get on well in the world without money. To be in want of money, is to pass through life with little credit or pleasure; it is to live out of the world, or to be despised if you come into it; it is not to be sent for to court, or asked out to dinner, or noticed in the street; it is not to have your opinion consulted or else rejected with contempt, to have your acquirements carped at and doubted, your good things disparaged, and at last to lose the wit and the spirit to say them; it is to be scrutinised by strangers, and neglected by friends; it is to be a thrall to circumstances, an exile in a foreign land; to forego leisure, freedom, ease of body and mind, to be dependent on the good-will and caprice of others, or earn a precarious and irksome livelihood by some laborious employment: it is to be compelled to stand behind a counter, or to sit at a desk in some public office, or to marry your landlady, or not the person you would wish; or to go out to the East or West-Indies, or to get a situation as judge abroad, and return home with a liver-complaint; or to be a law-stationer, or a scrivener or scavenger, or newspaper reporter; or to read law and sit in court without a brief, or to be deprived of the use of your fingers by transcribing Greek manuscripts, or to be a seal engraver and pore yourself blind; or to go upon the stage, or try some of the Fine Arts; with all your pains, anxiety, and hopes, most probably to fail, or, if you succeed, after the exertions of years, and undergoing constant distress of mind and fortune, to be assailed on every side with envy, back-biting, and falsehood, or to be a favourite with the public for a while, and then thrown into the back-ground – or a jail, by the fickleness of taste and some new favourite; to be full of enthusiasm and extravagance in youth, of chagrin and disappointment in after-life; to be jostled by the rabble because you do not ride in your coach, or avoided by those who know your worth and shrink from it as a claim on their respect or their purse; to be a burden to your relations, or unable to do any thing for them; to be ashamed to venture into crowds; to have cold comfort at home; to lose by degrees your confidence and any talent you might possess; to grow crabbed, morose, and querulous, dissatisfied with every one, but most so with yourself; and plagued out of your life, to look about for a place to die in, and quit the world without any one's asking after your will. The *wiseacres* will possibly, however, crowd round your coffin, and raise a monument at a considerable expense, and after a lapse of time, to commemorate your genius and your misfortunes!

The only reason why I am disposed to envy the professions of the church or army is, that men can afford to be poor in them without being subjected to insult. A girl with a handsome fortune in a country town may marry a poor lieutenant without degrading herself. An officer is always a gentleman; a clergyman is something more. Echard's book *On the Contempt of the Clergy* is unfounded. It is surely sufficient for any set of individuals, raised above actual want, that their characters are not merely respectable, but sacred. Poverty, when it is voluntary, is never despicable, but takes an heroical aspect. What are the begging friars? Have they not put their base feet upon the necks of princes? Money as a luxury is valuable only as a passport to respect. It is one instrument of power. Where there are other admitted and ostensible claims to this, it becomes superfluous, and the neglect of it is even admired and looked up to as a mark of superiority over it. Even a strolling beggar is a popular character, who makes an open profession of his craft and calling, and who is neither worth a doit nor in want of one. The Scotch are proverbially poor and proud: we know they can remedy their poverty when they set about it. No one is sorry for them. The French emigrants were formerly peculiarly situated in England.[14] The priests were obnoxious to the common people on account of their religion; both they and the nobles, for their politics. Their poverty and dirt subjected them to many rebuffs; but their privations being voluntarily incurred, and also borne with the characteristic patience and good-humour of the nation, screened them from contempt. I little thought, when I used to meet them walking out in the summer's-evenings at Somers' Town, in their long great-coats, their beards covered with snuff, and their eyes gleaming with mingled hope and regret in the rays of the setting sun, and regarded them with pity bordering on respect, as the last filmy vestige of the ancient regime, as shadows of loyalty and superstition still flitting about the earth and shortly to disappear from it for ever, that they would one day return over the bleeding corpse of their country, and sit like harpies, a polluted triumph, over the tomb of human liberty! To be a lord, a papist, and poor, is perhaps to some temperaments a consummation devoutly to be wished. There is all the subdued splendour of external rank, the pride of self-opinion, irritated and goaded on by petty privations and vulgar obloquy to a degree of morbid acuteness. Private and public annoyances must perpetually remind him of what he is, of what his ancestors were (a circumstance which might otherwise be forgotten); must narrow the circle of conscious dignity more and more, and the sense of personal worth and pretension must be exalted by habit and contrast into a refined abstraction – 'pure in the last recesses of the mind' – unmixed with, or unalloyed by 'baser matter'! – It was an hypothesis of the late Mr Thomas Wedgewood, that there is a principle of compensation in the human mind which equalises all situations, and by which the absence of any thing only gives us a more intense and intimate perception of the reality, that insult adds to pride, that pain looks forward to ease with delight, that hunger already enjoys the unsavoury morsel that is to save it from perishing; that want is surrounded with imaginary riches, like the poor poet in Hogarth, who has a map of the mines of Peru hanging on his garret walls;

in short, that 'we can hold a fire in our hand by thinking on the frosty Caucasus' – but this hypothesis, though ingenious and to a certain point true, is to be admitted only in a limited and qualified sense.

There are two classes of people that I have observed who are not so distinct as might be imagined – those who cannot keep their own money in their hands, and those who cannot keep their hands from other people's. The first are always in want of money, though they do not know what they do with it. They *muddle* it away, without method or object, and without having any thing to show for it. They have not, for instance, a fine house, but they hire two houses at a time; they have not a hot-house in their garden, but a shrubbery within doors; they do not gamble, but they purchase a library, and dispose of it when they move house. A princely benefactor provides them with lodgings, where, for a time, you are sure to find them at home: and they furnish them in a handsome style for those who are to come after them. With all this sieve-like economy, they can only afford a leg of mutton and a bottle of wine, and are glad to get a lift in a common stage; whereas with a little management and the same disbursements, they might entertain a round of company and drive a smart tilbury. But they set no value upon money, and throw it away on any object or in any manner that first presents itself, merely to have it off their hands, so that you wonder what has become of it. The second class above spoken of not only make away with what belongs to themselves, but you cannot keep any thing you have from their rapacious grasp. If you refuse to lend them what you want, they insist that you *must*: if you let them have any thing to take charge of for a time (a print or a bust) they swear that you have given it them, and that they have too great a regard for the donor ever to part with it. You express surprise at their having run so largely in debt; but where is the singularity while others continue to lend? And how is this to be helped, when the manner of these sturdy beggars amounts to dragooning you out of your money, and they will not go away without your purse, any more than if they came with a pistol in their hand? If a person has no delicacy, he has you in his power, for you necessarily feel some towards him; and since he will take no denial, you must comply with his peremptory demands, or send for a constable, which out of respect for his character you will not do. These persons are also poor – *light come, light go* – and the bubble bursts at last. Yet if they had employed the same time and pains in any laudable art or study that they have in raising a surreptitious livelihood, they would have been respectable, if not rich. It is their facility in borrowing money that has ruined them. No one will set heartily to work, who has the face to enter a strange house, ask the master of it for a considerable loan, on some plausible and pompous pretext, and walk off with it in his pocket. You might as well suspect a highway-man of addicting himself to hard study in the intervals of his profession.

There is only one other class of persons I can think of, in connexion with the subject of this Essay – those who are always in want of money from the want of spirit to make use of it. Such persons are perhaps more to be pitied than all the rest. They live in want, in the midst of plenty – dare not touch what belongs to them, are afraid to say that their soul is their own, have their wealth locked up from them by fear and meanness as effectually as by bolts and bars, scarcely allow themselves a coat to their backs or a morsel to eat, are in dread of coming to the parish all their lives, and are not sorry when they die, to think that they shall no longer be an expense to themselves – according to the old epigram:

> Here lies Father Clarges,
> Who died to save charges!

On the Feeling of Immortality in Youth

First published in *The Monthly Magazine* in March 1827, then reprinted by Hazlitt's son from an alternative text in *Literary Remains* (1836).

The opening quotation is from *Urn Burial*, and like Sir Thomas Browne's extraordinary essay on burial practices through the ages, 'On the Feeling of Immortality in Youth' has a sublimely detached, even mystical air. In the best Romantic style it is at once deeply personal and yet universal, philosophically rigorous and yet full of imaginative feeling. Of our world-view when young, Hazlitt comments that 'like a rustic at a fair, we are full of amazement and rapture, and have no thoughts of going home, or that it will soon be night'. Such an entropic and solipsistic narrative of life might well have been profoundly depressing, were it not for Hazlitt's continuing insistence upon the shared nature of our experience, the peculiar feeling of togetherness-in-isolation that is conjured up by that expressive 'we'.

Life is a pure flame, and we live by an invisible sun within us.
Sir Thomas Browne

No young man believes he shall ever die. It was a saying of my brother's, and a fine one. There is a feeling of Eternity in youth, which makes us amends for every thing. To be young is to be as one of the Immortal Gods. One half of time indeed is flown – the other half remains in store for us with all its countless treasures; for there is no line drawn, and we see no limit to our hopes and wishes. We make the coming age our own. –

The vast, the unbounded prospect lies before us.[1]

Death, old age, are words without a meaning, that pass by us like the idle air which we regard not. Others may have undergone, or may still be liable to them – we 'bear a charmed life', which laughs to scorn all such sickly fancies. As in setting out on a delightful journey, we strain our eager gaze forward –

Bidding the lovely scenes at distance hail,[2] –

and see no end to the landscape, new objects presenting themselves
as we advance; so, in the commencement of life, we set no bounds
to our inclinations, nor to the unrestricted opportunities of
gratifying them. We have as yet found no obstacle, no disposition
to flag; and it seems that we can go on so for ever. We look round
in a new world, full of life, and motion, and ceaseless progress; and
feel in ourselves all the vigour and spirit to keep pace with it, and
do not foresee from any present symptoms how we shall be left
behind in the natural course of things, decline into old age, and
drop into the grave. It is the simplicity, and as it were *abstractedness*
of our feelings in youth, that (so to speak) identifies us with nature,
and (our experience being slight and our passions strong) deludes
us into a belief of being immortal like it. Our short-lived connection
with existence, we fondly flatter ourselves, is an indissoluble and
lasting union – a honey-moon that knows neither coldness, jar, nor
separation. As infants smile and sleep, we are rocked in the cradle
of our wayward fancies, and lulled into security by the roar of the
universe around us – we quaff the cup of life with eager haste
without draining it, instead of which it only overflows the more –
objects press around us, filling the mind with their magnitude and
with the throng of desires that wait upon them, so that we have no
room for the thoughts of death. From that plenitude of our being,
we cannot change all at once to dust and ashes, we cannot imagine
'this sensible, warm motion, to become a kneaded clod '– we are
too much dazzled by the brightness of the waking dream around
us to look into the darkness of the tomb. We no more see our end
than our beginning: the one is lost in oblivion and vacancy, as the
other is hid from us by the crowd and hurry of approaching events.
Or the grim shadow is seen lingering in the horizon, which we are
doomed never to overtake, or whose last, faint, glimmering outline
touches upon Heaven and translates us to the skies! Nor would the
hold that life has taken of us permit us to detach our thoughts from
present objects and pursuits, even if we would. What is there more
opposed to health, than sickness; to strength and beauty, than
decay and dissolution; to the active search of knowledge than mere
oblivion? Or is there none of the usual advantage to bar the
approach of Death, and mock his idle threats; Hope supplies their
place, and draws a veil over the abrupt termination of all our
cherished schemes. While the spirit of youth remains unimpaired,

ere the 'wine of life is drank up', we are like people intoxicated or in a fever, who are hurried away by the violence of their own sensations: it is only as present objects begin to pall upon the sense, as we have been disappointed in our favourite pursuits, cut off from our closest ties, that passion loosens its hold upon the breast, that we by degrees become weaned from the world, and allow ourselves to contemplate, 'as in a glass, darkly', the possibility of parting with it for good. The example of others, the voice of experience, has no effect upon us whatever. Casualties we must avoid: the slow and deliberate advances of age we can play at *hide-and-seek* with. We think ourselves too lusty and too nimble for that blear-eyed decrepit old gentleman to catch us. Like the foolish fat scullion, in Sterne, when she hears that Master Bobby is dead, our only reflection is – 'So am not I!'[3] The idea of death, instead of staggering our confidence, rather seems to strengthen and enhance our possession and our enjoyment of life. Others may fall around us like leaves, or be mowed down like flowers by the scythe of Time: these are but tropes and figures to the unreflecting ears and overweening presumption of youth. It is not till we see the flowers of Love, Hope, and Joy, withering around us, and our own pleasures cut up by the roots, that we bring the moral home to ourselves, that we abate something of the wanton extravagance of our pretensions, or that the emptiness and dreariness of the prospect before us reconciles us to the stillness of the grave!

> Life! thou strange thing, that hast a power to feel
> Thou art, and to perceive that others are.*

Well might the poet begin his indignant invective against an art, whose professed object is its destruction, with this animated apostrophe to life. Life is indeed a strange gift, and its privileges are most miraculous. Nor is it singular that when the splendid boon is first granted us, our gratitude, our admiration, and our delight should prevent us from reflecting on our own nothingness, or from thinking it will ever be recalled. Our first and strongest impressions are taken from the mighty scene that is opened to us, and we very innocently transfer its durability as well as magnificence to ourselves. So newly found, we cannot make up our minds to parting with it yet and at least put off that consideration to an indefinite term. Like a rustic[4] at a fair, we are

---

* Fawcett's *Art of War*, a poem, 1794.

full of amazement and rapture, and have no thoughts of going home, or that it will soon be night. We know our existence only from external objects, and we measure it by them. We can never be satisfied with gazing; and nature will still want us to look on and applaud. Otherwise, the sumptuous entertainment, 'the feast of reason and the flow of soul', to which we were invited, seems little better than a mockery and a cruel insult. We do not go from a play till the scene is ended, and the lights are ready to be extinguished. But the fair face of things still shines on; shall we be called away, before the curtain falls, or ere we have scarce had a glimpse of what is going on? Like children, our step-mother Nature holds us up to see the raree-show of the universe; and then, as if life were a burthen to support, lets us instantly down again. Yet in that short interval, what 'brave sublunary things' does not the spectacle unfold; like a bubble, at one minute reflecting the universe, and the next, shook to air! – To see the golden sun and the azure sky, the outstretched ocean, to walk upon the green earth, and to be lord of a thousand creatures, to look down giddy precipices or over distant flowery vales, to see the world spread out under one's finger in a map, to bring the stars near, to view the smallest insects in a microscope, to read history, and witness the revolutions of empires and the succession of generations, to hear of the glory of Sidon and Tyre, of Babylon and Susa, as of a faded pageant, and to say all these were, and are now nothing, to think that we exist in such a point of time, and in such a corner of space, to be at once spectators and a part of the moving scene, to watch the return of the seasons, of spring and autumn, to hear

> – The stockdove plain amid the forest deep
> That drowsy rustles to the sighing gale[5] –

to traverse desert wildernesses, to listen to the midnight choir, to visit lighted halls, or plunge into the dungeon's gloom, or sit in crowded theatres and see life itself mocked, to feel heat and cold, pleasure and pain, right and wrong, truth and falsehood, to study the works of art and refine the sense of beauty to agony, to worship fame and to dream of immortality, to have read Shakespear and belong to the same species as Sir Isaac Newton;* to be and to do all

---

* Lady Wortley Montague[6] says, in one of her letters, that 'she would much rather be a rich *effendi*, with all his ignorance, than Sir Isaac Newton, with all his knowledge'. This was not perhaps an impolitic choice, as she had a better chance of becoming one than the other, there being many rich *effendis* to one Sir Isaac

this, and then in a moment to be nothing, to have it all snatched
from one like a juggler's ball or a phantasmagoria; there is

Newton. The wish was not a very intellectual one. The same petulance of rank
and sex breaks out every where in these *Letters*. She is constantly reducing the
poets or philosophers who have the misfortune of her acquaintance, to the figure
they might make at her Ladyship's levee or toilette, not considering that the
public mind does not sympathise with this process of a fastidious imagination.
In the same spirit, she declares of Pope and Swift, that 'had it not been for the
good-nature of mankind, these two superior beings were entitled, by their birth
and hereditary fortune, to be only a couple of link-boys.' Gulliver's Travels, and
the Rape of the Lock, go for nothing in this critical estimate, and the world raised
the authors to the rank of superior beings, in spite of their disadvantages of birth
and fortune, *out of pure good-nature!* So, again, she says of Richardson, that he
had never got beyond the servants' hall, and was utterly unfit to describe the
manners of people of quality; till in the capricious workings of her vanity, she
persuades herself that Clarissa is very like what she was at her age, and that Sir
Thomas and Lady Grandison strongly resembled what she had heard of her
mother and remembered of her father. It is one of the beauties and advantages
of literature, that it is the means of abstracting the mind from the narrowness of
local and personal prejudices, and of enabling us to judge of truth and excellence
by their inherent merits alone. Woe be to the pen that would undo this fine
illusion (the only reality), and teach us to regulate our notions of genius and
virtue by the circumstances in which they happen to be placed! You would not
expect a person whom you saw in a servants' hall, or behind a counter, to write
Clarissa; but after he had written the work, to *pre-judge* it from the situation of
the writer, is an unpardonable piece of injustice and folly. His merit could only
be the greater from the contrast. If literature is an elegant accomplishment, which
none but persons of birth and fashion should be allowed to excel in, or to exercise
with advantage to the public, let them by all means take upon them the task of
enlightening and refining mankind: if they decline this responsibility as too
heavy for their shoulders, let those who do the drudgery in their stead, however
inadequately, for want of their polite example, receive the meed that is their due,
and not be treated as low pretenders who have encroached on the province of
their betters. Suppose Richardson to have been acquainted with the great man's
steward, or valet, instead of the great man himself, I will venture to say that there
was more difference between him who lived in an *ideal world*, and had the genius
and felicity to open that world to others, and his friend the steward, than
between the lacquey and the mere lord, or between those who lived in different
rooms of the same house, who dined on the same luxuries at different tables,
who rode outside or inside of the same coach, and were proud of wearing or of
bestowing the same tawdry livery. If the lord is distinguished from his valet by
any thing else, it is by education and talent, which he has in common with our
author. But if the latter shews these in the highest degree, it is asked what are
his pretensions? Not birth or fortune, for neither of these would enable him to
write a Clarissa. One man is born with a title and estate, another with genius.
That is sufficient; and we have no right to question the genius for want of the
gentility, unless the former ran in families, or could be bequeathed with a fortune,
which is not the case. Were it so, the flowers of literature, like jewels and

something revolting and incredible to sense in the transition, and no wonder that, aided by youth and warm blood, and the flush of enthusiasm, the mind contrives for a long time to reject it with disdain and loathing as a monstrous and improbable fiction, like a monkey on a house-top, that is loath, amidst its fine discoveries and specious antics, to be tumbled head-long into the street, and crushed to atoms, the sport and laughter of the multitude!

The change, from the commencement to the close of life, appears like a fable, after it has taken place; how should we treat it otherwise than as a chimera before it has come to pass? There are some things that happened so long ago, places or persons we have formerly seen, of which such dim traces remain, we hardly know whether it was sleeping or waking they occurred; they are like dreams within the dream of life, a mist, a film before the eye of memory, which, as we try to recall them more distinctly, elude our notice altogether. It is but natural that the lone interval that we thus look back upon, should have appeared long and endless in prospect. There are others so distinct and fresh, they seem but of

embroidery, would be confined to the fashionable circles; and there would be no pretenders to taste or elegance but those whose names were found in the court list. No one objects to Claude's Landscapes as the work of a pastrycook, or withholds from Raphael the epithet of *divine*, because his parents were not rich. This impertinence is confined to men of letters; the evidence of the senses baffles the envy and foppery of mankind. No quarter ought to be given to this aristocratic tone of criticism whenever it appears. People of quality are not contented with carrying all the external advantages for their own share, but would persuade you that all the intellectual ones are packed up in the same bundle. Lord Byron was a later instance of this double and unwarrantable style of pretension – *monstrum ingens, biforme*. He could not endure a lord who was not a wit, nor a poet who was not a lord. Nobody but himself answered to his own standard of perfection. Mr Moore carries a proxy in his pocket from some noble persons to estimate literary merit by the same rule. Lady Mary calls Fielding names, but she afterwards makes atonement by doing justice to his frank, free, hearty nature, where she says 'his spirits gave him raptures with his cook-maid, and cheerfulness when he was starving in a garret, and his happy constitution made him forget every thing when he was placed before a venison-pasty or over a flask of champagne'. She does not want shrewdness and spirit when her petulance and conceit do not get the better of her, and she has done ample and merited execution on Lord Bolingbroke. She is, however, very angry at the freedoms taken with the Great; *smells a rat* in this indiscriminate scribbling, and the familiarity of writers with the reading public; and inspired by her Turkish costume, foretells a French or English revolution as the consequence of transferring the patronage of letters from the *quality* to the mob, and of supposing that ordinary writers or readers can have any notions in common with their superiors.

yesterday – their very vividness might be deemed a pledge of their permanence. Then, however far back our impressions may go, we find others still older (for our years are multiplied in youth); descriptions of scenes that we had read, and people before our time, Priam and the Trojan war; and even then, Nestor was old and dwelt delighted on his youth, and spoke of the race of heroes that were no more; – what wonder that, seeing this long line of being pictured in our minds, and reviving as it were in us, we should give ourselves involuntary credit for an indeterminate period of existence? In the Cathedral at Peterborough there is a monument to Mary, Queen of Scots, at which I used to gaze when a boy, while the events of the period, all that had happened since, passed in review before me.[7] If all this mass of feeling and imagination could be crowded into a moment's compass, what might not the whole of life be supposed to contain? We are heirs of the past; we count upon the future as our natural reversion. Besides, there are some of our early impressions so exquisitely tempered, it appears that they must always last – nothing can add to or take away from their sweetness and purity – the first breath of spring, the hyacinth dipped in the dew, the mild lustre of the evening-star, the rainbow after a storm – while we have the full enjoyment of these, we must be young; and what can ever alter us in this respect? Truth, friendship, love, books, are also proof against the canker of time; and while we live, but for them, we can never grow old. We take out a new lease of existence from the objects on which we set our affections, and become abstracted, impassive, immortal in them. We cannot conceive how certain sentiments should ever decay or grow cold in our breasts; and, consequently, to maintain them in their first youthful glow and vigour, the flame of life must continue to burn as bright as ever, or rather, they are the fuel that feed the sacred lamp, that kindle 'the purple light of love', and spread a golden cloud around our heads! Again, we not only flourish and survive in our affections (in which we will not listen to the possibility of a change, any more than we foresee the wrinkles on the brow of a mistress), but we have a farther guarantee against the thoughts of death in our favourite studies and pursuits, and in their continual advance. Art we know is long; life, we feel, should be so too. We see no end of the difficulties we have to encounter: perfection is slow of attainment, and we must have time to accomplish it in. Rubens complained that when he had just learnt his art, he was snatched away from it: we trust we shall be more fortunate! A wrinkle in an old head takes whole days to finish it properly: but to catch 'the Raphael grace, the Guido air', no limit should be put to our endeavours. What a prospect for the future! What a task we have entered upon! and shall we be arrested in the middle of it? We do not reckon our time thus employed lost, or our pains thrown away, or our progress slow – we do not droop or grow tired, but 'gain new vigour at our endless task'; – and shall Time grudge us the opportunity to finish what we have auspiciously begun, and have formed a sort of compact with nature to achieve? The fame of the great names we look up to is also imperishable; and shall not we, who contemplate it with such intense yearnings, imbibe a portion of ethereal fire, the *divinæ particula auræ*, which nothing can extinguish? I remember to have looked at a print of Rembrandt for hours together, without being conscious of the flight of time, trying to resolve it into its component parts, to connect its strong and sharp gradations, to learn the secret of its reflected lights, and found neither satiety nor pause in the prosecution of my studies. The print over which I was poring would last long enough; why should the idea in my mind, which was finer, more impalpable, perish before it? At this, I redoubled the ardour of my pursuit, and by the very subtlety and refinement of my inquiries, seemed to bespeak for them an exemption from corruption and the rude grasp of Death.*

Objects, on our first acquaintance with them, have that singleness and integrity of impression that it seems as if nothing could destroy or obliterate them, so firmly are they stamped and rivetted on the brain. We repose on them with a sort of voluptuous indolence, in full faith and boundless confidence. We are absorbed in the present moment, or return to the same point – idling away a great deal of time in youth, thinking we have enough and to spare. There is often a local feeling in the air, which is as fixed as if it were of marble; we loiter in dim cloisters, losing ourselves in thought and in their glimmering arches; a winding road before us seems as long as the journey of life, and as full of events. Time and experience dissipate this illusion; and by reducing them to detail, circumscribe the limits of our expectations. It is only as the pageant of life passes by and the masques turn their backs upon us, that we

---

* Is it not this that frequently keeps artists alive so long, *viz.*, the constant occupation of their minds with vivid images, with little of the *wear-and-tear* of the body?

see through the deception, or believe that the train will have an end. In many cases, the slow progress and monotonous texture of our lives, before we mingle with the world and are embroiled in its affairs, has a tendency to aid the same feeling. We have a difficulty, when left to ourselves, and without the resource of books or some more lively pursuit, to 'beguile the slow and creeping hours of time', and argue that if it moves on always at this tedious snail's-pace, it can never come to an end. We are willing to skip over certain portions of it that separate us from favourite objects, that irritate ourselves at the unnecessary delay. The young are prodigal of life from a superabundance of it; the old are tenacious on the same score, because they have little left, and cannot enjoy even what remains of it.

For my part, I set out in life with the French Revolution, and that event had considerable influence on my early feelings, as on those of others. Youth was then doubly such. It was the dawn of a new era, a new impulse had been given to men's minds, and the sun of Liberty rose upon the sun of Life in the same day, and both were proud to run their race together. Little did I dream, while my first hopes and wishes went hand in hand with those of the human race, that long before my eyes should close, that dawn would be overcast, and set once more in the night of despotism – 'total eclipse'! Happy that I did not. I felt for years, and during the best part of my existence, *heart-whole* in that cause, and triumphed in the triumphs over the enemies of man! At that time, while the fairest aspirations of the human mind seemed about to be realised, ere the image of man was defaced and his breast mangled in scorn, philosophy took a higher, poetry could afford a deeper range. At that time, to read the *Robbers*[8] was indeed delicious, and to hear

> From the dungeon of the tower time-rent,
> That fearful voice, a famish'd father's cry,

could be borne only amidst the fulness of hope, the crash of the fall of the strong holds of power, and the exulting sounds of the march of human freedom. What feelings the death-scene in *Don Carlos* sent into the soul! In that headlong career of lofty enthusiasm, and the joyous opening of the prospects of the world and our own, the thought of death crossing it, smote doubly cold upon the mind; there was a stifling sense of oppression and confinement, an impatience of our present knowledge, a desire to grasp the whole of our existence in one strong embrace, to sound the mystery of life and death, and in order to put an end to the agony of doubt and dread, to burst through our prison-house, and confront the King of Terrors in his grisly palace! ... As I was writing out this passage, my miniature-picture when a child lay on the mantle-piece, and I took it out of the case to look at it. I could perceive few traces of myself in it; but there was the same placid brow, the dimpled mouth, the same timid, inquisitive glance as ever. But its careless smile did not seem to reproach me with having become a recreant to the sentiments that were then sown in my mind, or with having written a sentence that could call up a blush in this image of ingenuous youth!

'That time is past with all its giddy raptures.'[9] Since the future was barred to my progress, I have turned for consolation to the past, gathering up the fragments of my early recollections, and putting them into a form that might live. It is thus, that when we find our personal and substantial identity vanishing from us, we strive to gain a reflected and substituted one in our thoughts: we do not like to perish wholly, and wish to bequeath our names at least to posterity. As long as we can keep alive our cherished thoughts and nearest interests in the minds of others, we do not appear to have retired altogether from the stage, we still occupy a place in the estimation of mankind, [and] exercise a powerful influence over them, and it is only our bodies that are trampled into dust or dispersed to air. Our darling speculations still find favour and encouragement, and we make as good a figure in the eyes of our descendants, nay, perhaps, a better than we did in our life-time. This is one point gained; the demands of our self-love are so far satisfied. Besides, if by the proofs of intellectual superiority we survive ourselves in this world, by exemplary virtue or unblemished faith, we are taught to ensure an interest in another and a higher state of being, and to anticipate at the same time the applauses of men and angels.

> Even from the tomb the voice of nature cries;
> Even in our ashes live their wonted fires.[10]

As we advance in life, we acquire a keener sense of the value of time. Nothing else, indeed, seems of any consequence; and we become misers in this respect. We try to arrest its few last tottering steps, and to make it linger on the brink of the grave. We can never leave off wondering how that which has ever been should cease to be, and would still live on, that we may wonder at our own shadow, and when 'all the life of life is flown', dwell on the retrospect of the past. This is accompanied by a mechanical tenaciousness of whatever we possess, by a distrust and a sense of fallacious hollowness in all we see. Instead of the full, pulpy feeling of youth, every thing is flat and insipid. The world is a painted witch, that puts us off with false shews and tempting appearances. The ease, the jocund gaiety, the unsuspecting security of youth are fled: nor can we, without flying in the face of common sense,

> From the last dregs of life, hope to receive
> What its first sprightly runnings could not give.[11]

If we can slip out of the world without notice or mischance, can tamper with bodily infirmity, and frame our minds to the becoming composure of *still-life*, before we sink into total insensibility, it is as much as we ought to expect. We do not in the regular course of nature die all at once: we have mouldered away gradually long before; faculty after faculty, attachment after attachment, we are torn from ourselves piece-meal while living; year after year takes something from us; and death only consigns the last remnant of what we were to the grave. The revulsion is not so great, and a quiet *euthanasia* is a winding-up of the plot, that is not out of reason or nature.

That we should thus in a manner outlive ourselves, and dwindle imperceptibly into nothing, is not surprising, when even in our prime the strongest impressions leave so little traces of themselves behind, and the last object is driven out by the succeeding one. How little effect is produced on us at any time by the books we have read, the scenes we have witnessed, the sufferings we have gone through! Think only of the variety of feelings we experience in reading an interesting romance, or being present at a fine play – what beauty, what sublimity, what soothing, what heart-rending emotions! You would suppose these would last for ever, or at least subdue the mind to a correspondent tone and harmony – while we turn over the page, while the scene is passing before us, it seems as if nothing could ever after shake our resolution, that 'treason domestic, foreign levy, nothing could touch us farther!' The first splash of mud we get, on entering the street, the first pettifogging shop-keeper that cheats us out of twopence, and the whole vanishes clean out of our remembrance, and we become the idle prey of the most petty and annoying circumstances. The mind soars by an effort to the grand and lofty: it is at home in the grovelling, the disagreeable, and the little. This happens in the height and hey-day of our existence, when novelty gives a stronger impulse to the blood and takes a faster hold of the brain (I have known the impression on coming out of a gallery of pictures then last half a day) – as we grow old, we become more feeble and querulous, every object 'reverbs its own hollowness', and both worlds are not enough to satisfy the peevish importunity and extravagant presumption of our desires! There are a few superior, happy beings, who are born with a temper exempt from every trifling annoyance. This spirit sits serene and smiling as in its native skies, and a divine harmony (whether heard or not) plays around them. This is to be at peace. Without this, it is in vain to fly into deserts, or to build a hermitage on the top of rocks, if regret and ill-humour follow us there: and with this, it is needless to make the experiment. The only true retirement is that of the heart; the only true leisure is the repose of the passions. To such persons it makes little difference whether they are young or old; and they die as they have lived, with graceful resignation.

Of Persons One Would Wish to Have Seen

First published in *The New Monthly Magazine*, January 1826, then reprinted by Hazlitt's son in *Literary Remains* (1836). Coleridge famously described the young Hazlitt as 'brow-hanging, shoe-contemplative, strange', and throughout his life the essayist had a lingering reputation for being shy and suspicious in company. But in fact, as many of his friends were quick to testify, in the right environment, that is, among people he loved and trusted, he was one of the most delightful and considerate of conversationalists. 'Though odd and quaint,' said Thomas Bewick, 'he was not a misanthrope; he loved the companionship of man and the exchange of intellectual thought.' Of all social settings, Hazlitt's favourite was undoubtedly No. 16 Mitre Court in the Temple, for many years the home of his friends Charles and Mary Lamb. Though of modest means, the Lambs were great entertainers, and between 1806 and 1814 they held a kind of literary salon, which took place once a week. This salon was attended by, among others, Captain James Burney, who had sailed with Captain Cook to the Pacific; his son Martin; William Ayrton, the music impressario; Coleridge; Hazlitt; Mary's friend Mrs Reynolds; John Lamb; Edward Phillips; John Rickman and George Dyer. These soirées were very informal, but with a decidedly literary emphasis, and they provided Hazlitt with some of the happiest moments of his life. 'Of Persons One Would Wish To Have Seen' is a retrospective transcript of one of these evenings, and offers a vivid, affectionate picture of the antiquarian passions it indulged.

Come like shadows – so depart.[1]

L[amb] it was, I think, who suggested this subject, as well as the defence of Guy Faux, which I urged him to execute. As, however, he would undertake neither, I suppose I must do both – a task for which he would have been much fitter, no less from the temerity than the felicity of his pen –

Never so sure our rapture to create
As when it touch'd the brink of all we hate.[2]

Compared with him I shall, I fear, make but a common-place piece
of business of it; but I should be loth the idea was entirely lost, and
besides I may avail myself of some hints of his in the progress of
it. I am sometimes, I suspect, a better reporter of the ideas of other
people than expounder of my own. I pursue the one too far into
paradox or mysticism; the others I am not bound to follow farther
than I like, or than seems fair and reasonable.

On the question being started, A[yrton] said, 'I suppose the two
first persons you would choose to see would be the two greatest
names in English literature, Sir Isaac Newton and Mr Locke?' In
this A[yrton], as usual, reckoned without his host. Every one burst
out a laughing at the expression of L[amb]'s face, in which
impatience was restrained by courtesy. 'Yes, the greatest names,'
he stammered out hastily, 'but they were not persons – not
persons.' – 'Not persons?' said A[yrton], looking wise and foolish
at the same time, afraid his triumph might be premature. 'That is,'
rejoined L[amb], 'not characters, you know. By Mr Locke and Sir
Isaac Newton, you mean the *Essay on the Human Understanding*, and
the *Principia*, which we have to this day. Beyond their contents
there is nothing personally interesting in the men. But what we
want to see any one *bodily* for, is when there is something peculiar,
striking in the individuals, more than we can learn from their
writings, and yet are curious to know. I dare say Locke and Newton
were very like Kneller's portraits of them. But who could paint
Shakespear?' – 'Ay,' retorted A[yrton], 'there it is; then I suppose
you would prefer seeing him and Milton instead?' – 'No,' said
L[amb], 'neither. I have seen so much of Shakespear on the stage
and on book-stalls, in frontispieces and on mantle-pieces, that I am
quite tired of the everlasting repetition: and as to Milton's face, the
impressions that have come down to us of it I do not like; it is too
starched and puritanical; and I should be afraid of losing some of
the manna of his poetry in the leaven of his countenance and the
precisian's band and gown.' – 'I shall guess no more,' said A[yrton].
'Who is it, then, you would like to see "in his habit as he lived," if
you had your choice of the whole range of English literature?'
L[amb] then named Sir Thomas Brown and Fulke Greville, the
friend of Sir Philip Sidney, as the two worthies whom he should
feel the greatest pleasure to encounter on the floor of his apartment

in their nightgown and slippers, and to exchange friendly greeting with them. At this A[yrton] laughed outright, and conceived L[amb] was jesting with him; but as no one followed his example, he thought there might be something in it, and waited for an explanation in a state of whimsical suspense. L[amb] then (as well as I can remember a conversation that passed twenty years ago – how time slips!) went on as follows. 'The reason why I pitch upon these two authors is, that their writings are riddles, and they themselves the most mysterious of personages. They resemble the soothsayers of old, who dealt in dark hints and doubtful oracles; and I should like to ask them the meaning of what no mortal but themselves, I should suppose, can fathom. There is Dr Johnson, I have no curiosity, no strange uncertainty about him: he and Boswell together have pretty well let me into the secret of what passed through his mind. He and other writers like him are sufficiently explicit: my friends, whose repose I should be tempted to disturb, (were it in my power), are implicit, inextricable, inscrutable.

> And call up him who left half-told
> The story of Cambuscan bold.[3]

When I look at that obscure but gorgeous prose-composition (the *Urn-burial*)[4] I seem to myself to look into a deep abyss, at the bottom of which are hid pearls and rich treasure; or it is like a stately labyrinth of doubt and withering speculation, and I would invoke the spirit of the author to lead me through it. Besides, who would not be curious to see the lineaments of a man who, having himself been twice married, wished that mankind were propagated like trees! As to Fulke Greville,[5] he is like nothing but one of his own "Prologues spoken by the ghost of an old king of Ormus," a truly formidable and inviting personage: his style is apocalyptical, cabalistical, a knot worthy of such an apparition to untie; and for the unravelling a passage or two, I would stand the brunt of an encounter with so portentous a commentator!' – 'I am afraid in that case,' said A[yrton], 'that if the mystery were once cleared up, the merit might be lost'; – and turning to me, whispered a friendly apprehension, that while L[amb] continued to admire these old crabbed authors, he would never become a popular writer. Dr Donne[6] was mentioned as a writer of the same period, with a very interesting countenance, whose history was singular, and whose meaning was often quite as *uncomeatable*, without a personal citation from the dead, as that of any of his contemporaries. The volume was produced; and while some one was expatiating on the exquisite simplicity and beauty of the portrait prefixed to the old edition, A[yrton] got hold of the poetry, and exclaiming 'What have we here?' read the following:

> Here lies a She-Sun and a He-Moon there,
> She gives the best light to his sphere,
> Or each is both and all, and so
> They unto one another nothing owe.

There was no resisting this, till L[amb], seizing the volume, turned to the beautiful 'Lines to his Mistress,' dissuading her from accompanying him abroad, and read them with suffused features and a faltering tongue.

> By our first strange and fatal interview,
> By all desires which thereof did ensue,
> By our long starving hopes, by that remorse
> Which my words' masculine persuasive force
> Begot in thee, and by the memory
> Of hurts, which spies and rivals threaten'd me,
> I calmly beg. But by thy father's wrath,
> By all pains which want and divorcement hath,
> I conjure thee, and all the oaths which I
> And thou have sworn to seal joint constancy
> Here I unswear, and overswear them thus,
> Thou shalt not love by ways so dangerous.
> Temper, oh fair Love! love's impetuous rage,
> Be my true mistress still, not my feign'd Page;[7]
> I'll go, and, by thy kind leave, leave behind
> Thee, only worthy to nurse in my mind.
> Thirst to come back; oh, if thou die before,
> My soul from other lands to thee shall soar.
> Thy (else Almighty) beauty cannot move
> Rage from the seas, nor thy love teach them love,
> Nor tame wild Boreas' harshness; thou hast read
> How roughly he in pieces shiver'd
> Fair Orithea, whom he swore he lov'd.[8]
> Fall ill or good 'tis madness to have prov'd
> Dangers unurg'd: Feed on this flattery,
> That absent lovers one with th'other be.

Dissemble nothing, not a boy; nor change
Thy body's habit, nor mind's; be not strange
To thyself only. All will spy in thy face
A blushing, womanly, discovering grace.
Richly cloth'd apes are called apes, and as soon
Eclips'd as bright we call the moon the moon.[9]
Men of France, changeable cameleons,
Spittles of diseases, shops of fashions,
Love's fuellers, and the rightest company
Of players, which upon the world's stage be,
Will quickly know thee… O stay here! for thee
England is only a worthy gallery,
To walk in expectation; till from thence
Our greatest King call thee to his presence.
When I am gone, dream me some happiness,
Nor let thy looks our long hid love confess,
Nor praise, nor dispraise me, nor bless, nor curse
Openly love's force, nor in bed fright thy nurse
With midnight starlings, crying out, Oh, oh,
Nurse, oh, my love is slain, I saw him go
O'er the white Alps alone; I saw him, I,
Assail'd, fight, taken, stabb'd, bleed, fall, and die.
Augur me better chance, except dread Jove
Think it enough for me to have had thy love.

Some one then inquired of L[amb] if we could not see from the window the Temple-walk in which Chaucer used to take his exercise; and on his name being put to the vote, I was pleased to find that there was a general sensation in his favour in all but A[yrton], who said something about the ruggedness of the metre, and even objected to the quaintness of the orthography. I was vexed at this superficial gloss, pertinaciously reducing every thing to its own trite level, and asked 'if he did not think it would be worth while to scan the eye that had first greeted the Muse in that dim twilight and early dawn of English literature; to see the head, round which the visions of fancy must have played like gleams of inspiration or a sudden glory; to watch those lips that "lisped in numbers, for the numbers came" – as by a miracle, or as if the dumb should speak? Nor was it alone that he had been the first to tune his native tongue (however imperfectly to modern ears); but he was himself a noble, manly character, standing before his age and striving to advance it; a pleasant humourist withal, who has not only handed down to us the living manners of his time, but had, no doubt, store of curious and quaint devices, and would make as hearty a companion as Mine Host of Tabard. His interview with Petrarch is fraught with interest. Yet I would rather have seen Chaucer in company with the author of the Decameron,[10] and have heard them exchange their best stories together, the *Squire's Tale* against the *Story of the Falcon*, the *Wife of Bath's Prologue* against the *Adventures of Friar Albert*. How fine to see the high mysterious brow which learning then wore, relieved by the gay, familiar tone of men of the world, and by the courtesies of genius. Surely, the thoughts and feelings which passed through the minds of these great revivers of learning, these Cadmuses who sowed the teeth of letters, must have stamped an expression on their features, as different from the moderns as their books, and well worth the perusal. Dante,' I continued, 'is as interesting a person as his own Ugolino, one whose lineaments curiosity would as eagerly devour in order to penetrate his spirit, and the only one of the Italian poets I should care much to see. There is a fine portrait of Ariosto by no less a hand than Titian's; light, Moorish, spirited, but not answering our idea. The same artist's large colossal profile of Peter Aretine is the only likeness of the kind that has the effect of conversing with "the mighty dead", and this is truly spectral, ghastly, necromantic.' L[amb] put it to me if I should like to see Spenser as well as Chaucer; and I answered without hesitation, 'No; for that his beauties were ideal, visionary, not palpable or personal, and therefore connected with less curiosity about the man. His poetry was the essence of romance, a very halo round the bright orb of fancy; and the bringing in the individual might dissolve the charm. No tones of voice could come up to the mellifluous cadence of his verse; no form but of a winged angel could vie with the airy shapes he has described. He was (to our apprehensions) rather "a creature of the element, that lived in the rainbow and played in the plighted clouds", than an ordinary mortal. Or if he did appear, I should wish it to be as a mere vision, like one of his own pageants, and that he should pass by unquestioned like a dream or sound –

> *That* was Arion crown'd:
> So went he playing on the watery plain![11]

Captain B[urney] muttered something about Columbus, and

M[artin Burney] hinted at the Wandering Jew; but the last was set aside as spurious, and the first made over to the New World.

'I should like,' said Miss L[amb], 'to have seen Pope talking with Patty Blount; and I *have* seen Goldsmith.' Every one turned round to look at Miss L[amb], as if by so doing they too could get a sight of Goldsmith.

'Where,' asked a harsh croaking voice, 'was Dr Johnson in the years 1745–6? He did not write any thing that we know of, nor is there any account of him in Boswell during those two years. Was he in Scotland with the Pretender? He seems to have passed through the scenes in the Highlands in company with Boswell many years after "with lack-lustre eye", yet as if they were familiar to him, or associated in his mind with interests that he durst not explain. If so, it would be an additional reason for my liking him; and I would give something to have seen him seated in the tent with the youthful Majesty of Britain, and penning the Proclamation to all true subjects and adherents of the legitimate Government.'

'I thought,' said A[yrton], turning short round upon L[amb], 'that you of the Lake School did not like Pope?' – 'Not like Pope! My dear sir, you must be under a mistake – I can read him over and over for ever!' – 'Why certainly, the *Essay on Man* must be allowed to be a master-piece.' – 'It may be so, but I seldom look into it.' – 'Oh! then it's his Satires you admire?' – 'No, not his Satires, but his friendly Epistles and his compliments.' – 'Compliments! I did not know he ever made any.' – 'The finest,' said L[amb], 'that were ever paid by the wit of man. Each of them is worth an estate for life – nay, is an immortality. There is that superb one to Lord Cornbury:

> Despise low joys, low gains;
> Disdain whatever Cornbury disdains;
> Be virtuous, and be happy for your pains.[12]

'Was there ever more artful insinuation of idolatrous praise? And then that noble apotheosis of his friend Lord Mansfield (however little deserved), when, speaking of the House of Lords, he adds –

> Conspicuous scene! another yet is nigh,
> (More silent far) where kings and poets lie;
> Where Murray (long enough his country's pride)
> Shall be no more than Tully or than Hyde!

'And with what a fine turn of indignant flattery he addresses Lord Bolingbroke –

> Why rail they then, if but one wreath of mine,
> Oh! all accomplish'd St John, deck thy shrine?[13]

'Or turn,' continued L[amb], with a slight hectic on his cheek and his eye glistening, 'to his list of early friends:

> But why then publish? Granville the polite,
> And knowing Walsh, would tell me I could write;
> Well-natured Garth inflamed with early praise,
> And Congreve loved and Swift endured my lays:
> The courtly Talbot, Somers, Sheffield read,
> Ev'n mitred Rochester would nod the head;
> And St John's self (great Dryden's friend before)
> Received with open arms one poet more.
> Happy my studies, if by these approved!
> Happier their author, if by these beloved!
> From these the world will judge of men and books
> Not from the Burnets, Oldmixons, and Cooks.'[14]

Here his voice totally failed him, and throwing down the book, he said, 'Do you think I would not wish to have been friends with such a man as this?'

'What say you to Dryden?' – 'He rather made a show of himself, and courted popularity in that lowest temple of Fame, a coffee-house, so as in some measure to vulgarise one's idea of him. Pope, on the contrary, reached the very *beau idéal* of what a poet's life should be; and his fame while living seemed to be an emanation from that which was to circle his name after death. He was so far enviable (and one would feel proud to have witnessed the rare spectacle in him) that he was almost the only poet and man of genius who met with his reward on this side of the tomb, who realised in friends, fortune, the esteem of the world, the most sanguine hopes of a youthful ambition, and who found that sort of patronage from the great during his lifetime which they would be thought anxious to bestow upon him after his death. Read Gay's verses to him on his supposed return from Greece, after his translation of Homer was finished, and say if you would not gladly join the bright procession that welcomed him home, or see it once more land at Whitehall-stairs.' – 'Still,' said Miss L[amb], 'I would rather have seen him talking with Patty Blount, or riding by in a coronet-coach with Lady Mary Wortley Montagu!'

P[hillips], who was deep in a game of piquet at the other end of the room, whispered to M[artin Burney] to ask if Junius would not be a fit person to invoke from the dead. 'Yes,' said L[amb], 'provided he would agree to lay aside his mask.'[15]

We were now at a stand for a short time, when Fielding was mentioned as a candidate: only one, however, seconded the proposition. 'Richardson?' – 'By all means, but only to look at him through the glass-door of his back-shop, hard at work upon one of his novels (the most extraordinary contrast that ever was presented between an author and his works), but not to let him come behind his counter lest he should want you to turn customer, nor to go upstairs with him, lest he should offer to read the first manuscript of *Sir Charles Grandison*, which was originally written in eight and twenty volumes octavo, or get out the letters of his female correspondents, to prove that *Joseph Andrews* was low.'[16]

There was but one statesman in the whole of English history that any one expressed the least desire to see – Oliver Cromwell, with his fine, frank, rough, pimply face, and wily policy; – and one enthusiast, John Bunyan, the immortal author of the *Pilgrim's Progress*. It seemed that if he came into the room, dreams would follow him, and that each person would nod under his golden cloud, 'nigh-sphered in Heaven,' a canopy as strange and stately as any in Homer.

Of all persons near our own time, Garrick's name[17] was received with the greatest enthusiasm, who was proposed by J[ohn Lamb]. He presently superseded both Hogarth and Handel, who had been talked of, but then it was on condition that he should act in tragedy and comedy, in the play and the farce, *Lear* and *Wildair* and *Abel Drugger*. What a *sight for sore eyes* that would be! Who would not part with a year's income at least, almost with a year of his natural life, to be present at it? Besides, as he could not act alone, and recitations are unsatisfactory things, what a troop he must bring with him – the silver-tongued Barry, and Quin, and Shuter and Weston, and Mrs Clive and Mrs Pritchard, of whom I have heard my father speak as so great a favourite when he was young! This would indeed be a revival of the dead, the restoring of art; and so much the more desirable, as such is the lurking scepticism mingled with our overstrained admiration of past excellence, that though we have the speeches of Burke, the portraits of Reynolds, the writings of Goldsmith, and the conversation of Johnson, to show what people could do at that period, and to confirm the universal testimony to the merits of Garrick; yet, as it was before our time, we have our misgivings, as if he was probably after all little better than a Bartlemy-fair actor, dressed out to play Macbeth in a scarlet coat and laced cocked-hat. For one, I should like to have seen and heard with my own eyes and ears. Certainly, by all accounts, if any one was ever moved by the true histrionic *æstus*,[18] it was Garrick. When he followed the Ghost in *Hamlet*, he did not drop the sword, as most actors do behind the scenes, but kept the point raised the whole way round, so fully was he possessed with the idea, or so anxious not to lose sight of his part for a moment. Once at a splendid dinner-party at Lord ———'s, they suddenly missed Garrick, and could not imagine what was become of him, till they were drawn to the window by the convulsive screams and peals of laughter of a young negro boy, who was rolling on the ground in an ecstacy of delight to see Garrick mimicking a turkey-cock in the court-yard, with his coat-tail stuck out behind, and in a seeming flutter of feathered rage and pride. Of our party only two persons present had seen the British Roscius; and they seemed as willing as the rest to renew their acquaintance with their old favourite.

We were interrupted in the hey-day and mid-career of this fanciful speculation, by a grumbler in a corner, who declared it was a shame to make all this rout about a mere player and farce-writer, to the neglect and exclusion of the fine old dramatists, the contemporaries and rivals of Shakespear. L[amb] said he had anticipated this objection when he had named the author of *Mustapha* and *Alaham*; and out of caprice insisted upon keeping him to represent the set, in preference to the wild hair-brained enthusiast Kit Marlowe; to the sexton of St Ann's, Webster, with his melancholy yew-trees and death's-heads; to Deckar, who was but a garrulous proser; to the voluminous Heywood; and even to Beaumont and Fletcher, whom we might offend by complimenting the wrong author on their joint productions. Lord Brook, on the contrary, stood quite by himself, or in Cowley's words, was 'a vast species alone'. Some one hinted at the circumstance of his being a lord, which rather startled L[amb], but he said a *ghost* would perhaps dispense with strict etiquette, on being regularly addressed by his title. Ben Jonson divided our suffrages pretty equally. Some were afraid he would begin to traduce Shakspear, who was not present to defend himself. 'If he grows disagreeable,' it was whispered aloud, 'there is H[azlitt] can match him.' At length, his romantic visit to Drummond of Hawthornden was mentioned, and turned the scale in his favour.

L[amb] inquired if there was any one that was hanged that I would choose to mention? And I answered, Eugene Aram.*¹⁹ The name of the 'Admirable Crichton' was suddenly started as a splendid example of *waste* talents, so different from the generality of his countrymen. This choice was mightily approved by a North-Briton present, who declared himself descended from that prodigy of learning and accomplishment, and said he had family-plate in his possession as vouchers for the fact, with the initials A.C. – *Admirable Crichton!* R[ickman] laughed or rather roared as heartily at this as I should think he has done for many years.

The last-named Mitre-courtier** then wished to know whether there were any metaphysicians to whom one might be tempted to apply the wizard spell? I replied, there were only six in modern times deserving the name – Hobbes, Berkeley, Butler, Hartley, Hume, Leibnitz; and perhaps Jonathan Edwards, a Massachusets man.*** As to the French, who talked fluently of having *created* this science, there was not a title in any of their writings, that was not to be found literally in the authors I had mentioned. (Horne Tooke, who might have a claim to come in under the head of Grammar, was still living.) None of these names seemed to excite much interest, and I did not plead for the re-appearance of those who might be thought best fitted by the abstracted nature of their studies for their present spiritual and disembodied state, and who, even while on this living stage, were nearly divested of common flesh and blood. As A[yrton] with an uneasy fidgetty face was about to put some question about Mr Locke and Dugald Stewart, he was prevented by M[artin Burney] who observed, 'If C[oleridge] was here, he would undoubtedly be for having up those profound and redoubted scholiasts, Thomas Aquinas and Duns Scotus.' I said this might be fair enough in him who had read or fancied he had read the original works, but I did not see how we

* See Newgate Calendar for 1758.
** L[amb] at this time occupied chambers in Mitre-court, Fleet Street.
*** Lord Bacon is not included in this list, nor do I know where he should come in. It is not easy to make room for him and his reputation together. This great and celebrated man in some of his works recommends it to pour a bottle of claret into the ground of a morning, and to stand over it, inhaling the perfumes. So he sometimes enriched the dry and barren soil of speculation with the fine aromatic spirit of his genius. His 'Essays' and his 'Advancement of Learning' are works of vast depth and scope of observation. The last, though it contains no positive discoveries, is a noble chart of the human intellect, and a guide to all future inquirers.

could have any right to call up these authors to give an account of themselves in person, till we had looked into their writings.

By this time it should seem that some rumour of our whimsical deliberation had got wind, and had disturbed the *irritabile genus* in their shadowy abodes, for we received messages from several candidates that we had just been thinking of. Gray declined our invitation, though he had not yet been asked: Gay offered to come and bring in his hand the Duchess of Bolton, the original Polly: Steele and Addison left their cards as Captain Sentry and Sir Roger de Coverley: Swift came in and sat down without speaking a word, and quitted the room as abruptly: Otway and Chatterton were seen lingering on the opposite side of the Styx, but could not muster enough between them to pay Charon his fare: Thomson fell asleep in the boat, and was rowed back again – and Burns sent a low fellow, one John Barleycorn, an old companion of his who had conducted him to the other world, to say that he had during his lifetime been drawn out of his retirement as a show, only to be made an exciseman of, and that he would rather remain where he was. He desired, however, to shake hands by his representative – the hand, thus held out, was in a burning fever, and shook prodigiously.

The room was hung round with several portraits of eminent painters. While we were debating whether we should demand speech with these masters of mute eloquence, whose features were so familiar to us, it seemed that all at once they glided from their frames, and seated themselves at some little distance from us. There was Leonardo with his majestic beard and watchful eye, having a bust of Archimedes before him; next him was Raphael's graceful head turned round to the Fornarina; and on his other side was Lucretia Borgia, with calm, golden locks; Michael Angelo had placed the model of St Peter's on the table before him; Corregio had an angel at his side; Titian was seated with his Mistress between himself and Giorgione; Guido was accompanied by his own Aurora, who took a dice-box from him; Claude held a mirror in his hand; Rubens patted a beautiful panther (led in by a satyr) on the head; Vandyke appeared as his own Paris, and Rembrandt was hid under furs, gold chains and jewels, which Sir Joshua eyed closely, holding his hand so as to shade his forehead. Not a word was spoken; and as we rose to do them homage, they still presented the same surface to the view. Not being *bonâ-fide* representations of living people, we got rid of the splendid apparitions by signs and dumb show. As soon as they had melted into thin air, there was a loud noise at the outer door, and we found it was Giotto, Cimabue, and Ghirlandaio, who had been raised from the dead by their earnest desire to see their illustrious successors –

> Whose names on earth
> In Fame's eternal records live for aye!

Finding them gone, they had no ambition to be seen after them, and mournfully withdrew. 'Egad!' said L[amb], 'those are the very fellows I should like to have had some talk with, to know how they could see to paint when all was dark around them!'

'But shall we have nothing to say,' interrogated G[eorge] D[yer], 'to the *Legend of Good Women*?' – 'Name, name, Mr D[yer],' cried R[ickman] in a boisterous tone of friendly exultation, 'name as many as you please, without reserve or fear of molestation!' D[yer] was perplexed between so many amiable recollections, that the name of the lady of his choice expired in a pensive whiff of his pipe; and L[amb] impatiently declared for the Duchess of Newcastle.[20] Mrs Hutchinson was no sooner mentioned, than she carried the day from the Duchess.[21] We were the less solicitous on this subject of filling up the posthumous lists of Good Women, as there was already one in the room as good, as sensible, and in all respects as exemplary, as the best of them could be for their lives! 'I should like vastly to have seen Ninon de l'Enclos,'[22] said that incomparable person; and this immediately put us in mind that we had neglected to pay honour due to our friends on the other side of the Channel: Voltaire, the patriarch of levity, and Rousseau, the father of sentiment, Montaigne and Rabelais (great in wisdom and in wit), Molière and that illustrious group that are collected round him (in the print of that subject) to hear him read his comedy of the *Tartuffe* at the house of Ninon; Racine, La Fontaine, Rochefoucault, St Evremont, &c.

'There is one person,' said a shrill, querulous voice, 'I would rather see than all these – Don Quixote!'

'Come, come!' said R[ickman]; 'I thought we should have no heroes, real or fabulous. What say you, Mr L[amb]? Are you for eking out your shadowy list with such names as Alexander, Julius Caesar, Tamerlane, or Ghengis Khan?' – 'Excuse me,' said L[amb], 'on the subject of characters in active life, plotters and disturbers of the world, I have a crotchet of my own, which I beg leave to reserve.' – 'No, no! come, out with your worthies!' – 'What do you think of Guy Faux and Judas Iscariot?' R[ickman] turned an eye upon him like a wild Indian, but cordial and full of smothered glee. 'Your most exquisite reason!' was echoed on all sides; and A[yrton] thought that L[amb] had now fairly entangled himself. 'Why, I cannot but think,' retorted he of the wistful countenance, 'that Guy Faux, that poor fluttering annual scare-crow of straw and rags, is an ill-used gentleman. I would give something to see him sitting pale and emaciated, surrounded by his matches and his barrels of gunpowder, and expecting the moment that was to transport him to Paradise for his heroic self-devotion; but if I say any more, there is that fellow H[azlitt] will make something of it. And as to Judas Iscariot, my reason is different. I would fain see the face of him, who, having dipped his hand in the same dish with the Son of Man, could afterwards betray him. I have no conception of such a thing; nor have I ever seen any picture (not even Leonardo's very fine one) that gave me the least idea of it.' – 'You have said enough, Mr L[amb], to justify your choice.'

'Oh! ever right, Menenius, – ever right!'

'There is only one other person I can ever think of after this,' continued R[ickman]; but without mentioning a name that once put on a semblance of mortality. 'If Shakespear was to come into the room, we should all rise up to meet him; but if that person was to come into it, we should all fall down and try to kiss the hem of his garment!'

As a lady present seemed now to get uneasy at the turn the conversation had taken, we rose up to go. The morning broke with that dim, dubious light by which Giotto, Cimabue, and Ghirlandaio must have seen to paint their earliest works; and we parted to meet again and renew similar topics that night, the next night, and the night after that, till that night overspread Europe which saw no dawn. The same event, in truth, broke up our little Congress that broke up the great one.[23] But that was to meet again: our deliberations have never been resumed.

On Footmen

First published in *The New Monthly Magazine*, September 1830, then reprinted by Hazlitt's son in *Sketches and Essays* (1839). This is a brilliant *jeu d'esprit*, from a confirmed republican, on aristocratic performance, master–servant relationships, and liveried servility's perverse appeal.

Footmen are no part of Christianity; but they are a very necessary appendage to our happy Constitution in Church and State. What would the bishop's mitre be without these grave supporters to his dignity? Even the plain presbyter does not dispense with his decent serving-man to stand behind his chair and load his duly emptied plate with beef and pudding, at which the genius of Ude[1] turns pale. What would become of the coronet-coach filled with elegant and languid forms, if it were not for the triple row of powdered, laced, and liveried footmen, clustering, fluttering, and lounging behind it? What an idea do we not conceive of the fashionable *belle* who is making the most of her time and tumbling over silks and satins within at Sewell and Cross's, or at the Bazaar in Soho-square, from the tall lacquey in blue and silver with gold-headed cane, cocked-hat, white thread stockings and large calves to his legs, who stands as her representative without! The sleek shopman appears at the door, at an understood signal the livery-servant starts from his position, the coach-door flies open, the steps are let down, the young lady enters the carriage as young ladies are taught to step into carriages, the footman closes the door, mounts behind, and the glossy vehicle rolls off, bearing its lovely burden and her gaudy attendant from the gaze of the gaping crowd! Is there not a spell in beauty, a charm in rank and fashion, that one would almost wish to be this fellow – to obey its nod, to watch its looks, to breathe but by its permission, and to live but for its use, its scorn, or pride?

Footmen are in general looked upon as a sort of supernumeraries in society – they have no place assigned them in any Scotch Encyclopaedia – they do not come under any of the heads in Mr Mill's *Elements* or Mr Maculloch's *Principles of Political Economy*; and they nowhere have had impartial justice done them, except in Lady Booby's love for one of that order.[2] But if not 'the Corinthian capitals of polished society', they are 'a graceful ornament to the civil order'. Lords and ladies could not do without them. Nothing exists in this world but by contrast. A foil is necessary to make the plainest truths self-evident. It is the very insignificance, the non-entity as it were of the gentlemen of the cloth, that constitutes their importance, and makes them an indispensable feature in the social system, by setting off the pretensions of their superiors to the best advantage. What would be the good of having a will of our own, if we had not others about us who are deprived of all will of their own, and who wear a badge to say 'I serve'? How can we show that we are the lords of the creation but by reducing others to the condition of machines, who never move but at the beck of our caprices? Is not the plain suit of the master wonderfully relieved by the borrowed trappings and mock-finery of his servant? You see that man on horseback who keeps at some distance behind another, who follows him as his shadow turns as he turns, and as he passes or speaks to him, lifts his hand to his hat and observes the most profound attention – what is the difference between these two men? The one is as well mounted, as well fed, is younger and seemingly in better health than the other; but between these two there are perhaps seven or eight classes of society, each of whom is dependent on and trembles at the frown of the other – it is a nobleman and his lacquey. Let any one take a stroll towards the West-end of the town, South Audley or Upper Grosvenor-street; it is then he will feel himself first entering into the *beau-idéal* of civilised life, a society composed entirely of lords and footmen! Deliver me from the filth and cellars of St Giles's, from the shops of Holborn and the Strand, from all that appertains to middle and to low life; and commend me to the streets with the straw at the doors and hatchments overhead to tell us of those who are just born or who are just dead, and with groups of footmen lounging on the steps and insulting the passengers – it is then I feel the true dignity and imaginary pretensions of human nature realised! There is here none of the squalidness of poverty, none of the hardships of daily labour, none of the anxiety and petty artifice of trade; life's business is changed into a romance, a summer's-dream, and nothing painful, disgusting, or vulgar intrudes. All is on a liberal and handsome scale. The true ends and benefits of society are here enjoyed and bountifully lavished, and all the trouble and misery banished, and not even allowed so much as to exist in thought. Those who would find the real Utopia, should look for it somewhere about Park-lane or May Fair. It is there only any feasible approach to equality is made – for it is *like master like man*. Here, as I look down Curzon-street, or catch a glimpse of the taper spire of South Audley Chapel, or the family-arms on the gate of Chesterfield-House, the vista of years opens to me, and I recall the period of the triumph of Mr Burke's *Reflections on the French Revolution*, and the overthrow of *The Rights of Man*! You do not indeed penetrate to the interior of the mansion where sits the stately possessor, luxurious and refined; but you draw your inference from the lazy, pampered, motley crew poured forth from his portals. This mealy-coated, moth-like, butterfly-generation, seem to have no earthly business but to enjoy themselves. Their green liveries accord with the budding leaves and spreading branches of the trees in Hyde Park – they seem 'like brothers of the groves' – their red faces and powdered heads harmonise with the blossoms of the neighbouring almond-trees, that shoot their sprays over old-fashioned brick-walls. They come forth like grasshoppers in June, as numerous and as noisy. They bask in the sun and laugh in your face. Not only does the master enjoy an uninterrupted leisure and tranquillity – those in his employment have nothing to do. He wants drones, not drudges, about him, to share his superfluity, and give a haughty pledge of his exemption from care. They grow sleek and wanton, saucy and supple. From being independent of the world, they acquire the look of *gentlemen's gentlemen*. There is a cast of the aristocracy, with a slight shade of distinction. The saying, 'Tell me your company, and I'll tell you your manners', may be applied *cum grano salis* to the servants in great families. Mr N[orthcote][3] knew an old butler who had lived with a nobleman so long, and had learned to imitate his walk, look, and way of speaking, so exactly that it was next to impossible to tell them apart. See the porter in the great leather-chair in the hall – how big, and burly, and self-important he looks; while my Lord's gentleman (the politician of the family) is reading the second edition of *The Courier* (once more in request) at the side window, and the footman is romping, or taking tea with the maids in the kitchen below. A match-girl meanwhile plies her shrill trade at the railing; or a gipsey-woman passes with her rustic wares through the street, avoiding the closer haunts of the city. What a pleasant farce is that of 'High Life Below Stairs'! What a careless life do the domestics of the Great lead! For, not to speak of the reflected self-importance of their masters and mistresses, and the contempt with which they look down on the herd of mankind, they have only to eat and drink their fill, talk the scandal of the neighbourhood, laugh at the follies, or assist the intrigues of their betters, till they themselves fall in love, marry, set up a public house, (the only thing they are fit for,) and without habits of industry, resources in themselves, or self-respect, and drawing fruitless comparisons with the past, are, of all people, the most miserable! Service is no inheritance; and when it fails, there is not a more helpless, or more worthless set of devils in the world. Mr C[oleridge] used to say he should like to be a footman to some elderly lady of quality, to carry her prayer-book to church, and place her hassock right for her. There can be no doubt that this would have been better, and quite as useful as the life he has led, dancing attendance on Prejudice, but flirting with Paradox in such a way as to cut himself out of the old lady's will. For my part, if I had to choose, I should prefer the service of a young mistress, and might share the fate of the footman recorded in heroic verse by Lady Wortley Montagu.[4] Certainly it can be no hard duty, though a sort of *forlorn hope*, to have to follow three sisters, or youthful friends, (resembling the three Graces,) at a slow pace, and with grave demeanour, from Cumberland Gate to Kensington Gardens – to be there shut out, a privation enhancing the privilege, and making the sense of distant, respectful, idolatrous admiration more intense – and then, after a brief interval lost in idle chat, or idler reverie, to have to follow them back again, observing, not observed, to keep within call, to watch every gesture, to see the breeze play with the light tresses or lift the morning robe aside, to catch the half-suppressed laugh, and hear the low murmur of indistinct words and wishes, like the music of the spheres. An *amateur footman* would seem a more rational occupation than that of an amateur author, or an amateur artist. An insurmountable barrier, if it excludes passion, does not banish sentiment, but draws an atmosphere of superstitious, trembling apprehension round the object of so much attention and respect; nothing makes women seem so much like angels as always to see, never to converse with them; and those whom we have to dangle a cane after must, to a lacquey of any spirit, appear worthy to wield sceptres.

But of all situations of this kind, the most enviable is that of a lady's maid in a family travelling abroad. In the obtuseness of foreigners to the nice gradations of English refinement and manners, the maid has not seldom a chance of being taken for the mistress – a circumstance never to be forgot! See our Abigail mounted in the *dicky* with my Lord, or John, snug and comfortable – setting out on the grand tour as fast as four horses can carry her, whirled over the 'vine-covered hills and gay regions of France', crossing the Alps and Apennines in breathless terror and wonder – frightened at a precipice, laughing at her escape – coming to the inn, going into the kitchen to see what is to be had – not speaking a word of the language, except what she picks up, 'as pigeons pick up peas': – the bill paid, the passport *visé*, the horses put to, and *au route* again – seeing everything, and understanding nothing, in a full tide of health, fresh air, and animal spirits, and without one qualm of taste or sentiment, and arriving at Florence, the city of palaces, with its amphitheatre of hills and olives, without suspecting that such a person as Boccacio, Dante, or Galileo, had ever lived there, while her young mistress is puzzled with the varieties of the Tuscan dialect, is disappointed in the Arno, and cannot tell what to make of the statue of David by Michael Angelo, in the Great Square. The difference is, that the young lady, on her return, has something to think of; but the maid absolutely forgets every thing, and is only giddy and out of breath, as if she had been up in a balloon.

> No more: where ignorance is bliss
> 'Tis folly to be wise![5]

English servants abroad, notwithstanding the comforts they enjoy, and although travelling as it were *en famille*, must be struck with the ease and familiar footing on which foreigners live with their domestics, compared with the distance and reserve with which they are treated. The housemaid (*la bonne*) sits down in the room, or walks abreast with you in the street; and the valet who waits behind his master's chair at table, gives Monsieur his advice or opinion without being asked for it. We need not wonder at this familiarity and freedom, when we consider that those who allowed it could (formerly at least, when the custom began) send those who transgressed but in the smallest degree to the Bastille or the galleys at their pleasure. The licence was attended with perfect impunity. With us the law leaves less to discretion, and by interposing a real independence (and plea of right) between the servant and master, does away with the appearance of it on the surface of manners. The insolence and tyranny of the Aristocracy fell more on the tradespeople and mechanics than on their domestics, who were attached to them by a semblance of feudal ties. Thus an upstart lady of quality (an imitator of the old school) would not deign to speak to a milliner while fitting on her dress, but gave her orders to her waiting-women to tell her what to do. Can we wonder at twenty *reigns of terror* to efface such a feeling?

I have alluded to the inclination in servants in great houses to ape the manners of their superiors, and to their sometimes succeeding. What facilitates the metamorphosis is, that the Great, in their character of *courtiers*, are a sort of footmen in their turn. There is the same crouching to interest and authority in either case, with the same surrender or absence of personal dignity – the same submission to the trammels of outward form, with the same suppression of inward impulses – the same degrading finery, the same pretended deference in the eye of the world, and the same lurking contempt from being admitted behind the scenes, the same heartlessness, and the same eye-service – in a word, they are alike puppets governed by motives not their own, machines made of coarser or finer materials. It is not, therefore, surprising, if the most finished courtier of the day cannot, by a vulgar eye, be distinguished from a gentleman's servant. M. de Bausset, in his amusing and excellent *Memoirs*, makes it an argument of the legitimacy of Napoleon's authority, that from denying it, it would follow that his lords of the bed-chamber were valets, and he himself (as prefect of the palace) no better than head-cook. The inference is logical enough. According to the author's view, there was no other difference between the retainers of the court and the kitchen than the rank of the master!

I remember hearing it said that 'all men were equal but footmen.' But of all footmen the lowest class is *literary footmen*. These consist of persons who, without a single grain of knowledge, taste, or feeling, put on the livery of learning, mimic its phrases by rote, and are retained in its service by dint of quackery and assurance alone. As they have none of the essence, they have all the externals of men of gravity and wisdom. They wear green spectacles, walk with a peculiar strut, thrust themselves into the acquaintance of persons they hear talked of, get introduced into the clubs, are seen reading books they do not understand at the Museum and public libraries, dine (if they can) with lords or officers of the Guards, abuse any party as *low* to show what fine gentlemen they are, and the next week join the same party to raise their own credit and gain a little consequence, give themselves out as wits, critics, and philosophers (and as they have never done any thing, no man can contradict them), and have a great knack of turning editors, and not paying their contributors. If you get five pounds from one of them, he never forgives it. With the proceeds thus appropriated, the book-worm graduates a dandy, hires expensive apartments, sports a tandem, and it is inferred that he must be a great author who can support such an appearance with his pen, and a great genius who can conduct so many learned works while his time is devoted to the gay, the fair, and the rich. This introduces him to new editorships, to new and more select friendships, and to more frequent and importunate demands from debts and duns. At length the bubble bursts and disappears, and you hear no more of our classical adventurer, except from the invectives and self-reproaches of those who took him for a great scholar from his wearing green spectacles and Wellington-boots. Such a candidate for literary honours bears the same relation to the man of letters, that the valet with his second-hand finery and servile airs does to his master.

On a Sun-Dial

First published in *The New Monthly Magazine*, October 1827, then reprinted by Hazlitt's son in *Sketches and Essays* (1839). Between 1824 and 1827 Hazlitt spent two extended periods on the Continent, the first writing his *Notes of a Journey through France and Italy* (1826), the second in Paris researching his *Life of Napoleon* (1828–30). Hence the cosmopolitan air that surrounds this late essay 'On a Sun-Dial', which is a serene meditation on the different faces and voices of time.

To carve out dials quaintly, point by point.

Shakespear[1]

Horas non numero nisi serenas – is the motto of a sun-dial near Venice. There is a softness and a harmony in the words and in the thought unparalleled. Of all conceits it is surely the most classical. 'I count only the hours that are serene.' What a bland and care-dispelling feeling! How the shadows seem to fade on the dial-plate as the sky lours, and time presents only a blank unless as its progress is marked by what is joyous, and all that is not happy sinks into oblivion! What a fine lesson is conveyed to the mind – to take no note of time but by its benefits, to watch only for the smiles and neglect the frowns of fate, to compose our lives of bright and gentle moments, turning always to the sunny side of things, and letting the rest slip from our imaginations, unheeded or forgotten! How different from the common art of self-tormenting! For myself, as I rode along the Brenta,[2] while the sun shone hot upon its sluggish, slimy waves, my sensations were far from comfortable; but the reading this inscription on the side of a glaring wall in an instant restored me to myself; and still, whenever I think of or repeat it, it has the power of wafting me into the region of pure and blissful abstraction. I cannot help fancying it to be a legend of Popish superstition. Some monk of the dark ages must have invented and bequeathed it to us, who, loitering in trim gardens and watching the silent march of time, as his fruits ripened in the sun or his flowers scented the balmy air, felt a mild languor pervade his senses, and having little to do or to care for, determined (in imitation of his sun-dial) to efface that little from his thoughts or draw a veil over it, making of his life one long dream of quiet! *Horas non numero nisi serenas* – he might repeat, when the heavens were overcast and the gathering storm scattered the falling leaves, and turn to his books and wrap himself in his golden studies! Out of some such mood of mind, indolent, elegant, thoughtful, this exquisite device (speaking volumes) must have originated.

Of the several modes of counting time, that by the sun-dial is perhaps the most apposite and striking, if not the most convenient or comprehensive. It does not obtrude its observations, though it 'morals on the time', and, by its stationary character, forms a contrast to the most fleeting of all essences. It stands *sub dio* – under the marble air, and there is some connexion between the image of infinity and eternity. I should also like to have a sunflower growing near it with bees fluttering round.* It should be of iron to denote duration, and have a dull, leaden look. I hate a sun-dial made of wood, which is rather calculated to show the variations of the seasons, than the progress of time, slow, silent, imperceptible, chequered with light and shade. If our hours were all serene, we might probably take almost as little note of them, as the dial does of those that are clouded. It is the shadow thrown across, that gives us warning of their flight. Otherwise, our impressions would take the same undistinguishable hue; we should scarce be conscious of our existence. Those who have had none of the cares of this life to harass and disturb them, have been obliged to have recourse to the hopes and fears of the next to enliven the prospect before them. Most of the methods for measuring the lapse of time have, I believe, been the contrivance of monks and religious recluses, who, finding time hang heavy on their hands, were at some pains to see how they got rid of it. The hour-glass is, I suspect, an older invention; and it is certainly the most defective of all. Its creeping sands are not indeed an unapt emblem of the minute, countless portions of our existence; and the manner in which they gradually slide through the hollow glass and diminish in number till not a single one is left, also illustrates the way in which our years slip from us by stealth: but as a mechanical invention, it is rather a hindrance

---

*   Is this a verbal fallacy? Or in the close, retired, sheltered scene which I have imagined to myself, is not the sun-flower a natural accompaniment of the sun-dial?

than a help, for it requires to have the time, of which it pretends to count the precious moments, taken up in attention to itself, and in seeing that when one end of the glass is empty, we turn it round, in order that it may go on again, or else all our labour is lost, and we must wait for some other mode of ascertaining the time before we can recover our reckoning and proceed as before. The philosopher in his cell, the cottager at her spinning-wheel must, however, find an invaluable acquisition in this 'companion of the lonely hour,' as it has been called,* which not only serves to tell how the time goes, but to fill up its vacancies. What a treasure must not the little box seem to hold, as if it were a sacred deposit of the very grains and fleeting sands of life! What a business, in lieu of other more important avocations, to see it out to the last sand, and then to renew the process again on the instant, that there may not be the least flaw or error in the account! What a strong sense must be brought home to the mind of the value and irrecoverable nature of the time that is fled; what a thrilling, incessant consciousness of the slippery tenure by which we hold what remains of it! Our very existence must seem crumbling to atoms, and running down (without a miraculous reprieve) to the last fragment. 'Dust to dust and ashes to ashes' is a text that might be fairly inscribed on an hour-glass: it is ordinarily associated with the scythe of Time and a Death's-head, as a *Memento mori*; and has, no doubt, furnished many a tacit hint to the apprehensive and visionary enthusiast in favour of a resurrection to another life!

The French give a different turn to things, less *sombre* and less edifying. A common and also a very pleasing ornament to a clock, in Paris, is a figure of Time seated in a boat which Cupid is rowing along, with the motto, *L'Amour fait passer le Tems* – which the wits again have travestied into *Le Tems fait passer L'Amour*. All this is ingenious and well; but it wants sentiment. I like a people who have something that they love and something that they hate, and with whom every thing is not alike a matter of indifference or *pour passer le tems*. The French attach no importance to any thing, except for the moment; they are only thinking how they shall get rid of one sensation for another; all their ideas are *in transitu*. Every thing is detached, nothing is accumulated. It would be a million of years

---

* Once more, companion of the lonely hour,
  I'll turn thee up again.

  Bloomfield's Poems, 'The Widow to her Hour-glass'.

before a Frenchman would think of the *Horas non numero nisi serenas*. Its impassioned repose and *ideal* voluptuousness are as far from their breasts as the poetry of that line in Shakespear – 'How sweet the moonlight sleeps upon that bank!' They never arrive at the classical – or the romantic. They blow the bubbles of vanity, fashion, and pleasure; but they do not expand their perceptions into refinement, or strengthen them into solidity. Where there is nothing fine in the ground-work of the imagination, nothing fine in the superstructure can be produced. They are light, airy, fanciful (to give them their due) – but when they attempt to be serious (beyond mere good sense) they are either dull or extravagant. When the volatile salt has flown off, nothing but a *caput mortuum* remains. They have infinite crotchets and caprices with their clocks and watches, which seem made for any thing but to tell the hour – gold-repeaters, watches with metal covers, clocks with hands to count the seconds. There is no escaping from quackery and impertinence, even in our attempts to calculate the waste of time. The years gallop fast enough for me, without remarking every moment as it flies; and farther, I must say I dislike a watch (whether of French or English manufacture) that comes to me like a footpad with its face muffled, and does not present its clear, open aspect like a friend, and point with its finger to the time of day. All this opening and shutting of dull, heavy cases (under pretence that the glass-lid is liable to be broken, or lets in the dust or air and obstructs the movement of the watch) is not to husband time, but to give trouble. It is mere pomposity and self-importance, like consulting a mysterious oracle that one carries about with one in one's pocket, instead of asking a common question of an acquaintance or companion. There are two clocks which strike the hour in the room where I am. This I do not like. In the first place, I do not want to be reminded twice how the time goes (it is like the second tap of a saucy servant at your door when perhaps you have no wish to get up): in the next place, it is starting a difference of opinion on the subject, and I am averse to every appearance of wrangling and disputation. Time moves on the same, whatever disparity there may be in our mode of keeping count of it, like true fame in spite of the cavils and contradictions of the critics. I am no friend to repeating watches. The only pleasant association I have with them is the account given by Rousseau of some French lady, who sat up reading the *New Heloise* when it first came out, and ordering her maid to sound the repeater, found it was too late to go to bed, and continued reading on till morning. Yet how different is the interest excited by this story from the account which Rousseau somewhere else gives of his sitting up with his father reading romances, when a boy, till they were startled by the swallows twittering in their nests at day-break, and the father cried out, half angry and ashamed – '*Allons, mon fils; je suis plus enfant que toi!*'[3] In general, I have heard repeating watches sounded in stage-coaches at night, when some fellow-traveller suddenly awaking and wondering what was the hour, another has very deliberately taken out his watch, and pressing the spring, it has counted out the time; each petty stroke acting like a sharp puncture on the ear, and informing me of the dreary hours I had already passed, and of the more dreary ones I had to wait till morning.

The great advantage, it is true, which clocks have over watches and other dumb reckoners of time is, that for the most part they strike the hour – that they are as it were the mouth-pieces of time; that they not only point it to the eye, but impress it on the ear; that they 'lend it both an understanding and a tongue'. Time thus speaks to us in an audible and warning voice. Objects of sight are easily distinguished by the sense, and suggest useful reflections to the mind; sounds, from their intermittent nature, and perhaps other causes, appeal more to the imagination, and strike upon the heart. But to do this, they must be unexpected and involuntary – there must be no trick in the case – they should not be squeezed out with a finger and a thumb; there should be nothing optional, personal in their occurrence; they should be like stern, inflexible monitors, that nothing can prevent from discharging their duty. Surely, if there is any thing with which we should not mix up our vanity and self-consequence, it is with Time, the most independent of all things. All the sublimity, all the superstition that hang upon this palpable mode of announcing its flight, are chiefly attached to this circumstance. Time would lose its abstracted character, if we kept it like a curiosity or a jack-in-a-box: its prophetic warnings would have no effect, if it obviously spoke only at our prompting, like a paltry ventriloquism. The clock that tells the coming, dreaded hour – the castle bell, that 'with its brazen throat and iron tongue, sounds one unto the drowsy ear of night' – the curfew, 'swinging slow with sullen roar' o'er wizard stream or fountain, are like a voice from other worlds, big with unknown events. The last sound, which is still kept up as an old custom in many parts of England, is a great favourite with me. I used to hear it when a boy. It tells a tale of other times. The days that are past, the generations that are gone, the tangled forest glades and hamlets brown of my native country, the woodsman's art, the Norman warrior armed for the battle or in his festive hall, the conqueror's iron rule and peasant's lamp extinguished, all start up at the clamorous peal, and fill my mind with fear and wonder. I confess, nothing at present interests me but what has been – the recollection of the impressions of my early life, or events long past, of which only the dim traces remain in a smouldering ruin or half-obsolete custom. That *things should be that are now no more*, creates in my mind the most unfeigned astonishment. I cannot solve the mystery of the past, nor exhaust my pleasure in it. The years, the generations to come, are nothing to me. I do not wonder that Mrs Shelley did not succeed with her *Last Man*.[4] We care no more about the world in the year 2300 than we do about one of the planets. Even George IV is better than the Earl of Windsor. We might as well make a voyage to the moon as think of stealing a march upon Time with impunity. *De non apparentibus et non existentibus eadem est ratio*.[5] Those who are to come after us and push us from the stage seem like upstarts and pretenders, that may be said to exist *in vacuo*, we know not upon what, except as they are blown up with vain and self conceit by their patrons among the moderns. But the ancients are true and *bonâ-fide* people, to whom we are bound by aggregate knowledge and filial ties, and in whom seen by the mellow light of history we feel our own existence doubled and our pride consoled, as we ruminate on the vestiges of the past. The public in general, however, do not carry this speculative indifference about the future to what is to happen to themselves, or to the part they are to act in the busy scene. For my own part, I do; and the only wish I can form, or that ever prompts the passing sigh, would be to live some of my years over again – they would be those in which I enjoyed and suffered most!

The ticking of a clock in the night has nothing very interesting nor very alarming in it, though superstition has magnified it into an omen. In a state of vigilance or debility, it preys upon the spirits like the persecution of a teazing pertinacious insect; and haunting the imagination after it has ceased in reality, is converted into the death-watch. Time is rendered vast by contemplating its minute portions thus repeatedly and painfully urged upon our attention, as the ocean in its immensity is composed of water-drops. A clock striking with a clear and silver sound is a great relief in such circumstances, breaks the spell, and resembles a sylph-like and friendly spirit in the room. Foreigners, with all their tricks and contrivances upon clocks and time-pieces, are strangers to the sound of village-bells, though perhaps a people that can dance may dispense with them. They impart a pensive, wayward pleasure to the mind, and are a kind of chronology of happy events, often serious in the retrospect – births, marriages, and so forth. Coleridge calls them 'the poor man's only music'. A village spire in England peeping from its cluster of trees is always associated in imagination with this cheerful accompaniment, and may be expected to pour its joyous tidings on the gale. In Catholic countries, you are stunned with the everlasting tolling of bells to prayers or for the dead. In the Apennines, and other wild and mountainous districts of Italy, the little chapel-bell with its simple tinkling sound has a romantic and charming effect. The Monks in former times appear to have taken a pride in the construction of bells as well as churches; and some of those of the great cathedrals abroad (as at Cologne and Rouen) may be fairly said to be hoarse with counting the flight of ages. The chimes in Holland are a nuisance. They dance in the hours and the quarters. They leave no respite to the imagination. Before one set has done ringing in your ears, another begins. You do not know whether the hours move or stand still, go backwards or forwards, so fantastical and perplexing are their accompaniments. Time is a more staid personage, and not so full of gambols. It puts you in mind of a tune with variations, or of an embroidered dress. Surely, nothing is more simple than time. His march is straightforward; but we should have leisure allowed us to look back upon the distance we have come, and not be counting his steps every moment. Time in Holland is a foolish old fellow with all the antics of a youth, who 'goes to church in a coranto, and lights his pipe in a cinque-pace'. The chimes with us, on the contrary, as they come in every three or four hours, are like stages in the journey of the day. They give a fillip to the lazy, creeping hours, and relieve the lassitude of country-places. At noon, their desultory, trivial song is diffused through the hamlet with the odour of rashers of bacon; at the close of day they send the toil-worn sleepers to their beds. Their discontinuance would be a great loss to the thinking or unthinking public. Mr Wordsworth has painted their effect on the mind when he makes his friend Matthew, in a fit of inspired dotage,

> Sing those witty rhymes
> About the crazy old church-clock
> And the bewilder'd chimes.[6]

The tolling of the bell for deaths and executions is a fearful summons, though, as it announces, not the advance of time but the approach of fate, it happily makes no part of our subject. Otherwise, the 'sound of the bell' for Macheath's execution in the *Beggar's Opera*, or for that of the Conspirators in *Venice Preserved*, with the roll of the drum at a soldier's funeral, and a digression to that of my Uncle Toby, as it is so finely described by Sterne, would furnish ample topics to descant upon. If I were a moralist, I might disapprove the ringing in the new and ringing out the old year.

> Why dance ye, mortals, o'er the grave of Time?[7]

St Paul's bell tolls only for the death of our English kings, or a distinguished personage or two, with long intervals between.*

Those who have no artificial means of ascertaining the progress of time, are in general the most acute in discerning its immediate signs, and are most retentive of individual dates. The mechanical aids to knowledge are not sharpeners of the wits. The understanding of a savage is a kind of natural almanac, and more true in its prognostication of the future. In his mind's eye he sees what has happened or what is likely to happen to him, 'as in a map the voyager his course'. Those who read the times and seasons in the aspect of the heavens and the configurations of the stars, who count by moons and know when the sun rises and sets, are by no means ignorant of their own affairs or of the common concatenation of events. People in such situations have not their faculties distracted by any multiplicity of inquiries beyond what befalls themselves, and the outward appearances that mark the change. There is, therefore, a simplicity and clearness in the knowledge they possess, which often puzzles the more learned. I am sometimes surprised at a shepherd-boy by the road-side, who sees nothing but the earth and sky, asking me the time of day – he ought to know so much better than any one how far the sun is above the horizon. I suppose he wants to ask a question of a passenger, or to see if he has a watch. Robinson Crusoe lost his

---

* Rousseau has admirably described the effect of bells on the imagination in a passage in the *Confessions*, beginning *'Le son des cloches m'a toujours singulièrement affecté'*, &c.

reckoning in the monotony of his life and that bewildering dream of solitude, and was fain to have recourse to the notches in a piece of wood. What a diary was his! And how time must have spread its circuit round him, vast and pathless as the ocean!

For myself, I have never had a watch nor any other mode of keeping time in my possession, nor ever wish to learn how time goes. It is a sign I have had little to do, few avocations, few engagements. When I am in a town, I can hear the clock; and when I am in the country, I can listen to the silence. What I like best is to lie whole mornings on a sunny bank on Salisbury Plain, without any object before me, neither knowing nor caring how time passes, and thus 'with light-winged toys of feathered Idleness' to melt down hours to moments. Perhaps some such thoughts as I have here set down float before me like motes before my half-shut eyes, or some vivid image of the past by forcible contrast rushes by me – 'Diana and her fawn, and all the glories of the antique world'; then I start away to prevent the iron from entering my soul, and let fall some tears into that stream of time which separates me farther and farther from all I once loved! At length I rouse myself from my reverie, and home to dinner, proud of killing time with thought, nay even without thinking. Somewhat of this idle humour I inherit from my father, though he had not the same freedom from *ennui*, for he was not a metaphysician; and there were stops and vacant intervals in his being which he did not know how to fill up. He used in these cases, and as an obvious resource, carefully to wind up his watch at night, and 'with lack-lustre eye' more than once in the course of the day look to see what o'clock it was. Yet he had nothing else in his character in common with the elder Mr Shandy.[8] Were I to attempt a sketch of him, for my own or the reader's satisfaction, it would be after the following manner: – but now I recollect, I have done something of the kind once before,[9] and were I to resume the subject here, some bat or owl of a critic, with spectacled gravity, might swear I had stolen the whole of this Essay from myself – or (what is worse) from him! So I had better let it go as it is.

The Free Admission

First published in *The New Monthly Magazine*, July 1830. This essay was written in the last year of Hazlitt's life, when he was living in Frith Street, Soho, only a short walk from the Covent Garden play-house. Hazlitt reviewed many plays during his life, but this late essay is unusual, being a child-like celebration of theatre-going in general. 'But let me once reach, and fairly establish myself in this favourite seat', he writes, 'and I can bid a gay defiance to mischance, and leave debts and duns, friends and foes, objections and arguments far behind me.'

A free Admission is the *lotos* of the mind: the leaf in which your name is inscribed as having the privileges of the *entrée* for the season is of an oblivious quality – an antidote for half the ills of life. I speak here not of a purchased but of a gift-ticket, an emanation of the generosity of the Managers, a token of conscious desert. With the first you can hardly bring yourself to go to the theatre; with the last, you cannot keep away. If you have paid five guineas for a free-admission for the season, this *free-admission* turns to a mere slavery. You seem to have done a foolish thing, and to have committed an extravagance under the plea of economy. You are struck with remorse. You are impressed with a conviction that pleasure is not to be bought. You have paid for your privilege in the lump, and you receive the benefit in driblets. The five pounds you are out of pocket does not meet with an adequate compensation the first night, or on any single occasion – you must come again, and use double diligence to strike a balance to make up your large arrears; instead of an obvious saving, it hangs as a dead-weight on your satisfaction all the year; and the improvident price you have paid for them kills every ephemeral enjoyment, and poisons the flattering illusions of the scene. You have incurred a debt, and must go every night to redeem it; and as you do not like being tied to the oar, or making a toil of a pleasure, you stay away altogether; give up the promised luxury as a bad speculation; sit sullenly at home, or bend your loitering feet in any other direction; and putting up with the first loss, resolve never to be guilty of the like folly again. But it is not thus with the possessor of a Free Admission, truly so called. His is a pure pleasure, a clear gain. He feels none of these irksome qualms and misgivings. He marches to the theatre like a favoured lover; if he is compelled to absent himself, he feels all the impatience and compunction of a prisoner. The portal of the Temple of the Muses stands wide open to him, closing the vista of the day – when he turns his back upon it at night with steps gradual and slow, mingled with the common crowd, but conscious of a virtue which they have not, he says, 'I shall come again to-morrow!' In passing through the streets, he casts a sidelong, careless glance at the playbills: he reads the papers chiefly with a view to see what is the play for the following day, or the ensuing week. If it is something new, he is glad; if it is old, he is resigned – but he goes in either case. His steps bend mechanically that way – pleasure becomes a habit, and habit a duty – he fulfils his destiny – he walks deliberately along Long-acre (you may tell a man going to the play, and whether he pays or has a free admission) quickens his pace as he turns the corner of Bow-street, and arrives breathless and in haste at the welcome spot, where on presenting himself, he receives a passport that is a release from care, thought, toil, for the evening, and wafts him into the regions of the blest! What is it to him how the world turns round if the play goes on; whether empires rise or fall, so that Covent-Garden stands its ground? Shall he plunge into the void of politics, that volcano burnt-out with the cold, sterile, sightless lava, hardening all around? or con over the registers of births, deaths, and marriages, when he may be present at Juliet's wedding, and gaze on Juliet's tomb? or shall he wonder at the throng of coaches in Regent-street, when he can feast his eyes with the coach (the fairy-vision of his childhood) in which Cinderella rides to the ball? Here (by the help of that *Open Sessame!* a Free Admission), ensconced in his favourite niche, looking from the 'loop-holes of retreat' in the second circle, he views the pageant of the world played before him; melts down years to moments; sees human life, like a gaudy shadow, glance across the stage; and here tastes of all earth's bliss, the sweet without the bitter, the honey without the sting, and plucks ambrosial fruits and amaranthine flowers (placed by the enchantress Fancy within his reach,) without having to pay a tax for it at the time, or repenting of it afterwards. 'He is all ear and eye, and drinks in sounds or sights that might create a soul under the ribs of death.' 'The fly,' says Gay, 'that sips treacle, is lost in the sweets': so he that has a free-admission forgets every thing else. Why not? It is the chief and enviable transfer of his being from the real to the unreal world, and the changing half his life into a dream. 'Oh! leave me to my repose', in my beloved corner at Covent Garden Theatre! This (and not 'the arm-chair at an inn', though that too, at other times, and under different circumstances, is not without its charms,) is to me 'the throne of felicity'. If I have business that would detain me from this, I put it off till the morrow; if I have friends that call in just at the moment, let them go away under pain of bearing my maledictions with them. What is there in their conversation to atone to me for the loss of one quarter of an hour at the 'witching time of night'? If it is on indifferent subjects, it is flat and insipid; if it grows animated and interesting, it requires a painful effort, and begets a feverish excitement. But let me once reach, and fairly establish myself in this favourite seat, and I can bid a gay defiance to mischance, and leave debts and duns, friends and foes, objections and arguments, far behind me. I would, if I could, have it surrounded with a balustrade of gold, for it has been to me a palace of delight. There golden thoughts unbidden betide me, and golden visions come to me. There the dance, the laugh, the song, the scenic deception greet me; there are wafted Shakespear's winged words, or Otway's plaintive lines; and there how often have I heard young Kemble's voice,[1] trembling at its own beauty, and prolonging its liquid tones, like the murmur of the billowy surge on sounding shores! There I no longer torture a sentence or strain a paradox: the mind is full without an effort, pleased without asking why. It inhales an atmosphere of joy, and is steeped in all the luxury of woe. To show how much sympathy has to do with the effect, let us suppose any one to have a free admission to the rehearsals of a morning, what mortal would make use of it? One might as well be at the bottom of a well, or at the top of St Paul's for any pleasure we should derive from the finest tragedy or comedy. No, a play is nothing without an audience, it is a satisfaction too great and too general not to be shared with others. But reverse this cold and comfortless picture – let the eager crowd beset the theatre-doors 'like bees in spring-time, when the sun with Taurus rides' – let the boxes be filled with innocence and beauty like beds of lilies on the first night of *Isabella* or *Belvidera*,[2] see the flutter, the uneasy delight of expectation, see the big tear roll down the cheek of sensibility as the story proceeds – let us listen to the deep thunder of the pit, or catch the gallery's shout at some true master-stroke of passion; and we feel that a thousand hearts are beating in our bosoms, and hail the sparkling illusion reflected in a thousand eyes. The stage has, therefore, been justly styled 'a discipline of humanity'; for there is no place where the social principle is called forth with such strength and harmony, by a powerful interest in a common object. A crowd is everywhere else oppressive; but the fuller the play-house, the more intimately and cordially do we sympathise with every individual in it. Empty benches have as bad an effect on the spectator as on the players. This is one reason why so many mistakes are made with respect to plays and players, ere they come before the public. The taste is crude and uninformed till it is ripened by the blaze of lighted lamps and the sunshine of happy faces: the cold, critical faculty, the judgment of Managers and Committees asks the glow of sympathy and the buzz of approbation to prompt and guide it. We judge in a crowd with the sense and feelings of others; and from the very strength of the impression, fancy we should have come to the same unavoidable conclusion had we been left entirely to ourselves. Let any one try the experiment by reading a manuscript play, or seeing it acted – or by hearing a candidate for the stage rehearse behind the scenes, or *top* his part after the orchestra have performed their fatal prelude. Nor is the air of a play-house favourable only to social feeling – it aids the indulgence of solitary musing. The brimming cup of joy or sorrow is full; but it runs over to other thoughts and subjects. We can there (nowhere better) 'retire, the world shut out, our thoughts call home'. We hear the revelry and the shout, but 'the still, small voice' of other years and cherished recollections is not wanting. It is pleasant to hear Miss Ford repeat *Love's Catechism*, or Mrs Humby* sing 'I cannot marry Crout': but the ear is not therefore deaf to Mrs Jordan's laugh in *Nell*; Mrs Goodall's Rosalind still haunts the glades of Arden, and the echo of Amiens' song, 'Blow, blow, thou winter's wind', lingers through a lapse of thirty years. A pantomime (the *Little Red Riding-Hood*) recalls the innocence of our childish thoughts: a dance (the Minuet de la Cour) throws us back to the gorgeous days of Louis XIV and tells us that the age of chivalry is gone for ever. Who will be the Mrs Siddons of a distant age? What future Kean shall 'strut and fret his hour upon the stage', full of genius and free from errors? What favourite

* This lady is not, it is true, at Covent Garden: I wish she were!

actor or actress will be taking their farewell benefit a hundred years hence? What plays and what players will then amuse the town? Oh, many-coloured scenes of human life! where are ye more truly represented than in the mirror of the stage? or where is that eternal principle of vicissitude which rules over ye, the painted pageant and the sudden gloom, more strikingly exemplified than here? At the entrance to our great theatres, in large capitals over the front of the stage, might be written MUTABILITY! Does not the curtain that falls each night on the pomps and vanities it was withdrawn awhile to reveal (and the next moment all is dark) afford a fine moral lesson? Here, in small room, is crowded the map of human life; the lengthened, varied scroll is unfolded like rich tapestry with its quaint and flaunting devices spread out; whatever can be saved from the giddy whirl of ever-rolling time and of this round orb, which moves on and never stops,* all that can strike the sense, can touch the heart, can stir up laughter or call tears from their secret source, is here treasured up and displayed ostentatiously – here is Fancy's motley wardrobe, the masks of all the characters that were ever played – here is a glass set up clear and large enough to show us our own features and those of all mankind – here, in this enchanted mirror, are represented, not darkly, but in vivid hues and bold relief, the struggle of Life and Death, the momentary pause between the cradle and the grave, with charming hopes and fears, terror and pity in a thousand modes, strange and ghastly apparitions, the events of history, the fictions of poetry (warm from the heart); all these, and more than can be numbered in my feeble page, fill that airy space where the green curtain rises, and haunt it with evanescent shapes and indescribable yearnings.

> See o'er the stage the ghost of Hamlet stalks
> Othello rages, Desdemona mourns
> And poor Monimia pours her soul in love.[3]

Who can collect into one audible pulsation the thoughts and feelings that in the course of his life all these together have occasioned; or what heart, if it could recall them at once, and in their undiminished power and plenitude, would not burst with the load? Let not the style be deemed exaggerated, but tame and creeping, that attempts to do justice to this high and pregnant theme, and let tears blot out the unequal lines that the pen traces!

---

* 'Mais vois la rapidité de cet astre qui vole et ne s'arrête jamais.' – *New Eloise.*

Quaffing these delights, inhaling this atmosphere, brooding over these visions, this long trail of glory, is the possessor of a Free Admission to be blamed if 'he takes his ease' at the play; and turning theatrical recluse, and forgetful of himself and his friends, devotes himself to the study of the drama, and to dreams of the past? By constant habit (having nothing to do, little else to think of), he becomes a tippler of the dews of Castaly – a dram-drinker on Mount Parnassus. He tastes the present moment, while a rich sea of pleasure presses to his lip and engulfs him round. The noise, the glare, the warmth, the company, produce a sort of listless intoxication, and clothe the pathos and the wit with a bodily sense. There is a weight, a closeness even, in the air, that makes it difficult to breathe out of it. The custom of going to the play night after night becomes a relief, a craving, a necessity – one cannot do without it. To sit alone is intolerable, to be in company is worse; we are attracted with pleasing force to the spot where 'all that mighty heart is beating still'. It is not that perhaps there is any thing new or fine to see – if there is, we attend to it – but at any time, it kills time and saves the trouble of thinking. O, Covent Garden! 'thy *freedom* hath made me effeminate!' It has hardly left me power to write this description of it. I am become its slave, I have no other sense or interest left. There I sit and lose the hours I live beneath the sky, without the power to stir, without any determination to stay. *Teddy the Tiler* is become familiar to me, and, as it were, a part of my existence: *Robert the Devil* has cast his spell over me. I have seen both thirty times at least, (no offence to the Management!) and could sit them out thirty times more. I am bed-rid in the lap of luxury; am grown callous and inert with perpetual excitement.

> – What avails from iron chains
> Exempt, if rosy fetters bind as fast?[4]

I have my favourite box too, as Beau Brummell had his favourite leg, one must decide on something, not to be always deciding. Perhaps I may have my reasons too – perhaps into the box next to mine a Grace enters; perhaps from thence an air divine breathes a glance (of heaven's own brightness), kindles contagious fire; – but let us turn all such thoughts into the lobbies. These may be considered as an Arabesque border round the inclosed tablet of human life. If the Muses reign within, Venus sports heedless, but not unheeded without. Here a bevy of fair damsels, richly clad, knit with the Graces and the Hours in dance, lead on 'the frozen winter and the pleasant spring'! Would I were allowed to attempt a list of some of them, and Cowley's *Gallery* would blush at mine![5] But this is a licence which only poetry, and not even a Free Admission can give. I can now understand the attachment to a player's life, and how impossible it is for those who are once engaged in it ever to wean themselves from it. If the merely witnessing the bustle and the splendour of the scene as an idle spectator creates such a fascination, and flings such a charm over it, how much more must this be the case with those who have given all their time and attention to it – who regard it as the sole means of distinction – with whom even the monotony and mortifications must please – and who, instead of being passive, casual votaries, are the dispensers of the bounty of the gods, and the high-priests at the altar?

The Sick Chamber

First published in *The New Monthly Magazine*, August 1830. In
the summer of 1830, having suffered from digestive problems
for years, Hazlitt was fatally struck down with a terrible
stomach complaint, probably cancer. 'The Sick-Chamber' was
written during a brief moment of remission, when he clearly
thought he was going to get better. The first part of the essay
describes the demoralising effects of illness; the second part
is about how we feel when we start to convalesce. The last
section, which is in many ways the most moving of all, is all
about the pleasure of reading books again – and offers a mock-
recantation of the assertion he had made in 'The Free
Admission', that the theatre was 'the true pathos and sublime
of human life'.

What a difference between this subject and my last – a 'Free
Admission'! Yet from the crowded theatre to the sick chamber,
from the noise, the glare, the keen delight, to the loneliness, the
darkness, the dulness, and the pain, there is but one step. A breath
of air, an overhanging cloud effects it; and though the transition is
made in an instant, it seems as if it would last for ever. A sudden
illness not only puts a stop to the career of our triumphs and
agreeable sensations, but blots out and cancels all recollection of
and desire for them. We lose the relish of enjoyment; we are
effectually cured of our romance. Our bodies are confined to our
beds; nor can our thoughts wantonly detach themselves and take
the road to pleasure, but turn back with doubt and loathing at the
faint, evanescent phantom which has usurped its place. If the
folding-doors of the imagination were thrown open or left ajar, so
that from the disordered couch where we lay, we could still hail
the vista of the past or future, and see the gay and gorgeous visions
floating at a distance, however denied to our embrace, the contrast,
though mortifying, might have something soothing in it, the mock-
splendour might be the greater for the actual gloom: but the misery
is that we cannot conceive any thing beyond or better than the
present evil; we are shut up and spell-bound in that, the curtains

of the mind are drawn close, we cannot escape from 'the body of this death', our souls are conquered, dismayed, 'cooped and cabined in', and thrown with the lumber of our corporeal frames in one corner of a neglected and solitary room. We hate ourselves and every thing else; nor does one ray of comfort 'peep through the blanket of the dark' to give us hope. How should we entertain the image of grace and beauty, when our bodies writhe with pain? To what purpose invoke the echo of some rich strain of music, when we ourselves can scarcely breathe? The very attempt is an impossibility. We give up the vain task of linking delight to agony, of urging torpor into ecstasy, which makes the very heart sick. We feel the present pain, and an impatient longing to get rid of it. This were indeed 'a consummation devoutly to be wished'; on this we are intent, in earnest, inexorable: all else is impertinence and folly; and could we but obtain *ease* (that Goddess of the infirm and suffering) at any price, we think we could forswear all other joy and all other sorrows. *Hoc erat in votis.* All other things but our disorder and its cure seem less than nothing and vanity. It assumes a palpable form; it becomes a demon, a spectre, an incubus hovering over and oppressing us: we grapple with it: it strikes its fangs into us, spreads its arms round us, infects us with its breath, glares upon us with its hideous aspect; we feel it take possession of every fibre and of every faculty; and we are at length so absorbed and fascinated by it, that we cannot divert our reflections from it for an instant, for all other things but pain (and that which we suffer most acutely,) appear to have lost their pith and power to interest. They are turned to dust and stubble. This is the reason of the fine resolutions we sometimes form in such cases, and of the vast superiority of a sick bed to the pomps and thrones of the world. We easily renounce wine when we have nothing but the taste of physic in our mouths: the rich banquet tempts us not, when 'our very gorge rises' within us: Love and Beauty fly from a bed twisted into a thousand folds by restless lassitude and tormenting cares: the nerve of pleasure is killed by the pains that shoot through the head or rack the limbs: an indigestion seizes you with its leaden grasp and giant force (down, Ambition!) – you shiver and tremble like a leaf in a fit of the ague (Avarice, let go your palsied hold!). We then are in the mood, without ghostly advice, to betake ourselves to the life of 'hermit poor,

In pensive place obscure,'[1] –

and should be glad to prevent the return of a fever raging in the blood by feeding on pulse, and slaking our thirst at the limpid brook. These sudden resolutions, however, or 'vows made in pain as violent and void,' are generally of short duration; the excess and the sorrow for it are alike selfish; and those repentances which are the most loud and passionate are the surest to end speedily in a relapse; for both originate in the same cause, the being engrossed by the prevailing feeling (whatever it may be), and an utter incapacity to look beyond it.

> The Devil was sick, the Devil a monk would be:
> The Devil grew well, the Devil a monk was he![2]

It is amazing how little effect physical suffering or local circumstances have upon the mind, except while we are subject to their immediate influence. While the impression lasts, they are every thing: when it is gone, they are nothing. We toss and tumble about in a sick bed; we lie on our right side, we then change to the left; we stretch ourselves on our backs, we turn on our faces; we wrap ourselves up under the clothes to exclude the cold, we throw them off to escape the heat and suffocation; we grasp the pillow in agony, we fling ourselves out of bed, we walk up and down the room with hasty or feeble steps; we return into bed; we are worn out with fatigue and pain, yet can get no repose for the one, or intermission for the other; we summon all our patience, or give vent to passion and petty rage: nothing avails; we seem wedded to our disease, 'like life and death in disproportion met'; we make new efforts, try new expedients, but nothing appears to shake it off, or promise relief from our grim foe: it infixes its sharp sting into us, or overpowers us by its sickly and stunning weight: every moment is as much as we can bear, and yet there seems no end of our lengthening tortures; we are ready to faint with exhaustion, or work ourselves up to frenzy: we 'trouble deaf Heaven with our bootless prayers': we think our last hour is come, or peevishly wish it were, to put an end to the scene; we ask questions as to the origin of evil and the necessity of pain; we 'moralise our complaints into a thousand similes'; we deny the use of medicine *in toto*, we have a full persuasion that all doctors are mad or knaves, that our object is to gain relief, and theirs (out of the perversity of human nature, or to seem wiser than we) to prevent it; we catechise the apothecary, rail at the nurse, and cannot so much as conceive the possibility that this state of things should not last for ever; we are even angry at those who would give us encouragement, as if they would make dupes or children of us; we might seek a release by poison, a halter, or the sword, but we have not strength of mind enough – our nerves are too shaken – to attempt even this poor revenge – when lo! a change comes, the spell falls off, and the next moment we forget all that has happened to us. No sooner does our disorder turn its back upon us than we laugh at it. The state we have been in, sounds like a dream, a fable; health is the order of the day, strength is ours *de jure* and *de facto*; and we discard all uncalled-for evidence to the contrary with a smile of contemptuous incredulity, just as we throw our physic-bottles out of the window! I see (as I awake from a short, uneasy doze) a golden light shine through my white window-curtains on the opposite wall: – is it the dawn of a new day, or the departing light of evening? I do not well know, for the opium 'they have drugged my posset with' has made strange havoc with my brain, and I am uncertain whether time has stood still, or advanced, or gone backward. By 'puzzling o'er the doubt', my attention is drawn a little out of myself to external objects; and I consider whether it would not administer some relief to my monotonous languour, if I could call up a vivid picture of an evening sky I witnessed a short while before, the white fleecy clouds, the azure vault, the verdant fields and balmy air. In vain! The wings of fancy refuse to mount from my bed-side. The air without has nothing in common with the closeness within: the clouds disappear, the sky is instantly overcast and black. I walk out in this scene soon after I recover; and with those favourite and well-known objects interposed, can no longer recall the tumbled pillow, the juleps or the labels, or the unwholesome dungeon in which I was before immured. What is contrary to our present sensations or settled habits, amalgamates indifferently with our belief: the imagination rules over imaginary themes, the senses and custom have a narrower sway, and admit but one guest at a time. It is hardly to be wondered at that we dread physical calamities so little beforehand: we think no more of them the moment after they have happened. *Out of sight, out of mind.* This will perhaps explain why all actual punishment has so little effect; it is a state contrary to nature, alien to the will. If it does not touch honour and conscience (and where these are not, how can it touch them?) it goes for nothing: and where these are, it rather sears and hardens them. The gyves, the cell, the meagre fare, the hard labour are abhorrent to the mind of the culprit on whom they are imposed, who carries the love of liberty or indulgence to licentiousness; and who throws the thought of them behind him (the moment he can evade the penalty,) with scorn and laughter,

Like Samson his green wythes.*[3]

So, in travelling, we often meet with great fatigue and inconvenience from heat or cold, or other accidents, and resolve never to go a journey again; but we are ready to set off on a new excursion to-morrow. We remember the landscape, the change of scene, the romantic expectation, and think no more of the heat, the noise, and dust. The body forgets its grievances, till they recur; but imagination, passion, pride, have a longer memory and quicker apprehensions. To the first the pleasure or the pain is nothing when once over; to the last it is only then that they begin to exist. The line in *Metastasio*,

The worst of every evil is the fear,[4]

is true only when applied to this latter sort. – It is curious that, on coming out of a sick-room, where one has been pent some time, and grown weak and nervous, and looking at Nature for the first time, the objects that present themselves have a very questionable and spectral appearance, the people in the street resemble flies crawling about, and seem scarce half-alive. It is we who are just risen from a torpid and unwholesome state, and who impart our imperfect feelings of existence, health, and motion to others. Or it may be that the violence and exertion of the pain we have gone through make common everyday objects seem unreal and unsubstantial. It is not till we have established ourselves in form in the sitting-room, wheeled round the arm-chair to the fire (for this makes part of our re-introduction to the ordinary modes of being in all seasons,) felt our appetite return, and taken up a book, that we can be considered as at all restored to ourselves. And even then our first sensations are rather empirical than positive; as after sleep we stretch out our hands to know whether we are awake. This is the time for reading. Books are then indeed 'a world, both

---

* The thoughts of a captive can no more get beyond his prison-walls than his limbs, unless they are busied in planning an escape; as, on the contrary, what prisoner, after effecting his escape, ever suffered them to return there, or took common precautions to prevent his own? We indulge our fancy more than we consult our interest. The sense of personal identity has almost as little influence in practice as it has foundation in theory.

pure and good', into which we enter with all our hearts, after our revival from illness and respite from the tomb, as with the freshness and novelty of youth. They are not merely acceptable as without too much exertion they pass the time and relieve *ennui*; but from a certain suspension and deadening of the passions, and abstraction from worldly pursuits, they may be said to bring back and be friendly to the guileless and enthusiastic tone of feeling with which we formerly read them. Sickness has weaned us *pro tempore* from contest and cabal; and we are fain to be docile and children again. All strong changes in our present pursuits throw us back upon the past. This is the shortest and most complete emancipation from our late discomfiture. We wonder that any one who has read *The History of a Foundling*⁵ should labour under an indigestion; nor do we comprehend how a perusal of the *Faery Queen* should not ensure the true believer an uninterrupted succession of halcyon days. Present objects bear a retrospective meaning, and point to 'a foregone conclusion'. Returning back to life with half-strung nerves and shattered strength, we seem as when we first entered it with uncertain purposes and faltering aims. The machine has received a shock, and it moves on more tremulously than before, and not all at once in the beaten track. Startled at the approach of death, we are willing to get as far from it as we can by making a proxy of our former selves; and finding the precarious tenure by which we hold existence, and its last sands running out, we gather up and make the most of the fragments that memory has stored up for us. Every thing is seen through a medium of reflection and contrast. We hear the sound of merry voices in the street; and this carries us back to the recollections of some country-town or village-group –

> We see the children sporting on the shore
> And hear the mighty waters roaring evermore.⁶

A cricket chirps on the hearth, and we are reminded of Christmas gambols long ago. The very cries in the street seem to be of a former date; and the dry toast eats very much as it did – twenty years ago. A rose smells doubly sweet, after being stifled with tinctures and essences; and we enjoy the idea of a journey and an inn the more for having been bed-rid. But a book is the secret and sure charm to bring all these implied associations to a focus. I should prefer an old one, Mr Lamb's favourite, the *Journey to Lisbon*; or the *Decameron*, if I could get it; but if a new one, let it be *Paul Clifford*.⁷

That book has the singular advantage of being written by a gentleman, and not about his own class. The characters he commemorates are every moment at fault between life and death, hunger and *a forced loan* on the public; and therefore the interest they take in themselves, and which we take in them, has no cant or affectation in it, but is 'lively, audible, and full of vent.' A set of well-dressed gentlemen picking their teeth with a graceful air after dinner, endeavouring to keep their cravats from the slightest discomposure, and saying the most insipid things in the most insipid manner, do not make a *scene*. Well, then, I have got the new paraphrase on the *Beggar's Opera*, am fairly embarked on it; and at the end of the first volume, where I am galloping across the heath with the three highwaymen, while the moon is shining full upon them, feel my nerves so braced, and my spirits so exhilarated, that, to say truth, I am scarce sorry for the occasion that has thrown me upon the work and the author – have quite forgot my *Sick Room*, and am more than half ready to recant the doctrine that a *Free-Admission* to the theatre is

> – The true pathos and sublime
> Of human life:[8] –

for I feel as I read that if the stage shows us the masks of men and the pageant of the world, books let us into their souls and lay open to us the secrets of our own. They are the first and last, the most home-felt, the most heart-felt of all our enjoyments.

The Letter-Bell

First published in *The Monthly Magazine*, March 1831 'by the late William Hazlitt'. The essay was then republished (with omissions) by Hazlitt's son in *Sketches and Essays* (1839). Probably the last essay Hazlitt wrote, this piece uses the letter-bell as a symbol for the way in which memory works by association, making distant connections, chiming the present with the past. 'It has a lively, pleasant sound with it,' Hazlitt writes, 'and not only fills the street with its importunate clamour, but rings clear through the length of many half-forgotten years.' Reminding Hazlitt of his childhood in Wem, his subsequent move to London, his first experience of the theatre, and of learning to paint, the letter-bell is also a powerful reminder of the fundamental constancy of his feelings, their faithful, consistent tone; and this is something he can't help mentioning in his final gibe against Coleridge, who has not been steadfast at all: 'This is the reason I can write an article on the *Letter-Bell*, and other such subjects; I have never given the lie to my own soul. If I have felt any impression once, I feel it more strongly a second time; and I have no wish to revile or discard my best thoughts.'

Complaints are frequently made of the vanity and shortness of human life, when, if we examine its smallest details, they present a world by themselves. The most trifling objects, retraced with the eye of memory, assume the vividness, the delicacy, and importance of insects seen through a magnifying glass. There is no end of the brilliancy or the variety. The habitual feeling of the love of life may be compared to 'one entire and perfect chrysolite', which, if analysed, breaks into a thousand shining fragments. Ask the sum-total of the value of human life, and we are puzzled with the length of the account and the multiplicity of items in it: take any one of them apart, and it is wonderful what matter for reflection will be found in it! As I write this, the *Letter-Bell* passes: it has a lively, pleasant sound with it, and not only fills the street with its importunate clamour, but rings clear through the length of many half-forgotten years. It strikes upon the ear, it vibrates to the brain, it wakes me from the dream of time, it flings me back upon my first entrance into life, the period of my first coming up to town,[1] when all around was strange, uncertain, adverse – a hubbub of confused noises, a chaos of shifting objects – and when this sound alone, startling me with the recollection of a letter I had to send to the friends I had lately left, brought me as it were to myself, made me feel that I had links still connecting me with the universe, and gave me hope and patience to persevere. At that loud-tinkling, interrupted sound (now and then), the long line of blue hills[2] near the place where I was brought up waves in the horizon, a golden sunset hovers over them, the dwarf-oaks rustle their red leaves in the evening-breeze, and the road from [Wem] to [Shrewsbury], by which I first set out on my journey through life, stares me in the face as plain, but from time and change not less visionary and mysterious, than the pictures in the *Pilgrim's Progress*. I should notice, that at this time the light of the French Revolution circled my head like a glory, though dabbled with drops of crimson gore: I walked comfortable and cheerful by its side –

> And by the vision splendid
> Was on my way attended.[3]

It rose then in the east: it has again risen in the west.[4] Two suns in one day, two triumphs of liberty in one age, is a miracle which I hope the Laureate will hail in appropriate verse.[5] Or may not Mr Wordsworth give a different turn to the fine passage, beginning –

> What though the radiance which was once so bright,
> Be now for ever vanished from my sight;
> Though nothing can bring back the hour
> Of glory in the grass, of splendour in the flower?[6]

For is it not brought back, 'like morn risen on mid-*night*'; and may he not yet greet the yellow light shining on the evening bank with eyes of youth, of genius, and freedom, as of yore?[7] No, never! But what would not these persons give for the unbroken integrity of their early opinions – for one unshackled, uncontaminated strain – one *Io pæan* to Liberty – one burst of indignation against tyrants and sycophants, who subject other countries to slavery by force, and prepare their own for it by servile sophistry, as we see the huge serpent lick over its trembling, helpless victim with its slime and poison, before it devours it! On every stanza so penned should be written the word RECREANT! Every taunt, every reproach, every note of exultation at restored light and freedom, would recall to them how their hearts failed them in the Valley of the Shadow of Death. And what shall we say to *him*[8] – the sleep-walker, the dreamer, the sophist, the word-hunter, the craver after sympathy, but still vulnerable to truth, accessible to opinion, because not sordid or mechanical? The Bourbons being no longer tied about his neck, he may perhaps recover his original liberty of speculating; so that we may apply to him the lines about his own *Ancient Mariner* –

> And from his neck so free
> The Albatross fell off, and sank
> Like lead into the sea.[9]

This is the reason I can write an article on the *Letter-Bell*, and other such subjects; I have never given the lie to my own soul. If I have felt any impression once, I feel it more strongly a second time; and I have no wish to revile or discard my best thoughts. There is at least a thorough *keeping* in what I write – not a line that betrays a principle or disguises a feeling. If my wealth is small, it all goes to enrich the same heap; and trifles in this way accumulate to a tolerable sum. Or if the Letter-Bell does not lead me a dance into the country, it fixes me in the thick of my town recollections, I know not how long ago. It was a kind of alarm to break off from my work when there happened to be company to dinner or when I was going to the play. *That* was going to the play, indeed, when I went twice a year, and had not been more than half a dozen times in my life. Even the idea that any one else in the house was going, was a sort of reflected enjoyment, and conjured up a lively anticipation of the scene. I remember a Miss D——, a maiden lady from Wales (who in her youth was to have been married to an earl), tantalised me greatly in this way, by talking all day of going to see Mrs Siddons' 'airs and graces' at night in some favourite part; and when the Letter-Bell announced that the time was approaching, and its last receding sound lingered on the ear, or was lost in silence, how anxious and uneasy I became, lest she and her companion should not be in time to get good places – lest the curtain should draw up before they arrived – and lest I should lose one line or look in the intelligent report which I should hear the next morning! The punctuating of time at that early period – every thing that gives it an articulate voice – seems of the utmost consequence; for we do not know what scenes in the *ideal* world may run out of them: a world of interest may hang upon every instant, and we can hardly sustain the weight of future years which are contained in embryo in the most minute and inconsiderable passing events. How often have I put off writing a letter till it was too late! How often had to run after the postman with it – now missing, now recovering the sound of his bell – breathless, angry with myself – then hearing the welcome sound come full round a corner – and seeing the scarlet costume which set all my fears and self-reproaches at rest! I do not recollect having ever repented giving a letter to the postman, or wishing to retrieve it after he had once deposited it in his bag. What I have once set my hand to, I take the consequences of, and have been always pretty much of the same humour in this respect. I am not like the person who, having sent off a letter to his mistress, who resided a hundred and twenty miles in the country, and disapproving, on second thoughts, of some expressions contained in it, took a post-chaise and four to follow and intercept it the next morning. At other times, I have sat and watched the decaying embers in a little *back* painting-room (just as the wintry day declined), and brooded over the half-finished copy of a Rembrandt, or a landscape by Vangoyen, placing it where it might catch a dim gleam of light from the fire; while the Letter-Bell was the only sound that drew my thoughts to the world without, and reminded me that I had a task to perform in it. As to that landscape, methinks I see it now –

> The slow canal, the yellow-blossomed vale,
> The willow-tufted bank, the gliding sail.[10]

There was a windmill, too, with a poor low clay-built cottage beside it: – how delighted I was when I had made the tremulous, undulating reflection in the water, and saw the dull canvas become a lucid mirror of the commonest features of nature! Certainly, painting gives one a strong interest in nature and humanity (it is not the *dandy-school* of morals or sentiment) –

> While with an eye made quiet by the power
> Of harmony and the deep power of joy,
> We see into the life of things.[11]

Perhaps there is no part of a painter's life (if we must tell 'the secrets of the prison-house') in which he has more enjoyment of himself and his art, than that in which after his work is over, and with furtive, sidelong glances at what he has done, he is employed in washing his brushes and cleaning his pallet for the day. Afterwards, when he gets a servant in livery to do this for him, he may have other and more ostensible sources of satisfaction – greater splendour, wealth, or fame; but he will not be so wholly in his art, nor will his art have such a hold on him as when he was too poor to transfer its meanest drudgery to others – too humble to despise aught that had to do with the object of his glory and his pride, with that on which all his projects of ambition or pleasure were founded. 'Entire affection scorneth nicer hands.' When the professor is above this mechanical part of his business, it may have become a *stalking-horse* to other worldly schemes, but is no longer his *hobby-horse* and the delight of his inmost thoughts –

His shame in crowds, his solitary pride![12]

I used sometimes to hurry through this part of my occupation, while the Letter-Bell (which was my dinner-bell) summoned me to the fraternal board,[13] where youth and hope

Made good digestion wait on appetite
And health on both[14] –

or oftener I put it off till after dinner, that I might loiter longer and with more luxurious indolence over it, and connect it with the thoughts of my next day's labours.

The dustman's-bell, with its heavy, monotonous noise, and the brisk, lively tinkle of the muffin-bell, have something in them, but not much. They will bear dilating upon with the utmost licence of inventive prose. All things are not alike *conductors* to the imagination. A learned Scotch professor found fault with an ingenious friend and arch-critic for cultivating a rookery on his grounds: the professor declared 'he would as soon think of encouraging *a froggery*'. This was barbarous as it was senseless. Strange, that a country that has produced the Scotch novels and *Gertrude of Wyoming* should want sentiment!

The postman's double knock at the door the next morning is 'more germain to the matter'. How that knock often goes to the heart! We distinguish to a nicety the arrival of the Two-penny or the General Post.[15] The summons of the latter is louder and heavier, as bringing news from a greater distance, and as, the longer it has been delayed, fraught with a deeper interest. We catch the sound of what is to be paid – eight-pence, nine-pence, a shilling – and our hopes generally rise with the postage. How we are provoked at the delay in getting change – at the servant who does not hear the door! Then if the postman passes, and we do not hear the expected knock, what a pang is there! It is like the silence of death – of hope! We think he does it on purpose, and enjoys all the misery of our suspense. I have sometimes walked out to see the Mail-Coach pass, by which I had sent a letter, or to meet it when I expected one. I never see a Mail-Coach, for this reason, but I look at it as the bearer of glad tidings – the messenger of fate. I have reason to say so. The finest sight in the metropolis is that of the Mail-Coaches setting off from Piccadilly.[16] The horses paw the ground, and are impatient to be gone, as if conscious of the precious burden they convey. There is a peculiar secresy and despatch, significant and full of meaning, in all the proceedings concerning them. Even the outside passengers have an erect and supercilious air, as if proof against the accidents of the journey. In fact, it seems indifferent whether they are to encounter the summer's heat or winter's cold, since they are borne on through the air in a winged chariot. The Mail-Carts drive up; the transfer of packages is made; and, at a signal given, they start off, bearing the irrevocable scrolls that give wings to thought, and that bind or sever hearts for ever. How we hate the Putney and Brentford stages that draw up in a line after they are gone! Some persons think the sublimest object in nature is a ship launched on the bottom of the ocean: but give me, for my private satisfaction, the Mail-Coaches that pour down Piccadilly of an evening, tear up the pavement, and devour the way before them to the Land's-End!

In Cowper's time, Mail-Coaches were hardly set up;[17] but he has beautifully described the coming in of the Post-Boy:

> Hark! 'tis the twanging horn o'er yonder bridge,
> That with its wearisome but needful length
> Bestrides the wintry flood, in which the moon
> Sees her unwrinkled face reflected bright: –
> He comes, the herald of a noisy world,
> With spattered boots, strapped waist, and frozen locks
> News from all nations lumbering at his back.
> True to his charge, the close-packed load behind.
> Yet careless what he brings, his one concern
> Is to conduct it to the destined inn;
> And having dropped the expected bag, pass on.
> He whistles as he goes, light-hearted wretch!

Cold and yet cheerful; messenger of grief
Perhaps to thousands, and of joy to some;
To him indifferent whether grief or joy.
Houses in ashes and the fall of stocks,
Births, deaths, and marriages, epistles wet
With tears that trickled down the writer's cheeks
Fast as the periods from his fluent quill,
Or charged with amorous sighs of absent swains
Or nymphs responsive, equally affect
His horse and him, unconscious of them all.[18]

And yet, notwithstanding this, and so many other passages that seem like the very marrow of our being, Lord Byron denies that Cowper was a poet! – The Mail-Coach is an improvement on the Post-Boy; but I fear it will hardly bear so poetical a description. The picturesque and dramatic do not keep pace with the useful and mechanical. The telegraphs that lately communicated the intelligence of the new revolution to all France within a few hours, are a wonderful contrivance; but they are less striking and appalling than the beacon-fires (mentioned by Æschylus), which, lighted from hill-top to hill-top, announced the taking of Troy, and the return of Agamemnon.[19]

Notes

The Indian Jugglers

1. A recollection of Oliver Goldsmith, *The Deserted Village*, ll. 211–12.
2. The Juggernaut was 'the uncouth idol of Krishna at Puri in Orissa, annually dragged in procession on an enormous car, under the wheels of which many devotees are said to have formerly thrown themselves to be crushed' (*OED*).
3. From the poet Thomas Gray's letter to Horace Walpole, September 1737.
4. A reference to the journey Milton's Satan makes through hell in Book II of *Paradise Lost*, ll. 941–2.
5. Leigh Hunt (1784–1859), radical editor of the *Examiner* newspaper, essayist, polemicist, critic and poet. A great friend of Hazlitt's, especially during the 1810s.
6. John Napier (1550–1617), mathematician, and inventor of logarithms. Jedediah Buxton (1707–72), a farm labourer, was briefly famous for his stupendous untaught skill at arithmetic (*DNB*).
7. Sarah Siddons (1755–1831), the most celebrated actress of the Romantic period, renowned particularly for her tragic roles.
8. Fives is 'a game in which a ball is struck by the hand against the front wall of a three-sided court' (*OED*).
9. Henry Peter Brougham (1778–1868) lawyer and Whig politician; George Canning (1770–1827), satirist and Tory politician; the *Quarterly Review* was the leading Tory magazine of the period, the *Edinburgh Review* was the corresponding organ of the Whigs.
10. Robert Stewart Castlereagh (1769–1822) British foreign minister 1812–22; John Wilson Croker (1780–1857) Secretary of the Admiralty, 1810–30. Both eminent Tory politicians.
11. Both debtor's prisons. The Fleet Prison in Farringdon Street and the King's Bench in Southwark were both equipped with open-air yards where inmates could play rackets, fives, skittles, etc.
12. From William Wordsworth, *Ellen Irwin*, ll. 55–6.

On Living to One's-Self

1. Goldsmith, *The Traveller*, ll. 1–2.
2. A reminiscence of Hazlitt's friend Keats's *Hyperion*, II, ll. 36–8.
3. A reference to the insufferably virtuous hero of Samuel Richardson's epistolary novel *Sir Charles Grandison* (1754).
4. 'The loop-holes of retreat' and 'He hears the tumult, and is still' are both lifted from the meditation on virtuous retirement in Book IV of William Cowper's blank verse poem of 1785 *The Task* (IV, ll. 88, 99–100). Cowper (1731–1800) was Jane Austen's favourite poet, as well as being a regular touchstone of Hazlitt's.
5. Wordsworth, *Lines left upon a Seat in a Yew-Tree*, ll. 51–5.
6. Wordsworth again, this time the famous *Ode on Intimations of Immortality*, one of Hazlitt's favourite poems, ll. 169–70.
7. Claude Lorrain, real name Claude Gelée (1600–82), French painter, especially of idealised landscapes, noted particularly for his subtle depiction of light.
8. Oliver Goldsmith (1728–74), Irish poet, dramatist and novelist. Author of *The Vicar of Wakefield* and *She Stoops to Conquer*.
9. William Shakespeare (1564–1616), *Cymbeline*, III. iii. 47–9.
10. Both this and the line quoted a few sentences later on, 'the heart-aches and the thousand natural pangs', are reminiscences of the 'to be or not to be' soliloquy from *Hamlet* (III. i. 73, 62).
11. That is, a painting by Richard Wilson (1713–82), the first British artist to concentrate on landscape.
12. From the play of *Mirandola* (1821) by Hazlitt's friend 'Barry Cornwall' (Bryan Waller Proctor, 1787–1874). In *Liber Amoris* these same lines are used to describe Hazlitt's inamorata, Sarah Walker.
13. From John Gay's *The Beggar's Opera*, II. viii, 5–7.
14. *Paradise Lost*, X, ll. 898–908.
15. Lord Byron, *Childe Harold's Pilgrimage*, Canto III, ll. 1049–66.
16. The Brocken Spectre is an atmospheric phenomenon in which an observer, when the sun is low, may see his enlarged shadow against the clouds, often surrounded by coloured lights.
17. Hazlitt was convinced that the virulent attack on his *Characters of Shakespeare's Plays* that appeared in the January 1818 edition of the *Quarterly Review* had all but destroyed the book's sales. And, as with *Blackwood's Magazine's* stigmatisation of him as one of Leigh Hunt's 'Cockney School', he knew that violent political prejudice lay at the heart of it.
18. Shakespeare, *Romeo and Juliet*, I. i. 151–3.

On Going a Journey

1. Robert Bloomfield, *The Farmer's Boy, Spring,* l. 32.
2. Cowper, *Retirement,* ll. 741–2.
3. Milton, *Comus,* ll. 377–9.
4. A reminiscence of the summer of 1798, when the twenty-year-old Hazlitt made a pilgrimage from his home in Shropshire to stay with Wordsworth and Coleridge in Allfoxden in Somerset. The fullest and most famous recollection of this is in the essay 'On My First Acquaintance with Poets', first published in 1823.
5. By Shakespeare's contemporary, the poet and dramatist John Fletcher (1579–1625).
6. Cowper, *The Task,* IV, ll. 39–40. Hazlitt was himself a great tea drinker.
7. The engraved copies of Raphael's Cartoons by Simon Gribelin (1661–1733).
8. *Julie, ou La Nouvelle Heloise* (1758) by Jean-Jacques Rousseau, one of the most celebrated novels of the eighteenth century, and a personal favourite of Hazlitt's. The letter in question describes Saint-Preux's return to his home country after a long period of exile.
9. Itself a quotation from Coleridge's translation of Schiller's *Death of Wallenstein,* V. i. 68.
10. A recollection of the 'sylvan Wye' in Wordsworth's great poem of revisitation, *Tintern Abbey* (1798). The phrase 'in youth and gladness' is also an echo of a line in the same poet's *Resolution and Independence*: 'we poets in our youth begin in gladness'.
11. Sir Fopling Flutter is a character from George Etherege's Restoration comedy *The Man of Mode* (1676). However, the line in question is delivered by Harriet Woodvill to Dorimant in Act V, scene ii: 'Whatever you say, I know all beyond Hyde Park's a desert to you, and that no gallantry can draw you farther'.
12. *Paradise Lost,* III, ll. 550.
13. Nobody has been able to identify this quotation.

On Coffee-House Politicians

1. Shakespeare, *Macbeth,* IV. iii. 175.
2. John Cam Hobhouse (1786–1869) liberal politician and friend of Byron, who composed the notes to Canto IV of *Childe Harold's Pilgrimage.* A good classical scholar (*DNB*).
3. From Francis Beaumont, *Mr Francis Beaumont's Letter to Ben Jonson,* first

published in 1647.

4. The Southampton Coffee House, Southampton Buildings, Chancery Lane. This was Hazlitt's local, off and on, for a number of years between 1807 and 1823.

5. Hazlitt's son identified this man as George Mounsey of Mounsey and Gray, solicitors in Staple Inn, next to Southampton Buildings. Signor Friscobaldo is a character in Thomas Dekker's play *The Honest Whore* (1604–5).

6. The Globe and the Rainbow are both on Fleet Street. The Mitre, Dr Johnson's local, is in Mitre Court, just off the main thoroughfare.

7. *The Tickler, A Monthly Compendium of Good Things in Prose and Verse* (London 1818–24), an aspirational magazine for Cockney dandies.

8. Master Stephen is a type of fashion victim in Ben Jonson's play *Every Man in his Humour* (1598).

9. Gotham was the name of a village, proverbial for the folly of its inhabitants (*OED*).

10. Sarratt was one of the leading amateur chess players of the period. Hume is Joseph Hume (1767–1843), who published a bad verse translation of Dante's *Inferno* and invited Lamb, Hazlitt and Godwin to his residence at Montpellier Terrace, Notting Hill. Ayrton is William Ayrton (1777–1858) the musical writer, director of the King's Theatre, and editor of the *Harmonicon* (*DNB*).

11. William Mudford (1782–1848), editor of the *Courier*, a Tory newspaper of the time, and a regular contributor to the equally conservative *Blackwood's Magazine*. *Coelebs in Search of a Wife* was a novel by Hannah More (1745–1833).

12. The Holy Alliance was a counter-revolutionary alliance formed in 1815 after the defeat of Napoleon by the kings of Russia, Prussia and Austria.

13. William Cobbett (1762–1835) loyalist then radical journalist, politician, agriculturalist and reformer. Hazlitt was a great admirer of his direct, combative style.

14. Hazlitt's friend Charles Lamb's delightful Elia essay 'Mrs Battle's Opinions on Whist' appeared in the *London Magazine* in February 1821.

15. John Tobin (1770–1804), playwright; William Wordsworth (1770–1850), poet; John Wilson (1785–1854), *Blackwood's* contributor; Richard Porson (1759–1808), classical scholar and textual critic; William Paley (1743–1805), theologian; Thomas Erskine (1750–1823), advocate and Lord Chancellor.

16. Porson was a notorious drinker. The Cider Cellar, a celebrated Cockney haunt, was at No. 20 Maiden Lane, Covent Garden.

17. Charles Jeremiah Wells (1800–79), poet and solicitor, a friend of Keats as well as Hazlitt. He paid for a tomb to be erected over Hazlitt's grave at St Anne's, Soho.
18. See Anthony Hamilton, *Memoirs of the Life of Count de Gramont* (London: 1714).
19. A reference to the kindly, bumbling, pipe-smoking Uncle Toby from Laurence Sterne's *Tristram Shandy* (1759)
20. Elia, alias Charles Lamb, was afflicted throughout his life by a very bad stutter, hence Hazlitt's comment on the painfulness of his manner.
21. Shakespeare, *Troilus and Cressida*, III. iii. 121.
22. 'Barry Cornwall' was the pen name of the poet and dramatist Bryan Waller Proctor (1787–1874).

On the Aristocracy of Letters

1. Shakespeare, *King Lear*, III. iv. 110.
2. Holland House in West London, the home of Henry Richard Vassall Fox (1773–1840), third Baron, Lord Holland, a leading Whig peer and patron of the arts in this period.
3. Richard Brinsley Sheridan (1751–1816), Irish dramatist and Whig politician. From 1776 to 1809, Sheridan was manager and owner of Drury Lane, where his plays *The Rivals* (1775) and *The School for Scandal* (1777) were produced.
4. Samuel Butler (1613–80) *Satire upon the Abuse of Human Learning*, ll. 67–70.
5. Shakespeare, *Othello*, III. iii. 158.
6. Dr Charles Burney (1726–1814) who wrote a four-volume *History of Music* between 1776 and 1789, and was a friend of Dr Johnson. Madame D'Arblay, alias Fanny Burney, was Dr Burney's daughter, and the author of several significant novels, including *Evelina* and *Cecilia*. The other Burneys include Charles Burney the younger (1757–1817), a Greek scholar; Captain James Burney (1750–1821), author of *A Chronological History of the Discoveries in the South Sea or Pacific Ocean* (1803–17); Sarah Harriet Burney (1770–1844), Dr Burney's youngest daughter, author of *Clarentine*; and Martin Burney, son of Captain Burney, a great friend of Lamb and Hazlitt's, who makes a cameo appearance in 'On Coffee-House Politicians'.
7. i.e. Sir Walter Scott (1771–1832).
8. Alexander Pope, *Essay on Criticism*, ll. 420–1.
9. Byron's *Letter to [John Murray] on the Rev. Wm. L. Bowles's Strictures on*

the Life and Writings of Pope was published in 1821.

10. Hazlitt pointed out a borrowed line in Thomas Campbell's *The Pleasures of Hope* (1799) in his lecture 'On the Living Poets' of 1818. According to Cyrus Redding, sub-editor of the *New Monthly Magazine* under Campbell, the poet never forgave Hazlitt for this, and only published his contributions with extreme reluctance thereafter.

11. Francis Beaumont and John Fletcher, *Philaster*, V. i.

12. Hazlitt rehearses the argument, already voiced by Byron, Shelley, Leigh Hunt and others, that it was hostile reviews from conservative magazines that shortened the life of the young poet John Keats. Keats had died of tuberculosis in Rome in 1821, at the age of twenty-five. The references are to Perdita's speech from Act IV of Shakespeare's *The Winter's Tale* and to the dismemberment of the poet Orpheus by Bacchic women as described by Milton in *Paradise Lost* VII, l. 37.

13. The shop of John Murray (1778–1843), publisher of Byron, and of the *Quarterly Review*.

14. Isaac D'Israeli (1766–1848), father of Benjamin Disraeli and author of *Curiosities of Literature*; William Jacob (1762–1851), traveller and miscellaneous writer.

15. A toad-eater was originally the attendant of a charlatan, employed to eat toads (held to be poisonous) to enable his master to exhibit his skill in expelling poison, hence the phrase signifies a fawning flatterer, parasite or sycophant.

16. Thomas 'Tommy' Hill (1760–1840), dry-salter, book-collector and *bon-vivant*.

17. An RA was a member of the Royal Academy of Arts, an extremely exclusive organisation established in London in 1786 to protect and promote the arts in Britain.

18. 'The Jackals of the North' were the anonymous (and therefore, Hazlitt considered, cowardly) reviewers who attacked Keats, Hunt and himself repeatedly in the Scottish literary journal *Blackwood's Edinburgh Magazine*.

19. John Britton (1771–1857), the antiquary and topographer, author or part author of *Architectural Antiquities of Great Britain* (1805–14).

20. John Taylor (1757–1832), convivial man of the theatre, friend of James Boswell, and proprietor of the violently Tory newspaper *The Sun*.

21. Thomas Tomkins (1743–1816) calligrapher, friend of Reynolds and Johnson.

Why Distant Objects Please

1. William Collins (1721–59) *The Passions, an Ode for Music*, ll. 29–32.
2. A reference to Wordsworth's poem 'Yarrow Unvisited', which was published in 1807.
3. Shakespeare, *A Midsummer Night's Dream*, V. i. 18.
4. From Wordsworth's *Ode on Intimations of Immortality*, ll. 180–1.
5. Shakespeare, *Twelfth Night*, I. i. 5–7 (Alexander Pope's text).
6. See Leigh Hunt's essay, 'A Nearer View of Some of the Shops', *The Indicator*, 7 June 1820.
7. Hazlitt's family resided briefly in North America between 1785 and 1786.
8. *The Blind Fiddler* by David Wilkie (1785–1841), a very popular genre painting, now hanging in the National Gallery.
9. John Fearn (1768–1837) was a minor philosopher of the period. His *Essay on Consciousness, or a Series of Evidences of a Distinct Mind* was published in 1810.
10. The reference here is almost certainly to 'Z', the anonymous assailant of Hazlitt, Hunt and Keats in the *Blackwood's Magazine* 'Cockney School' articles. These articles were written by John Gibson Lockhart (1794–1854).
11. John Sheffield, Duke of Buckingham, *An Essay Upon Poetry* (1682).
12. Shakespeare, *All's Well That Ends Well*, IV. iii. 71–4.

On Mr Wordsworth's Excursion

1. In Henry Fielding's novel *Joseph Andrews* (1742).
2. From Wordsworth, *The Excursion* (1814), VII. vi. 763–4; 777–93.

On Londoners and Country People

1. A reference to the notorious series of articles published by *Blackwood's Magazine* between October 1817 and October 1819 'On the Cockney School of Poetry'. These articles viciously attacked a number of London-based writers loosely associated with the liberal *Examiner* newspaper, most notably Leigh Hunt, Keats and Hazlitt.
2. Thule was the name given by the classical writer Polybius to a land six days' sail north of Britain, possibly Shetland, which was then thought to be the most northerly point of the the world.

3. A barker was a shop tout; a slop-seller sold cheap ready-made clothing in the streets; a tapster was a barman, and a drab was a low prostitute.

4. Three popular pleasure gardens in Islington. White Conduit House was a tavern beside the White Conduit, the site of a water supply in Islington. There is still a pub on the site, but it is now called the Penny Farthing. Rosemary Gardens, a small modern park, approximately marks the site of the old Rosemary Branch pleasure grounds, and the old tavern's name is retained by a Victorian public house at No. 2 Shepperton Road, near Hoxton. Bagnigge Wells had been a relatively genteel spa in the eighteenth century, but by the early nineteenth century it was more or less the sole preserve of the Cockney classes. It was located just east of what is now Gray's Inn Road and north of the Clerkenwell House of Correction.

5. John Braham and J.B. Duruset were two of the most celebrated singers of the period.

6. Richard Pinch, hosier. The original has not been identified.

7. Anthony Collins (1676–1729), English deist and free-thinker. The tract Goodman kept in secret was probably Collins's *A Discourse of Free-Thinking* (1713).

8. A marker is an old slang word for that member of a pick-pocketing team who takes the stolen item from the person who actually picks the pocket.

9. *Evelina*, which was published anonymously in 1778, was the first novel of Fanny Burney, later Fanny D'Arblay (1752–1840).

10. Ring-taw is a game where marbles are put in a ring and played at.

11. i.e. the *Blackwoodsmen*, who were based in Edinburgh.

12. This is the review piece 'On Mr Wordsworth's Excursion', which precedes this essay.

13. From Sheridan's *The Duenna*, III. v. 1.

14. All of these people were actors, hence the rusticated Cockney is imagining himself back at the theatre.

15. In Shakespeare's *Henry IV Part Two*, III. ii.

16. Hazlitt refers to Wordsworth's Prospectus to *The Recluse*, first published in the Preface to *The Excursion* (1814) where Wordsworth says he

> must hang
> Brooding above the fierce confederate storm
> Of sorrow, barricadoed evermore
> Within the walls of cities ...

(ll. 77–80)

Brummelliana

1. A line from Act V, scene i of *Virginius* (1820) by Hazlitt's friend James Sheridan Knowles (1784–1862).
2. Edmund Spenser, *The Faerie Queene*, II. xii. 77.
3. Theodore Hook (1788–1841) novelist, poet and dramatist, and editor of the ultra-Tory *John Bull*. For many years Hook was patronised by Regency high society as a wit and spontaneous extemporiser of light verse.
4. Brummell had been forced to leave England and live in Calais, because of his gambling debts.
5. Sir Lumley Skeffington (1771–1850) was a playwright and a fop.

On Fashion

1. Spenser, *The Faerie Queene*, III. xii. 8.
2. Lord Foppington is a character in John Vanbrugh's Restoration comedy *The Relapse* (1696).
3. As told in *The Fudge Family in Paris* (1818), a collection of comic verses by the Irish writer Thomas Moore (1779–1852).
4. Linsey-woolsey was a dress material of coarse inferior wool, woven upon a cotton warp.
5. In Tobias Smollett's *Peregrine Pickle* (1751), ch. lxxxvii.
6. John Dryden, *Absalom and Achitophel*, I, l. 164.
7. In Fanny Burney's *Evelina*. See also the reference to these characters in 'On Londoners and Country People'.

On the Want of Money

1. See 'On the Aristocracy of Letters', note 3.
2. Dryden, *The Hind and the Panther*, I, l. 271.
3. William Wilberforce (1759–1833) an evangelical Christian, philanthropist, and leading campaigner for the abolition of the slave trade.
4. Both economists. Thomas Robert Malthus's *Essay on Population* (1798) was notorious for its hard-hearted sermonising towards the poor.
5. *Gil Blas* (1715–35) was a novel by the French novelist and playwright Alain-René Lesage (1668–1747).
6. In Henry Fielding's *Amelia* (1752), Book X, ch. v.

7. *The Bride of Lammermoor* (1819) by Sir Walter Scott. One of the central figures in the novel is Edgar Ravenswood's servant Caleb, who is so proud of the family name that rather than let guests see the enforced poverty of Edgar's hospitality, he continually invents far-fetched excuses – storms, fires, acts of God – in order to avoid feeding them.
8. A quotation from Milton's celebrated poem *L'Allegro*, ll. 133–6.
9. *The City Madam*, by Philip Massinger (1583–1640), acted 1632, printed 1658.
10. Mateo Alcman's *Guzman d'Alfarache* (1599), referred to in Charles Lamb's *Specimens of English Dramatic Poets who lived about the time of Shakespeare* (1808).
11. In Hazlitt's day, the cost of postage was paid by the recipient. It was not until 1840, with the reforms of Rowland Hill, that a uniform Penny Post was established, and delivery was paid for by the sender.
12. A dun is a demanding creditor, or their agent.
13. To raise the wind is to obtain money, get a loan.
14. During the 1790s many French aristocrats and Catholic priests fled to England to escape persecution from the Jacobins. A significant number of them settled in Somers Town, then a new suburb of London, situated just north of where St Pancras Station and the British Library now stand.

On the Feeling of Immortality in Youth

1. Joseph Addison, *Cato*, V. i.
2. Collins, *The Passions*, l. 32.
3. From *Tristram Shandy*, Book V, ch. vii.
4. In the first draft Hazlitt wrote 'like a rustic at a fair' but then changed it to 'clown' in the final, published version. Hence it is clear that, in spite of the carnivalesque context, the word 'clown' was not meant to indicate a comic circus performer, but was being used in the old, Shakespearean sense, to refer to a simple-minded country person. With that meaning of clown having been completely lost today, I have decided that it might be less confusing for the modern reader if I revert briefly to the original manuscript.
5. James Thomson, *The Castle of Indolence*, I, ll. 33–4.
6. Lady Mary Wortley Montagu (1689–1762) daughter of the fifth earl and first duke of Kingston. Poet, wit and letter-writer, Lady Mary was a leading member of English society between 1715 and 1739.
7. Hazlitt's mother's family, the Loftuses, lived in Peterborough.
8. Highly revolutionary both in form and content, Friedrich Schiller's *The

Robbers and *Don Carlos* had a great reputation in England during the 1790s. The quotation is from Coleridge's Sonnet to Schiller, itself a product of that decade.

9. Wordsworth, *Tintern Abbey*.
10. Thomas Gray, *Elegy Written in a Country Churchyard*, ll. 91–2.
11. John Dryden, *Aurengzebe*, IV. i. 41–2.

Of Persons One Would Wish to Have Seen

1. Shakespeare, *Macbeth* IV. i. 111.
2. Alexander Pope, *Epistle to a Lady*, ll. 51–2.
3. Milton, *Il Penseroso*, ll. 109–10.
4. *Hydriotaphia, or Urn Burial*, an extraordinary essay on burial practices, life, death and immortality by the seventeenth-century writer Sir Thomas Browne (1605–82).
5. Sir Fulke Greville (1554–1628) dramatist, poet and biographer of Sir Philip Sidney.
6. John Donne (1572–1631), metaphysical poet in his youth, in later life Dean of St Paul's; famous even in his own time for the difficulty and far-fetchedness of his poetic conceits.
7. The poet requests his lover not to accompany him abroad disguised as a servant-boy. The poem is entitled in two manuscripts 'On his mistress's desire to be disguised and to go like a page with him'.
8. The ill-natured north wind Boreas, courting the nymph Orithyia, overcame her by resorting to brute force.
9. i.e. whether it is in eclipse, or at its brightest, we still call the moon the moon.
10. Giovanni Boccaccio (1313–75).
11. Spenser, *The Faerie Queene*, IV. xi. 23.
12. The tribute to Lord Cornbury, and that to Lord Mansfield which follows it, are both from Alexander Pope's *Imitations of Horace, Epistles*, I. vi. 60–2, 50–3.
13. Pope, *Epilogue to the Satires*, II, ll. 138–9.
14. Pope, *Epistle to Dr Arbuthnot*, ll. 135–46.
15. 'Junius' was the pseudonymous author of a series of Whiggish pro-Wilkesite letters that appeared in the *Public Advertiser* between 1769–72, attacking the duke of Grafton, Lord Mansfield and George III. To this day, Junius's identity has never been definitely established, although the consensus is that the letters were written by Sir Philip Francis.

16. Samuel Richardson was a printer as well as an author. Henry Fielding's *Joseph Andrews* (1742), like the same author's *Apology for the Life of Mrs Shamela Andrews* (1741), was a kind of parody of Richardson's celebrated first novel, *Pamela, or Virtue Rewarded*, the story of a virtuous young servant girl called Pamela Andrews (1740).
17. David Garrick (1717–79), the most celebrated actor of the eighteenth century.
18. *æstus* = heat.
19. Eugene Aram (1704–59), the famous scholar-murderer, was hanged in 1759 for the killing of Daniel Clark several years earlier at Knaresborough in Yorkshire.
20. Margaret, Duchess of Newcastle (1623–73), poet, dramatist and biographer of her husband William Cavendish.
21. Mrs Lucy Hutchinson (b. 1620), author of the *Memoirs of the Life of Colonel Hutchinson*, first published in 1806, a vivid and valuable account of the outbreak of the English Civil War told from the Puritan point of view.
22. Anne, known as Ninon de l'Enclos (1620–1705), a Frenchwoman known for her beauty and wit.
23. This is a reference to the temporary dissolution of the Congress of Vienna in 1814 after Napoleon's dramatic return from Elba.

On Footmen

1. Louis-Eustache Ude, whose book *The French Cook; or the Art of Cookery developed in all its branches*, was published in 1813.
2. In Henry Fielding's *Joseph Andrews* (1742).
3. James Northcote (1746–1831) was a painter friend of Hazlitt's, and a former pupil and assistant of Sir Joshua Reynolds.
4. A reference to Lady Mary Wortley Montagu's 'Epistle from Arthur Grey, the Footman, to Mrs Murray'.
5. Thomas Gray, *Ode on a Distant Prospect of Eton College*, ll. 99–100.

On a Sun-Dial

1. From *Henry VI Part III*, II. v. 24.
2. See Hazlitt's *Notes of a Journey through France and Italy* (1826) in Volume X of P.P. Howe's *Complete Works*, p. 266.
3. From Book I of Rousseau's *Confessions* (1782).

4. Mary Shelley's *The Last Man* was published in January 1826, and is set in the future. The King of England has been demoted to Earl of Windsor in Shelley's novel, which explains Hazlitt's subsequent reference.
5. A Latin tag, 'things that don't appear count the same as things that don't exist'.
6. Wordsworth, *The Fountain*, ll. 70–2.
7. A reminiscence of some lines from Hazlitt's friend the poet Joseph Fawcett's *Elegy VIII, Written on New Year's Day*, ll. 1–4.
8. Walter Shandy, the father of Tristram in Sterne's novel *Tristram Shandy*.
9. In the essay 'My First Acquaintance with Poets' from 1823.

The Free Admission

1. Fanny (Frances Anne) Kemble (1809–93) was the daughter of Charles Kemble the actor, and niece of Sarah Siddons. The season of 1829–30 was Fanny Kemble's first on the London stage, and the last which Hazlitt would live to see.
2. Fanny Kemble's first appearance in these parts was on 9 December 1829, and 28 April 1830 respectively.
3. James Thomson (1700–48), *Winter*, from *The Seasons*, ll. 646–8.
4. From Sneyd Davies, *To the Worthy, Humane, Generous, Reverend, and Noble, Mr Frederick Cornwallis, now Archbishop of Canterbury*, ll. 79–80.
5. The reference is to *The Chronicle: A Ballad* by Abraham Cowley (1618–67).

The Sick Chamber

1. Sir Walter Raleigh, 'Like to a Hermite poore in place obscure,' quoted in Charles Lamb's *John Woodvil*, Act V.
2. François Rabelais (c. 1494–c. 1553), *Gargantua and Pantagruel*, IV, l. 24.
3. An allusion to Cowper, *The Task*, V, l. 737.
4. Pietro Metastasio (1698–1782), *Themistocles*, III. ii.
5. i.e. Henry Fielding's *Tom Jones*.
6. William Wordsworth, *Ode on Intimations of Immortality*, ll. 169–70.
7. The *Journey of a Voyage to Lisbon* is by Henry Fielding; *The Decameron* is by Boccaccio. *Paul Clifford*, a novel about a gentleman highwayman, was first published in 1830, by Hazlitt's friend Edward Bulwer-Lytton.
8. Robert Burns, *Epistle to Dr Blacklock*, ll. 53–4.

The Letter-Bell

1. Hazlitt first came up to London in September 1793 to attend the Unitarian New College in Hackney.
2. The village of Wem in Shropshire, where Hazlitt was brought up, is within sight of the Welsh mountains. On the blue hills of Hazlitt's boyhood see also 'Why Distant Objects Please', reprinted earlier in this volume.
3. Wordsworth, *Ode on Intimations of Immortality*, ll. 73–4.
4. Hazlitt refers to recent events in France, specifically the July Revolution of 1830, when Charles X abdicated in favour of the Duc D'Orléans Louis-Philippe, and ended the Bourbon *régime* in France. This was a victory for popular sovereignty and constitutional monarchy.
5. The Poet Laureate was Robert Southey (1774–1843), a great friend of Wordsworth and Coleridge, who had begun his career as an ardent republican, only to turn violently reactionary when he reached his thirties.
6. Wordsworth, *Ode on Intimations of Immortality*, ll. 178–81.
7. In 'My First Acquaintance With Poets' (1823) Hazlitt remembers Wordsworth pointing out a particularly beautiful yellow bank to him during his historic pilgrimage to Somerset in 1798.
8. Samuel Taylor Coleridge. One of Hazlitt's pet theories was that the main reason why the three Lake Poets, Wordsworth, Coleridge and Southey, had abandoned their early radicalism was because poets were intrinsically less independent-minded than philosophers or reformers, and that it was in their very nature to crave sympathy, patronage and public approval.
9. Coleridge, *The Rime of the Ancient Mariner*, ll. 289–91.
10. Oliver Goldsmith, *The Traveller*, ll. 293–4.
11. Wordsworth, *Tintern Abbey*, ll. 48–50.
12. Goldsmith, *The Deserted Village*, l. 412.
13. Hazlitt is recalling the period when he lodged in the house of his brother, the painter John Hazlitt, who lived at 12 Rathbone Place, off Oxford Street.
14. Shakespeare, *Macbeth*, III. iv. 37–8.
15. The Two-Penny Post was for deliveries within London, the General Post was national.
16. In Hazlitt's day the mail coaches from London to the provinces carried a limited number of passengers, and an armed guard, and they ran to a strict schedule. The horses were changed at coaching inns, and if a

passenger was not ready in time he was left behind. From 1830 the development of the railways led to a gradual decline of the mail-coach service.

17. The mail-coach system first saw the light of day in 1784, Cowper's *The Task* in 1785.
18. Cowper, *The Task*, IV, ll. 1–22.
19. Hazlitt is recalling Clytemnestra's speech near the beginning of Aeschylus's *Agamemnon*, ll. 281–316.

Select Bibliography

Scholarly editions

The Complete Works of William Hazlitt, ed. P.P. Howe, 21 vols, London: Dent, 1930–4
The Selected Writings of William Hazlitt, ed. Duncan Wu, 9 vols, London: Pickering and Chatto, 1998

Paperback editions

The Fight and Other Writings, ed. Tom Paulin and David Chandler, Harmondsworth: Penguin, 2000
Selected Writings, ed. Jon Cook, Oxford: Oxford University Press, 1991

Biographies

P.P. Howe, *The Life of William Hazlitt*, Harmondsworth: Penguin, 1949
Stanley Jones, *Hazlitt: A Life: From Winterslow to Frith Street*, Oxford: Oxford University Press, 1989
A.C. Grayling, *The Quarrel of the Age: The Life and Times of William Hazlitt*, London: Phoenix Press, 2000

Criticism

David Bromwich, *William Hazlitt: The Mind of a Critic*, Oxford: Oxford University Press, 1983
Uttara Nattarajan, *William Hazlitt and the Reach of Sense: Criticism, Morals and the Metaphysics of Power*, Oxford: Oxford University Press, 1998
Tom Paulin, *The Day-Star of Liberty: William Hazlitt's Radical Style*, London: Faber, 1998

Historical background

Celine Fox, ed., *London: World City 1800–1840*, New Haven: Yale University Press, 1992

Lightning Source UK Ltd.
Milton Keynes UK
175063UK00001B/27/P